BEST ROAD TRIPS

NEW ENGLAND

ESCAPES ON THE OPEN ROAD

RAY BARTLETT,

ISABEL ALBISTON, AMY C BALFOUR, ROBERT BALKOVICH,

GREGOR CLARK, ADAM KARLIN, BRIAN KLUEPFEL,

REGIS ST LOUIS, MARA VORHEES, BENEDICT WALKER

Contents

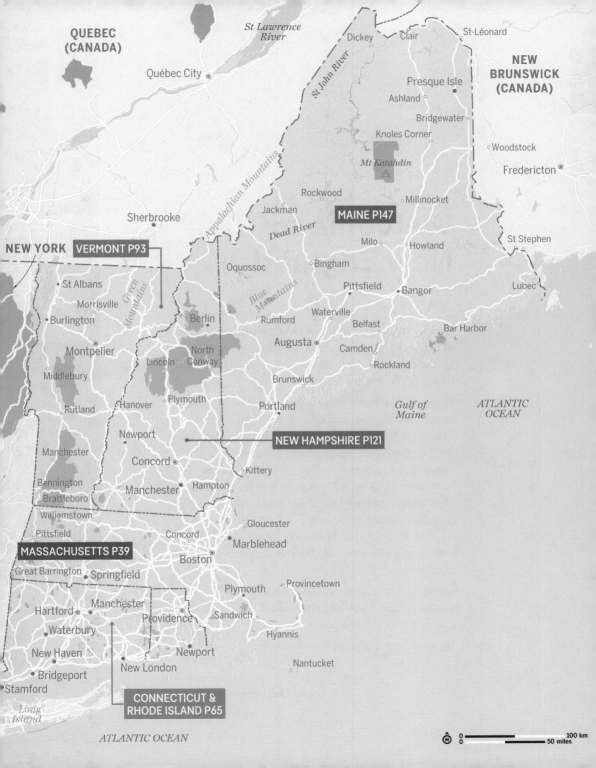

QUEBEC
(CANADA)

St Lawrence
River

Québec City

NEW
BRUNSWICK
(CANADA)

Dickey

Clair

St-Léonard

St John River

Presque Isle

Ashland

Bridgewater

Woodstock

Knoles Corner

Fredericton

Sherbrooke

Appalachian Mountains

Mt Katahdin

Millinocket

Rockwood

MAINE P147

St Stephen

NEW YORK   VERMONT P93

Jackman

Dead River

Milo

Howland

St Albans

Green Mountains

Blue Mountains

Bingham

Pittsfield

Bangor

Lubec

Morrisville

Burlington

Berlin

Rumford

Waterville

Belfast

Bar Harbor

Montpelier

North Conway

Augusta

Camden

Middlebury

Lincoln

Brunswick

Rockland

Hanover

Plymouth

Portland

Gulf of Maine

ATLANTIC OCEAN

Rutland

Newport

NEW HAMPSHIRE P121

Manchester

Concord

Kittery

Bennington

Manchester

Hampton

Brattleboro

Williamstown

Concord

Gloucester

Pittsfield

Marblehead

MASSACHUSETTS P39

Boston

Great Barrington

Springfield

Provincetown

Manchester

Plymouth

Hartford

Providence

Sandwich

Waterbury

Hyannis

New Haven

Newport

Bridgeport

New London

Nantucket

Stamford

CONNECTICUT & RHODE ISLAND P65

Long Island

ATLANTIC OCEAN

N   0   100 km
     0   50 miles

Welcome to New England

New England is one of America's best road-tripping regions: it's steeped in history and culture, chock-full of culinary and architectural delights, and crisscrossed by scenic byways from the ancient Appalachians to the shores of the mighty Atlantic.

The trips listed here are dreamy rides through well-known destinations and off-the-beaten-track treasures. Cruise the fabled coastlines of Maine and Cape Cod, thrill to the White Mountains' spectacular granite summits, and gawk at the fiery fall foliage of the Berkshires and Green Mountains. From historic sites like Plimoth Patuxet Museums and Nantucket to big cities and contemporary art museums, these trips traverse pumpkin patches and cranberry bogs, red barns and white-steepled churches, covered bridges and lighthouses.

Along the way, sample cuisine from the best clam shacks, lobster joints and farm-to-table eateries, and stay at cozy B&Bs, vintage hotels and classic roadside motels.

Turn the page and start the adventure.

Plimoth Patuxet Museums (p50), Massachusetts
ALEXANDER SVIRIDOV/SHUTTERSTOCK ©

Our Picks

BEST COASTAL VIEWS

Few things are prettier than the vistas you'll see while slowly driving along a coastal highway, zipping along a rushing river or gazing on the calm surface of a pristine lake. New England's got water views galore, and they'll have you stopping more often than not to take photographs. Adding to the enjoyment are the quaint fishing towns and zany tourist traps that give each drive its character.

SHIPWRECKS

More shipwrecks occurred off Cape Cod than any other part of the eastern seaboard...until the Cape Cod Canal was built.

 Maritime Maine

A delightful drive along some of the state's most scenic coastline.

P150

 Acadia National Park

One of America's wildest parks, with lighthouses, rugged coast, wildlife and blueberries.

P156

 Cape Cod & the Islands

The arm-like sandbar of the Cape holds great beaches, fantastic seafood and whale sightings.

P42

 Coastal New England

Seafood shanties, lighthouses, lobsters and more on a drive that encompasses New England's best coasts.

P20

 Around Cape Ann

This short but pretty tour takes you to art galleries, fishing villages and lobsters.

P52

FENG CHENG/SHUTTERSTOCK ©

Portland Head Light (p151), Maine

Right: Acadia National Park (p156), Maine

**FALL
FORECAST**

Check the forecast;
a dry year means
duller, less vibrant
colors and a shorter
window in which to
see them.

Our Picks

BEST FOLIAGE DRIVES

While New England is gorgeous any time of year, it's indescribable in autumn, when the maple, birch and beech trees turn the mountains into a palette of reds, golds, yellows and oranges that in certain years is simply breathtaking. Timing is tricky: it varies – sometimes by several weeks – year to year. Be aware that a poorly timed storm can leave the trees without leaves or dry them up too quickly.

Berkshire Back Roads

The Berkshires turn fiery red, yellow and gold every fall; this loop showcases them at their prettiest.

P56

Mohawk Trail

Follow in the footsteps of the pioneers as you pass striking hills, beautiful lakes and quaint villages.

P60

White Mountain National Forest (p127), New Hampshire

Vermont's Spine: Route 100

This drive is especially breathtaking in fall, taking you through the best of the state.

P96

White Mountains Loop

New Hampshire, and the White Mountains in particular, is a prime spot for leaf peepers.

P124

Litchfield Hills Loop

Connecticut stays out of the limelight, but this loop will have you rethinking it as a fall destination.

P88

The Berkshires (p28), Massachusetts

Our Picks

BEST HISTORY DRIVES

History buffs will delight in driving through many of America's famous sights, museums and historic homesteads. Revolutionary battles were fought here; Boston alone is filled with historic homes. To the south is where the Pilgrims landed on the continent for the first time, stopping in Provincetown before finally settling across Cape Cod Bay in Plymouth. You can see all this and more as you tour New England.

Pilgrim Trail

A mostly coastal route takes you to where the Pilgrims first landed: Cape Cod and Plymouth.

P48

Coastal New England

History, much of it maritime, is what's on display here in this delightful, surprise-filled trip.

P20

Ivy League Tour

The hallowed lecture halls are full of fascinating history, people and discoveries.

P32

Marblehead (p22), Massachusetts

Mohawk Trail

This inland route goes through historic Deerfield, where homes are restored to their original state.

P60

Rhode Island: East Bay

This pretty, short and historic drive helps you explore the founding of America.

P68

Right: Old State House, Boston (p51)

FREEDOM TRAIL

If you're in Boston check out the Freedom Trail, the historic route that Paul Revere took on his famous ride.

Our Picks

BEST LAKES & RIVER DRIVES

The coastline often hogs the spotlight in this region but there's something truly special about the inland waterways. Mist rising off a mirror-calm lake as a moose munches reeds. A bald eagle swooping down, talons outstretched, to pluck a trout from a river. Or a hike that crisscrosses the musical gurgle of a spring- or snow-fed stream.

ITCHING TO GO

Don't forget the insect repellent. Where there are lakes, there are bugs!

 1 Lower River Valley

Tour the Connecticut River, admiring castles and eagles along one of the region's greatest waterways.

P84

 2 Litchfield Hills Loop

A trip around the rolling hills and lakes of Connecticut's summer escape for the wealthy.

P88

 3 Lake Champlain Byway

Discover Burlington's urban attractions and the slower-paced charms of Lake Champlain's islands.

P112

 4 Lake Winnipesaukee

This family-friendly lakeside loop features trails, wildlife, drive-in movies and ice-cream shops.

P132

 5 Lakes Tour

A lovely zip around some of Maine's funnest lakes, with water sports and lots of kid-friendly activities.

P172

STAN DZUGAN/GETTY IMAGES ©

Lake Waramaug (p91), Connecticut

Our Picks

BEST FOOD & WINE DRIVES

New England is a tourist favorite for its incredible bounty of food and drink. Have a seafood lunch so fresh it was in the water hours earlier, then savor a farm-to-table dinner just a short drive away. Some regional delicacies, like Maine lobster (let's get real, everything else is just a big shrimp!) are found not only in their home state but throughout New England.

DRY RUN

Scallop-lovers should ask establishments if they are 'wet' or 'dry.' The latter is more expensive but not treated with preservatives.

Connecticut Wine Trail

Visit rural and coastal vineyards with a dose of modern architecture in between.

P80

RFONDREN PHOTOGRAPHY/SHUTTERSTOCK ©

Lobster roll

Around Cape Ann

Pull up a picnic table for succulent fried clams, steamers and mouthwatering lobster rolls.

P52

Cape Cod & the Islands

Feast on seafood at the region's best restaurants or the famous Wellfleet Oyster Festival.

P42

Cider Season Sampler

Sample Vermont's agricultural bounty and sip fresh-pressed cider during the state's most colorful season.

P102

Maritime Maine

Lobster rolls, haddock and chowder – look for shacks and no-frills eateries along the coast.

P150

When to Go

Each season has its highlights – it's always a good time to visit New England.

DRIVING THE KANCAMAGUS HIGHWAY

Ray Bartlett is a writer based in Boston. @kaisoradotcom

'I've driven this beautiful 34-mile stretch in New Hampshire on many occasions and each time it seems to be a different road. In the fall it's a slow but beautiful slog, as RVs chug up the inclines and dozens of cars wait for a chance to pass. In spring it's the opposite – sometimes I'm the only car. The rushing water, conifers and maple trees, and the chance to see deer or moose, are always thrilling. It's only a 30-minute drive if there's no traffic, but it's always a memorable part of any visit to the state.'

New England's four distinct seasons bring beauty throughout the year. Visit the same landscape in a different season and you may think you're seeing it for the first time. Autumn (September to November) is perhaps the most famous time to come, with its color-strewn mountainsides that light up in a blaze. Winter brings beautiful snow scenes, but also road closures and slick driving conditions. Spring is delightful, with its yellow-green leaves and rushing creeks, though biting insects and mud are a part of

SARAH MICHALS/SHUTTERSTOCK ©

Kancamagus Hwy (p127), New Hampshire

Weather Watch (Boston)

JANUARY	FEBRUARY	MARCH	APRIL	MAY	JUNE
Avg. daytime max: **37°F**. Days of precipitation: **9**	Avg. daytime max: **39°F**. Days of precipitation: **8**	Avg. daytime max: **46°F**. Days of precipitation: **11**	Avg. daytime max: **57°F**. Days of precipitation: **11**	Avg. daytime max: **67°F**. Days of precipitation: **12**	Avg. daytime max: **76°F**. Days of precipitation: **10**

> ✓
> ### WHERE TO STAY
> This region has just about every kind of accommodations you can think of, from cozy log cabins and beach-side shacks to funky Airstream hotels and high-end resorts. Book well in advance for the most flexibility.

St Paddy's Day Parade, Boston

the equation. Summer is drier and sometimes even downright sweltering, though the heat never lasts for too long. It's always easy to cool off with stops at refreshing swimming holes or ocean beaches.

Accommodations

If you're planning a visit in high season (eg 4th of July or fall), you'll need to book accommodations well in advance. At other times of year lodging is easier to find, though reservations are always recommended.

NEW ENGLAND'S THREE SEASONS

Locals like to joke that New England has only three seasons: mud, bugs and snow. You'll find trails are muddy in springtime, and after that you'll want to bring bug repellent. Once the bugs go there's a window of pure magic...and then the snow begins.

LOCAL FESTIVITIES

St Paddy's Day Parade Every St Patrick's Day Boston puts on a giant parade. Make merry and drink green beer (and other beverages) as floats roll by and spectators get boisterous. **March**

Tanglewood Music Festival Catching a summer performance at Tanglewood is a musical highlight. This long-running series ranges from classical music to jazz and is held in Lenox, Massachusetts (p58). **July & August**

Laconia Pumpkin Festival A tower of jack-o'-lanterns and other pumpkin-themed fun and festivities turn this New Hampshire town into the area's largest pumpkin festival (p123). **October**

First Night New Englanders head to Boston's City Hall for First Night celebrations on December 31. Screaming crowds and stolen kisses at midnight – it's a heck of a lot of fun. **December**

JULY	AUGUST	SEPTEMBER	OCTOBER	NOVEMBER	DECEMBER
Avg. daytime max: **82°F**. Days of precipitation: **9**	Avg. daytime max: **80°F**. Days of precipitation: **9**	Avg. daytime max: **73°F**. Days of precipitation: **8**	Avg. daytime max: **62°F**. Days of precipitation: **9**	Avg. daytime max: **51°F**. Days of precipitation: **10**	Avg. daytime max: **41°F**. Days of precipitation: **10**

Get Prepared for New England

Useful things to load in your bag, your ears and your brain.

WATCH

Jaws
(*Steven Spielberg;
1975*) Few movies have
gripped the psyche
like this one, set in the
fictional town of Amity.

Mystic River
(*Clint Eastwood; 2003*)
A haunting tale of
friendship, loss and
redemption, featuring
an all-star cast.

**Hotel New
Hampshire**
(*Tony Richardson; 1984*)
John Irving's incredible
novel comes to life in
this faithful adaptation.

Good Will Hunting
(*Gus Van Sant; 1997*)
The story of a brilliant
but troubled savant,
written by and starring
Ben Affleck and Matt
Damon.

Black Mass
(*Scott Cooper; 2015*)
A spectacular, chilling
movie on the infamous
mobster Whitey Bolger,
set in Boston's Southie
neighborhood.

Clothing

Layers: Weather in New England
can range from sunshine and blue
skies to a fog bank or snowstorm
in a matter of hours. Make like a
Scout and come prepared: avoid
emergency stops at the store to get
a sweatshirt in summer, or roasting
in the Arctic parka you brought
thinking it couldn't possibly reach
70°F in January. Synthetic layers
(which don't absorb moisture) are
preferred over cotton for strenuous
outdoor activities.

Watch out on the water: Know
that temps can be up to 20°F colder
on boat trips, especially if you factor
in clothes getting wet and the bitter
sea winds. Rain gear is wise.

Footwear and extra socks: Bring
a variety of shoes: flip-flops (thongs)
for the beach, grippy sneakers for a
hike, closed-toed sandals for water
sports and flats for that special dinner
you've got planned.

Fleece and windbreaker: Hikers
will find that the difference between
the trailhead and a mountain
summit can be quite dramatic,
especially when your only T-shirt
is clammy with sweat and there are
40mph gusts at the top.

Hat and sunscreen: Never
underestimate the power of the sun,
even in New England. Consider a hat
with a wide brim to protect your face
and slather on sunscreen regularly.

Clam chowder

Words

Boston in particular is famous for its accent, which often drops r's (and occasionally adds them elsewhere). 'Park the car in Harvard Yard' becomes 'Paak the caa in Haavaad Yaad.' 'Shower' becomes 'shao-aa.' Meanwhile, 'idea' becomes 'idear.' You get the picture.

Quahog: (KOE-hawg) A tasty clam from which chowder (chowda) is made. Rhymes with 'TOE-frog.'

Chowda: A thick, milk-based quahog stew that is markedly different from New York's tomato-based version.

Lobsta roll: Pieces of Maine lobster meat, often seasoned with mayo, celery and spices, served in a hot-dog bun.

Dunkin': Dunkin Donuts, a ubiquitous donut chain. Also Dunks.

Soda: A carbonated beverage. Never say 'pop.'

Coke: This does not mean cola generically, but rather the specific brand: Coca-Cola. If you ask for a Coke in New England, you will not be served Pepsi.

Pissah: Cool, great, amazing, awesome.

Wicked pissah: Really cool, great, amazing, awesome.

Leaf peepers: Tourists who arrive in time to see the autumn foliage.

Snowbirds: Summer-only residents who head south for the colder winter months, often to Florida.

Nor'easter: A major winter storm, often bringing significant snowfall.

Cherrystones: A small quahog, often eaten raw on the half shell, like an oyster.

Packie: A liquor store, short for 'Package Store.'

Blue laws: Laws limiting the purchase and consumption of alcohol, often to the frustration of both tourists and locals alike.

LISTEN

Best of Car Talk
(1977–2015) This hysterical NPR talk show gets under the hood with Boston natives Tom and Ray Magliozzi.

Bumblebee Radio
(2018–) Local radio personality Kristen Eck runs this indie music station (bumblebeeradio.com), with a 'Bumblebee Brunch' every Friday.

WBZ
(1921–) 1030AM radio station with news and vital traffic updates around Boston, the Cape and elsewhere, every 10 minutes.

READ

The Perfect Storm
(*Sebastian Junger; 1997*) The gripping account of the *Andrea Gail*, a fishing vessel lost during a storm in 1991.

Cape Cod
(*Henry David Thoreau; 1865*) This inspirational account of Thoreau's wanderings on Cape Cod is a must-read.

The Ruins of Woodman's Village
(*Albert Waitt; 2023*) LT Nichols investigates the disappearance of twin sisters in a quiet seaside town.

Moby Dick
(*Herman Melville; 1851*) 'Call me Ishmael': so begins the story of Captain Ahab's obsessive pursuit of the white whale.

ROAD TRIPS

White Mountain, New Hampshire (p124)
SONGQUAN DENG/SHUTTERSTOCK ©

Contents

01

Coastal New England

BEST 2 DAYS

The first 35 miles (stops one to four) showcase coastal New England, past and present.

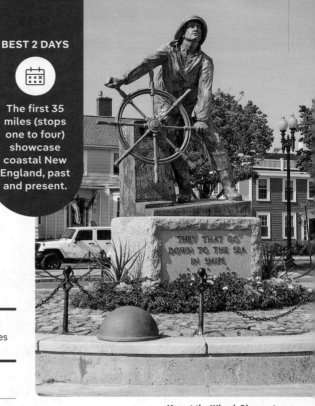

***Man at the Wheel**, Gloucester*

DURATION	DISTANCE	GREAT FOR
6–8 days	240 miles / 386km	History, families & nature

BEST TIME TO GO	
	May to September

From a pirate's perspective, there was no better base in Colonial America than Newport, given the easy access to trade routes and friendly local merchants. Until 1723, that is, when the new governor ceremoniously hanged 26 sea bandits at Gravelly Point. This classic trip highlights the region's intrinsic connection to the sea, from upstart pirates to upper-crust merchants, from Gloucester fisherfolk to New Bedford whalers, from clipper ships to submarines.

Link Your Trip

06 Around Cape Ann

Head north from Gloucester for more quaint coastal culture.

12 Connecticut Wine Trail

Continue south along the coast for a tasty tour through New England's wine country.

01 **GLOUCESTER**
Founded in 1623 by English fisherfolk, Gloucester is among New England's oldest towns. This port on Cape Ann has made its living from fishing for almost 400 years, and has inspired works like Rudyard Kipling's *Captains Courageous* and Sebastian Junger's *The Perfect Storm*. Visit the **Maritime Gloucester Museum** (maritime gloucester.org) to see the working waterfront in action. There is plenty of hands-on educational fun, including an outdoor aquarium and the excellent Stellwagen Bank National Marine Sanctuary (stellwagen.noaa.gov). **7 Seas Whale Watch**

Revere Beach

Cruising through Revere, MA 1A parallels the wide, sandy stretch of Revere Beach, which proudly proclaims itself America's first public beach, established in 1896. Scenic but soulless, the condo-fronted beach belies the history of this place, which was a raucous boardwalk and amusement park for most of the 20th century. Famous for roller coasters, dance halls and the Wonderland dog track, Revere Beach attracted hundreds of thousands of sunbathers and fun-seekers during summer months.

The area deteriorated in the 1970s due to crime and pollution. In 1978 a historic blizzard wiped out many of the remaining buildings and businesses, and the 'Coney Island of New England' was relegated to the annals of history.

Revere Beach benefited from a clean-up effort in the 1980s; nowadays, the beach itself is lovely to look at and a safe place to swim.

Unfortunately, dominated by high-end condominium complexes, the area retains nothing of its former charm. Only one vestige of 'old' Revere Beach remains: the world-famous **Kelly's Roast Beef** (kellysroastbeef.com), which has been around since 1951 and still serves up the best roast-beef sandwiches and clam chowder in town. There's no indoor seating, so pull up some sand and enjoy the view. Beware of the seagulls: they're crazy for roast beef.

(7seaswhalewatch.com) boats also depart from here.

Don't leave before you pay your respects at the **Gloucester Fishermen's Memorial**, where Leonard Craske's famous statue *Man at the Wheel* stands.

THE DRIVE
Head out of town on Western Ave (MA 127), cruising past *Man at the Wheel* and Stage Fort Park. This road follows the coastline south through swanky seaside towns like Manchester-by-the-Sea and Beverly Farms, with glimpses of the bay. After about 14 miles, cross Essex Bridge and continue south into Salem. For a quicker trip, take MA 128 S to MA 114.

02 SALEM
Salem's glory dates from the 18th century, when it was a center for clipper-ship trade with the Far East, thanks to the enterprising efforts of merchant Elias Hasket Derby. His namesake Derby Wharf is now the centre of the **Salem Maritime National Historic Site** (nps.gov/sama), which includes the 1871 lighthouse, the tall ship *Friendship* and the state custom house. Many Salem vessels followed Derby's ship *Grand Turk* around the Cape of Good Hope, and soon the owners founded the East India Marine Society to provide warehousing services for their ships' logs and charts.

The new company's charter required the establishment of 'a museum in which to house the natural and artificial curiosities, brought back by members' ships. The collection was the basis for what is now the world-class **Peabody Essex Museum** (pem.org), which contains an amazing collection of Asian art, among other treasures. A stroll around town reveals some impressive architecture – grand houses that were once sea captains' homes.

 THE DRIVE
Take Lafayette St (MA 114) south out of Salem center, driving past the campus of Salem State College. After crossing an inlet, the road bends east and becomes Pleasant St as it enters Marblehead center.

 03 **MARBLEHEAD**
First settled in 1629, Marblehead is a maritime village with winding streets, brightly painted Colonial houses, and sailing yachts bobbing at moorings in the harbor.

This is the Boston area's premier yachting port and one of New England's most prestigious addresses. Clustered around the harbor, Marblehead center is dotted with historic houses, art galleries and waterside parks.

 THE DRIVE
Drive south on MA 129, exiting Marblehead and continuing through the seaside town of Swampscott. At the traffic circle, take the first exit onto MA 1A, which continues south through Lynn and Revere. Take the VFW Pkwy (MA 1A) to the Revere Beach Pkwy (MA 16) to the Northeast Expwy (US 1), which goes over Tobin Bridge and into Boston.

04 **BOSTON**
Boston's seaside location has influenced every aspect of its history, but it's only in recent years that the waterfront has become an attractive and accessible destination for visitors. Now you can stroll along the **Rose Kennedy Greenway** (rose kennedygreenway.org), with the sea on one side and the city on the other. The focal point of the waterfront is the excellent **New England Aquarium** (neaq.org), home to seals, penguins, turtles and oodles of fish.

From Long Wharf, you can catch a ferry out to the **Boston Harbor Islands** (bostonharbor islands.org) for berry picking, beachcombing and sunbathing. Harbor cruises and trolley tours also depart from these docks. If you prefer to keep your feet on dry land, take a walk to explore Boston's flower-filled parks and shop-lined streets.

 THE DRIVE
Drive south out of Boston on I-93. You'll recognize the urban 'hood of Dorchester by pretty Savin Hill Cove and the landmark Rainbow Swash painted on the gas tank. At exit 4, take MA 24 S toward Brockton, then MA 140 S toward New Bedford. Take I-195 E for 2 miles, exiting onto MA 18 for New Bedford.

05 **NEW BEDFORD**
During its heyday as a whaling port (1765–1860), New Bedford commanded some 400 whaling ships – a vast fleet that brought in hundreds of thousands of barrels of whale oil for lighting lamps. Novelist Herman Melville worked on one of these ships for four years, and thus set his celebrated novel *Moby Dick* in New Bedford. The excellent, hands-on **New Bedford**

Parking in Boston

Parking in downtown Boston is prohibitively expensive. For more affordable rates, cross the Fort Point Channel and park in the Seaport District. There are some (relatively) reasonable deals to be found in the parking lots on Northern Ave (near the Institute of Contemporary Art); alternatively, head for the Necco Street Garage (further south, off A St), which charges only $14 per day on weekends and $14 for overnight parking on weekdays.

Whaling Museum (whaling museum.org) commemorates this history. A 66ft skeleton of a blue whale welcomes you at the entrance. Inside, you can tramp the decks of the *Lagoda*, a fully rigged, half-size replica of an actual whaling bark.

 THE DRIVE
Take I-195 W for about 10 miles. In Fall River, head south on MA 24, which becomes RI 24 as you cross into Rhode Island. Cross the bridge, with views of Mt Hope Bay to the north and Sakonnet River to the south, then merge onto RI 114, heading south into Newport.

06 **NEWPORT**
Blessed with a deep-water harbor, Newport has been a shipbuilding base since 1646. Bowen's Wharf and Bannister's Wharf, once working wharves, now typify Newport's transformation from a working

Right: Marblehead

city-by-the-sea to a resort town. Take a narrated cruise with **Classic Cruises of Newport** (sail-newport.com) on *Rum Runner II*, a Prohibition-era bootlegging vessel, or *Madeleine*, a 72ft schooner.

Although its pirate days are over, Newport's harbor remains one of the most active yachting centers in the country, while its waterfront boasts a standout lineup of other attractions. Make sure to tour at least one of the city's magnificent mansions, such as the **Breakers** or **Rosecliff** (newportmansions.org), then stop in for a visit at **Fort Adams** (fortadams.org), one of the largest seacoast fortifications in the USA. In summer it's the venue for the **Newport Jazz Festival**

Photo Opportunity

Pose for a snap alongside *Man at the Wheel*.

(newportjazz.org) and the **Newport Folk Festival** (newportfolk.org).

 THE DRIVE
Head west out of Newport on RI 138, swooping over Newport Bridge onto Conanicut Island and then over Jamestown Bridge to pick up US 1 for the drive into Mystic. The views of the bay from both bridges are a highlight.

07 MYSTIC

Many of Mystic's clipper ships launched from George Greenman & Co Shipyard, now the site of the **Mystic Seaport Museum** (mysticseaport.org). Today the museum covers 17 acres and includes more than 60 historic buildings, four tall ships and almost 500 smaller vessels. Interpreters staffing all the buildings are glad to discuss their crafts and trades. Most illuminating are the demonstrations on such topics as ship rescue, oystering and whaleboat launching. The museum's exhibits also include a replica of the 77ft slave ship *Amistad*.

If the call of the sea beckons, set sail on the ***Argia*** (argiamystic.com), a replica of a

Mystic Seaport Museum

ACTIUM/SHUTTERSTOCK ©

WHY THIS IS A CLASSIC TRIP

Isabel Albiston, writer

Pretty seaside towns and worthwhile museums are two highlights of this trip, but another is the drive itself. It's hard to beat the exhilaration of driving with the window down, hair whipping in the wind, with the Atlantic at your side and the open road ahead, grabbing glimpses of grand mansions that allow you to slip, for a moment, into a different life.

19th-century schooner, which cruises down the Mystic River to Fishers' Island Sound.

THE DRIVE

The 7-mile drive from Mystic to Groton along US 1 S is through built-up suburbs and light industrial areas. To hop across the Thames River to New London, head north along North St to pick up I-95 S.

08 GROTON & NEW LONDON

Groton is home to the US Naval Submarine Base, the first and the largest in the country. It is off-limits to the public, but you can visit the **Historic Ship Nautilus & Submarine Force Museum** (ussnautilus.org), which is home to *Nautilus*, the world's first nuclear-powered submarine and the first sub to transit the North Pole.

Across the river, New London has a similarly illustrious seafaring history, although these days it's built a reputation for itself as a budding creative center. Each summer it hosts **Sailfest** (sailfest.org), a three-day festival with free entertainment, topped off by the second-largest fireworks display in the Northeast. There's also a **Summer Concert Series**, organized by **Hygienic Art** (hygienic.org).

THE DRIVE

It's a 52-mile drive from Groton or New London to New Haven along I-95 S. The initial stages of the drive plow through the suburbs, but after that the interstate runs through old coastal towns such as Old Lyme, Old Saybrook and Guilford.

09 NEW HAVEN

Although most famous for its Ivy League university of Yale, New Haven also played an important role in the burgeoning antislavery movement when, in 1839, the trial of mutineering Mendi tribesmen was held in New Haven's District Court.

Following their illegal capture by Spanish slave traders, the tribesmen, led by Joseph Cinqué, seized the schooner *Amistad* and sailed to New Haven seeking refuge. Pending the successful outcome of the trial, the men were held in a jailhouse on the green, where a 14ft-high bronze memorial now stands. It was the first civil-rights case held in the country.

For a unique take on the New Haven shoreline, take the 3-mile round trip on the **Shore Line Trolley** (shorelinetrolley.org), the oldest operating suburban trolley in the country, which takes you from East Haven to Short Beach in Branford. A wealth of art and architecture is packed into the streets of downtown New Haven.

02

Fall Foliage Tour

DURATION	DISTANCE	GREAT FOR
5–7 days	375 miles / 603km	Families & nature

BEST TIME TO GO	Mid-September to late October

The brilliance of fall in New England is legendary. Scarlet and sugar maples, ash, birch, beech, dogwood, tulip tree, oak and sassafras all contribute to the carnival of autumn color. But this trip is about much more than just flora and fauna: the harvest spirit makes for family outings to seasonal fairs, leisurely walks along dappled trails and tables groaning beneath delicious seasonal produce.

Link Your Trip

08 Mohawk Trail

Pick up the Mohawk Trail at Williamstown for more spectacular mountain vistas and rural New England charm.

15 Vermont's Spine: Route 100

Branch off US 7 at Manchester and take Vermont's dazzlingly scenic VT 100 north along the eastern slopes of the Green Mountains.

01 CANDLEWOOD LAKE

With a surface area of 8.4 sq miles, Candlewood is the largest lake in Connecticut. On the western shore, the **Squantz Pond State Park** (ctparks.com) is popular with leaf peepers, who come to amble the pretty shoreline. In Brookfield and Sherman, quiet vineyards with acres of grapevines line the hillsides. Visitors can tour **White Silo Farm** (whitesilowinery.com), where the focus is on specialty wines made from farm-grown fruit. On the lake's further shore, **Lover's Leap State Park** allows a short walk over a classic iron bridge to a divine view of the Housatonic River.

BEST FOR OUTDOORS

Ziplining through the tree canopy in Bretton Woods.

Kent Falls

 THE DRIVE
From Danbury, at the southern tip of the lake, you have a choice of heading 28 miles north via US 7, taking in Brookfield and New Milford (or trailing the scenic eastern shoreline along Candlewood Lake Rd S); or heading 26 miles north along CT 37 and CT 39 via New Fairfield, Squantz Pond and Sherman, before reconnecting with US 7 to Kent.

02 KENT
Kent has previously been voted *the* spot in all of New England for fall foliage viewing. Situated prettily in the Litchfield Hills on the banks of the Housatonic River, it is surrounded by dense woodlands.

For a sweeping view, hike up Cobble Mountain in **Macedonia Brook State Park** (ctparks.com), a wooded oasis 2 miles north of town. The steep climb to the rocky ridge affords panoramic views of the foliage against a backdrop of the Taconic and Catskill Mountains.

The 250ft waterfall at **Kent Falls State Park** (ctparks.com) is spectacular, and not too challenging a climb, with plenty of viewing platforms along the way.

The 2175-mile Georgia-to-Maine **Appalachian National Scenic Trail** (appalachiantrail.com) also runs through Kent and up to Salisbury on the Massachusetts border. Unlike much of the trail,

LOCAL KNOWLEDGE

Kent Falls

Kent is a great place to base yourself in the fall, with lots of accessible spots for viewing the leaves and good amenities in the pretty town center. The best hiking trail in season is the section that connects with the Appalachian Trail at Caleb's Peak, with fantastic views. If you're less able to hike, the easiest way to get a beautiful vista is to head 5 miles south out of town on US 7 to Kent Falls State Park, which is unmissable on your right. The falls are right before you and there are lots of easy trails into the forest.

the Kent section offers a mostly flat 5-mile river walk alongside the Housatonic, the longest river walk along the entire length of the trail. The trailhead is accessed on River Rd, off CT 341.

 THE DRIVE
The 15-mile drive from Kent to Housatonic Meadows State Park along US 7 is one of the most scenic drives in Connecticut. The single-lane road weaves between thick stands of forest, past Kent Falls State Park with its waterfall (visible from the road), and through West Cornwall's picturesque covered bridge, which spans the Housatonic.

03 HOUSATONIC MEADOWS STATE PARK
During the spring thaw, the churning waters of the Housatonic challenge kayakers and canoeists. By summer the scenic waterway transforms into a lazy, flat river, perfect for fly-fishing.

Photo Opportunity

Kent Falls set against a backdrop of autumnal colors.

In **Housatonic Meadows State Park** (ctparks.com), campers vie for a spot on the banks of the river while hikers take to the hills on the Appalachian Trail. **Housatonic River Outfitters** (dryflies.com) runs guided fishing trips with gourmet picnics.

Popular with artists and photographers, one of the most photographed fall scenes is the (West Cornwall), an antique covered bridge that stretches across the broad river, framed by vibrantly colored foliage.

On Labor Day weekend, in the nearby town of Goshen, you can visit the **Goshen Fair** (goshenfair.org) – one of Connecticut's best old-fashioned fairs, with ox-pulling and wood-cutting contests.

 THE DRIVE
Continue north along US 7 toward the Massachusetts border and Great Barrington, 27 miles away. After a few miles you leave the forested slopes of the park behind and enter expansive rolling countryside dotted with large, red-and-white barns. Look out for hand-painted signs advertising farm produce and consider stopping overnight in Falls Village, which has an excellent B&B.

 04 BERKSHIRES
Blanketing the westernmost part of Massachusetts, the mountains of the Berkshires turn crimson and gold as early as mid-September.

HEIDI BESEN/SHUTTERSTOCK ©

War Veterans Memorial Tower, Mt Greylock

Northern Berkshire Fall Foliage Parade

If your timing is right, you can stop in North Adams for the Northern Berkshire Fall Foliage Parade (1berkshire. com) – and festival – held in late September or early October. Held for over 60 years, the event follows a changing theme, but it always features music, food and fun – and, of course, foliage.

The effective capital of the Berkshires is **Great Barrington**, a formerly industrial town whose streets are now lined with art galleries and upscale restaurants. It's the perfect place to pack your picnic or rest your legs before or after a hike in nearby **Beartown State Forest** (mass.gov). Crisscrossing some 12,000 acres, hiking trails yield spectacular views of wooded hillsides and pretty Benedict Pond.

Further north, **October Mountain State Forest** (mass. gov) is the state's largest tract of green space (16,127 acres), also interwoven with hiking trails. The name – attributed to Herman Melville – gives a good indication of when this park is at its loveliest, with its multicolored tapestry of hemlocks, birches and oaks.

THE DRIVE
Drive north on US 7, the spine of the Berkshires, cruising 11 miles through Great Barrington and Stockbridge. In Lee, the highway merges with scenic US 20, from where you can access October Mountain. Continue 16 miles north through Lenox and Pittsfield to Lanesborough. Turn right on N Main St and follow the signs to the Mt Greylock State Reservation entrance.

05 MT GREYLOCK STATE RESERVATION

At 3491ft, Massachusetts' highest peak is perhaps not very high, but a climb up the 92ft **War Veterans Memorial Tower** rewards you with a panorama stretching up to 100 verdant miles, across the Taconic, Housatonic and Catskill ranges, and over five states. If the weather seems drab, driving to the summit may well lift you above the gray blanket, and the view with a layer of cloud floating between trees and sky is magical.

Mt Greylock State Reservation (mass.gov) has some 45 miles of hiking trails, including a portion of the Appalachian Trail. Frequent trail pull-offs on the road up – including some that lead to waterfalls – make it easy to get at least a little hike in before reaching the top of Mt Greylock.

THE DRIVE
Return to US 7 and continue north through the quintessential college town of Williamstown. Cross the Vermont border and continue north through the historic village of Bennington. Just north of Bennington, turn left on VT 7A and continue north to Manchester (51 miles total).

06 MANCHESTER

Stylish Manchester is known for its magnificent New England architecture. For fall foliage views, head south of the center and take the **Mt Equinox Skyline Drive** (equinox mountain.com) to the summit of 3848ft Mt Equinox, the highest mountain accessible by car in the Taconic Range. Wind up the 5.2 miles – with gasp-inducing scenery at every turn – seemingly to the top of the world, where the 360-degree panorama unfolds, offering views of the Adirondacks, the lush Battenkill Valley and Montréal's Mt Royal.

If early snow makes Mt Equinox inaccessible, visit 412-acre **Hildene** (hildene.org), a Georgian Revival mansion that was once home to the Lincoln family. It's filled with presidential memorabilia and sits at the edge of the Green Mountains, with access to 8 miles of walking trails.

THE DRIVE
Take VT 7 north, following the western slopes of the Green Mountains through Rutland and Middlebury to reach Burlington (100 miles) on the shores of Lake Champlain.

07 LAKE CHAMPLAIN

With a surface area of 490 sq miles straddling New York, Vermont and Quebec, Lake Champlain is the largest freshwater lake in the US after the Great Lakes. On its eastern side, **Burlington** is a gorgeous base for enjoying the lake. Explore it on foot, then scoot down to the wooden promenade, take a swing on the four-person rocking benches and consider a bike ride along the 7.5-mile lakeside bike path.

Imagine you are a painter. Or a hiker. Or a writer (oh, that's me). As the hills of New England turn from the color of old broccoli to an autumnal range of browns, yellows, oranges and reds, you can't help but be inspired: to paint, hike, write or just gawk at this wonder as it frames waterfalls, christens the hummocks and hills, and is brilliantly reflected in awaiting lakes.

For the best offshore foliage views, we love the *Friend Ship* sailboat at **Whistling Man Schooner Company** (whistling man.com), a 43ft sloop that accommodates just 17 passengers. Next door, **Echo Leahy Center for Lake Champlain** (echo vermont.org) explores the history and ecosystem of the lake, including a famous snapshot of Lake Champlain's mythical sea creature.

 THE DRIVE
Take I-89 S to Montpelier, savoring gorgeous views of Vermont's iconic Mt Mansfield and Camel's Hump, then continue northeast on US 2 to St Johnsbury, where you can pick up I-93 S across the New Hampshire line to Littleton. Take the eastbound US 302 exit and continue toward Crawford Notch State Park and Bretton Woods. The drive is 115 miles.

 08 BRETTON WOODS
Unbuckle your seat belts and step away from the car. You're not just peeping at leaves today – you're swooping past them on ziplines that drop 1000ft at 30mph. The four-season **Bretton Woods Canopy Tour** (brettonwoods.com) includes a hike through the woods, a stroll over sky bridges and a swoosh down 10 cables to tree platforms.

If this leaves you craving even higher views, cross US 302 and drive 6 miles on Base Rd to the coal-burning, steam-powered **Mt Washington Cog Railway** (thecog.com) at the western base of Mt Washington, the highest peak in New England. This historic railway has been hauling sightseers to the mountain's 6288ft summit since 1869.

 THE DRIVE
Cross through Crawford Notch and continue 20 miles southeast on US 302, a gorgeous route through the White Mountains that parallels the Saco River and the Conway Scenic Railroad. At the junction of NH 16 and US 302, continue 5 miles on US 302 into North Conway.

09 NORTH CONWAY
Many restaurants, pubs and inns in North Conway come with expansive views of the nearby mountains, making it an ideal place to wrap up a fall foliage road trip. Consider an excursion on the antique steam Valley Train with the **Conway Scenic Railroad** (conway scenic.com); it's a short but sweet round-trip ride through Mt Washington Valley from North Conway to Conway, 11 miles south, with the Moat Mountains and the Saco River as a scenic backdrop.

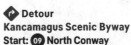 **Detour**
Kancamagus Scenic Byway
Start: 09 North Conway
Just south of North Conway, the 34.5-mile Kancamagus Scenic Byway, otherwise known as NH 112, passes through the White Mountains from Conway to Lincoln, NH. You'll drive alongside the Saco River and enjoy sweeping views of the Presidential Range from Kancamagus Pass. Inviting trailheads and pull-offs line the road. From Lincoln at the highway's western end, a short drive north on I-93 leads to **Franconia Notch State Park** (nhstateparks.org), where the foliage in September and October is simply spectacular.

03

Ivy League Tour

DURATION	DISTANCE	GREAT FOR
5 days	315 miles / 507km	History & families

BEST TIME TO GO	September to November

What's most surprising about a tour of the Ivy League? The distinct personalities of the different campuses, which are symbiotically fused with their surrounding landscapes. Compare fresh-faced Dartmouth, with its breezy embrace of New Hampshire's outdoors, to enclaved Yale, its Gothic buildings fortressed against the urban wilds of New Haven. But the schools all share one trait – vibrant, diverse and engaged students who dispel any notions that they're out-of-touch elites.

Link Your Trip

12 Connecticut Wine Trail

From New Haven, jump from grades to grapes by heading southwest along US 1.

21 Connecticut River Byway

From Hanover, drive south on NE 10 for riverside history.

 01

HANOVER, NEW HAMPSHIRE

When the first big snowfall hits **Dartmouth College** (dartmouth.edu), an email blasts across campus, calling everyone to the central **Green** for a midnight snowball fight. The Green is also the site of elaborate ice sculptures during Dartmouth's **Winter Carnival** (dartmouth.edu), a weeklong celebration that's been held annually for more than 100 years.

North of the Green is **Baker-Berry Library** (dartmouth.edu), which holds an impressive mural called the *Epic of American Civilization*. Painted by José

BEST FOR HISTORY

Learn about the USA's oldest university during a Harvard tour.

Baker-Berry Library, Dartmouth College

Clemente Orozco, it traces the course of civilization in the Americas from the Aztec era to modern times. At 4pm, stop by the adjacent **Sanborn Library**, where tea is served during the academic year for 10¢. This tradition honors a 19th-century English professor who invited students for chats and afternoon tea. For a free student-led **walking tour** (dartmouth.edu) of the campus, stop by the admissions office on the 2nd floor of McNutt Hall on the west side of the Green. Call or check online to confirm departure times.

The collection at Dartmouth's revamped **Hood Museum of Art** (hoodmuseum.dartmouth.edu) includes nearly 70,000 items. The collection is particularly strong in American pieces, including Native American art. One highlight is a set of Assyrian reliefs dating from the 9th century BCE.

From the museum, turn left onto E Wheelock St and walk toward the Hanover Inn. You'll soon cross the Appalachian Trail, which runs through downtown (from here, it's 431 miles to Mt Katahdin in Maine, the start/finish point for the trail).

THE DRIVE
From Hanover, follow NH 120 E to I-89 S. Take exit 117 to NH 4 E, following it to NH 4A. Turn right and follow NH 4A 3.5 miles to the museum.

02 ENFIELD SHAKER MUSEUM
The Enfield Shaker site sits in stark contrast to today's college campuses. In fact, the two couldn't be more different – except for the required communal housing with a bunch of nonrelatives. But a trip here is illuminating. Set in a valley overlooking Mascoma Lake, the Enfield Shaker site dates from the late 18th century. At its peak, some 300 members lived in Enfield. Farmers and craftspeople, they built impressive wood and brick

buildings and took in converts, orphans and children of the poor – essential for the Shaker future since sex was not allowed in the pacifist, rule-abiding community. By the early 1900s the community had gone into decline and the last family left in 1917.

The **museum** (shakermuseum. org) centers on the Great Stone Dwelling, the largest Shaker dwelling house ever built. You can also explore the gardens and grounds. The guide might even let you ring the rooftop bell. Spend the night on the 3rd and 4th floor of the building; **accommodations** feature traditional Shaker furniture, but not phones or TVs, although there is wi-fi.

🚗 **THE DRIVE**
Return to I-89 S. After 54 miles, take I-93 N 3 miles to exit 15E for I-393 E. From there, take exit 1 and follow the signs.

WHY THIS IS A CLASSIC TRIP

Amy Balfour, writer

America's most esteemed universities become less imposing as you explore their sprawling grounds. During the school year, the energy on the various campuses is downright invigorating, and you'll feel like a student yourself as you delve into each school's history and soak up the culture. The many quirky traditions prove that these smarty-pants students are just as weird as the rest of us.

---

03 CONCORD, NEW HAMPSHIRE

New Hampshire's capital is a trim and tidy city with a wide Main St dominated by the striking **State House** (gencourt.state. nh.us), a granite-hewed 19th-century edifice topped with a glittering dome.

Nearby, the New Hampshire schoolteacher Christa McAuliffe, chosen to be America's first teacher-astronaut, is honored at the **McAuliffe-Shepard Discovery Center** (starhop.com). She died in the *Challenger* explosion on January 28, 1986. The museum also honors New Hampshire native Alan B Shepard, a member of NASA's elite *Mercury* corps, who became America's first astronaut in 1961. Some exhibits feel a bit tired, but you can view a life-size replica of a NASA rocket and the *Mercury* capsule that transported Shepard to space. For hands-on adventure, you can try to land a *Discovery* space shuttle from inside a mock cockpit and learn about space travel to Mars and the power of the sun. There's also a planetarium.

🚗 **THE DRIVE**
Return to I-93 S, passing through Manchester before entering Massachusetts. Follow I-495 S toward Lowell.

---

04 LOWELL

In the early 19th century, textile mills in Lowell churned out cloth by the mile, driven by the abundant waterpower of Pawtucket Falls. Today, the historic buildings in the city center – connected by the trolley and canal boats – comprise the Lowell National Historic Park, which gives a fascinating peek at the workings of a 19th-century industrial town. Stop first at the

---

Market Mills Visitors Center (nps.gov/lowe) to pick up a map and check out the general exhibits. Five blocks northeast along the river, the **Boott Cotton Mills Museum** (nps.gov/lowe) has exhibits that chronicle the rise and fall of the industrial revolution in Lowell, including technological changes, labor movements and immigration. The highlight is a working weave room, with 88 power looms. A special exhibit on **Mill Girls & Immigrants** examines the lives of working people, while seasonal exhibits are sometimes on display in other historic buildings around town.

🚗 **THE DRIVE**
Take the Lowell Connector to US 3 heading south. In Billerica, exit to Concord Rd. Continue south on Concord Rd (MA 62) through Bedford. This road becomes Monument St and terminates at Monument Sq in Concord center. Walden Pond is about 3 miles south of Monument Sq, along Walden St (MA 126) south of MA 2.

---

05 CONCORD, MASSACHUSETTS

Tall, white church steeples rise above ancient oaks in Colonial Concord, giving the town a stateliness that belies the American Revolution drama that occurred centuries ago. It is easy to see how so many writers found their inspiration here in the 1800s.

Ralph Waldo Emerson was the paterfamilias of literary Concord and the founder of the transcendentalist movement (and, incidentally, a graduate of Harvard College).

His home of nearly 50 years, the **Ralph Waldo Emerson Memorial House**

(ralphwaldoemersonhouse.org), often hosted his renowned circle of friends.

One of them was Henry David Thoreau (another Harvard grad), who put transcendentalist beliefs into practice when he spent two years in a rustic cabin on the shores of **Walden Pond** (mass. gov/dcr). The glacial pond is now a state park, surrounded by acres of forest. A footpath circles the pond, leading to the site of Thoreau's cabin on the northeast side.

THE DRIVE
Take MA 2 east to its terminus in Cambridge. Go left on the Alewife Brook Pkwy (MA 16), then right on Massachusetts Ave and into Harvard Sq. Parking spaces are in short supply, but you can usually find one on the streets around the Cambridge Common.

06 CAMBRIDGE
Founded in 1636 to educate men for the ministry, Harvard is America's oldest **college** (harvard.edu). The geographic heart of the university – where redbrick buildings and leaf-covered paths exude academia – is **Harvard Yard**. For maximum visual impact, enter the yard through the wrought-iron Johnston Gate, which is flanked by the two oldest buildings on campus, **Harvard Hall** and **Massachusetts Hall**.

The focal point of the yard is the **John Harvard statue**, by Daniel Chester French. Inscribed 'John Harvard, Founder of Harvard College, 1638,' it is commonly known as the 'statue of three lies': John Harvard was not the college's founder but its first benefactor; Harvard was actually founded in 1636; and the man depicted isn't even Mr Harvard himself! This symbol hardly lives up to the university's motto, *Veritas* (truth).

Most Harvard hopefuls rub the statue's shiny foot for good luck; little do they know that campus pranksters regularly use the foot like dogs use a fire hydrant.

The revamped **Smith Campus Center** (commonspaces.harvard. edu/smith-campus-center/about) across from the yard is also worth a look. Hosting lectures, movies and several cafes, it's sure to be a campus hub. It's also home to 12,000 plants!

Overflowing with coffeehouses and pubs, bookstores and record

All About Haaahhhvaaahhhd
Want to know more? Get the inside scoop from savvy students on the unofficial Hahvahd Tour (harvardtour.com).

Johnston Gate, Harvard

stores, street musicians and sidewalk artists, panhandlers and professors, nearby **Harvard Square** exudes energy, creativity and nonconformity – and it's all packed into a handful of streets between the university and the river. Spend an afternoon browsing bookstores, riffling through records and trying on vintage clothing, then camp out in a local cafe.

 THE DRIVE
Hop on Memorial Dr and drive east along the Charles River. At Western Ave, cross the river and follow the signs to I-90 E (toll road). Cruise through the tunnel (product of the notorious Big Dig) and merge with I-93 S. Follow I-93 S to I-95 S. Take I-95 S to Providence.

07 PROVIDENCE
College Hill rises east of the Providence River, and atop it sits **Brown University** (brown.edu), the rambunctious younger child of an uptight New England household. Big brothers Harvard and Yale carefully manicure their public image, while the little black sheep of the family prides itself on staunch liberalism. Founded in 1764, Brown was the first American college to accept students regardless of religious affiliation, and the first to appoint an African American woman, Ruth Simmons, as

Photo Opportunity

Stand beside the statue of John Harvard, the man who didn't found Harvard.

president in 2001. Of its small 700-strong faculty, five Brown professors and two alumni have been honored as Nobel laureates.

The campus, consisting of 235 buildings, is divided into the Main Green and Lincoln Field. Enter through the wrought-iron **Van Wickle Gates** on College St. The oldest building on the campus is **University Hall**, a 1770 brick edifice that was used as a barracks during the Revolutionary War. Free tours of the campus begin from the **Brown University Admissions Office** (brown. edu/about/visit).

 THE DRIVE
Take Memorial Blvd out of Providence and merge with I-95 S. The generally pleasant tree-lined interstate will take you around the periphery of Groton, Old Lyme, Guilford and Madison, where you may want to stop for a coffee or snack. Exit at junction 47 for downtown New Haven.

08 NEW HAVEN
Gorgeous, Gothic Yale University is America's third-oldest college. Head to the **Yale University Visitor Center** (visitorcenter.yale.edu) to pick up a free map or take a free one-hour tour.

The tour does a good job of fusing historical and academic facts and passes by several standout monuments, including Yale's tallest building, **Harkness Tower**. Guides refrain, however, from mentioning the tombs scattered around the campus. No, these aren't filled with corpses: they're secret hang-outs for senior students. The most notorious **Tomb** (64 High St) is the HQ for the Skull & Bones Club, founded in 1832. Its list of members reads like a who's who of high-powered politicos and financiers over the last two centuries.

New Haven's spacious **Green** has been the spiritual center of the city since its Puritan fathers designed it in 1638 as the prospective site for Christ's second coming. Since then it has held the municipal burial grounds – graves were later moved to Grove St Cemetery – several statehouses and an array of churches, three of which still stand. A short walk along the Green also passes numerous spots for appreciating art and architecture.

Left: Brown University

BOXIC BOJAN/SHUTTERSTOCK ©

Nantucket (p43)

Massachusetts

Explore
Massachusetts

City streets and cow-dotted pastures, windswept beaches and forest-covered mountains: Massachusetts offers an incredible diversity of landscapes. The state is small, but the scenery is anything but.

When you're ready for a pit stop, the Commonwealth has you covered, with a tantalizing spread of local specialties, such as fruit and vegetables straight from the farm and succulent seafood fresh from the ocean. So fuel up, because you have a lot to do. Massachusetts trips show off four centuries of dramatic history, rich displays of artistry and creativity, and thrilling opportunities for outdoor adventure. Buckle up and enjoy the ride.

Boston

Boston's got it all: it's the capital of the state, the largest of its cities and has the area's largest airport, Logan International. While Boston and its suburbs are congested and the drivers are often rude (they don't call them 'Massholes' for nothing), 'the City' offers the best bookend for your New England drives, and you'll be able to find, rent or buy whatever you're looking for. If you're on a budget, consider staying at a hotel on the outskirts of town, as in-city prices are astronomical.

Hyannis

Whether you're driving, flying or taking the bus to Cape Cod, chances are you'll spend at least a little time in Hyannis, the Cape's largest town. It's got all the pluses and minuses that come with that: it's not as quaint as elsewhere, but it has the largest selection of hotels, restaurants, bars and nightlife, and there are malls and Main St if you need to stock up on goods or souvenirs before you hit the road.

Plymouth

One of America's oldest towns, Plymouth is a delightful mix of quaint and modern, with fried seafood shacks butting up against Asian fusion spots and boutique hotels neighboring places that look like they've been in business since the Pilgrims landed. There are nearby museums, lots of restaurants to choose from and, while it's off-Cape, you could easily use Plymouth as an overnight

WHEN TO GO

Drivers will enjoy just about any time of year in Massachusetts, though the winter can be dreary if there's no snow on the ground, while the ice means it's imperative to drive with caution.

Fall is hands down the best season, but you'll be here with crowds galore. Summers are nice, but humid and hot. Spring is also spectacular.

stopover while combining Cape drives with those in the rest of the state.

Great Barrington

Nestled between mountains in the western part of the state, Great Barrington is a beautiful hub town for folks wanting to drive around the Appalachians, or those hoping to combine some of the Massachusetts trips with others in New York, Connecticut or Vermont. You'll find a decent variety of B&Bs, a few hotels and motels, and a surprising selection of restaurants to choose from. If you're here in the fall, plan well in advance as the town will be packed with leaf peepers.

Greenfield

At the confluence of the Deerfield and Connecticut Rivers near the New Hampshire border, Greenfield is an old mill town that's gotten a new lease on life thanks to tourism and the revitalization of its warehouses and riverside. Poet's Seat Tower, a brick structure perched on a hill that overlooks the river and town below, is a popular viewpoint, and there are plenty of B&Bs, hotels and motels to choose from.

TRANSPORTATION

If you're flying in, chances are you'll arrive at Boston's Logan International Airport. From there you could hop a puddle jumper to Cape Cod's Gateway Airport or Springfield, MA, if you're headed further west. Renting a vehicle at the airport is the most convenient, though prices may be cheaper if you pick it up in town.

 WHAT'S ON

Boston Book Fair

A mega book fair attracting readers, writers and publishers from all over the world.

Wellfleet Oysterfest

Wellfleet is a September festival honoring the world's greatest oysters. Eat your fill, try your hand in the shucking contest and pair them with a local brew!

The Figawi

This regatta is held in Nantucket Sound every spring. Urban legend says the name comes from the sailor's expression, 'Where the fig are we?'

 WHERE TO STAY

The state has numerous campgrounds, rest areas, roadside motels and hotels, as well as fancier spots and cozy B&Bs. Book well in advance during the fall season (mid-September through October), when the roads flood with travelers. The cheapest time to book is winter. Spring is pretty, but if you're camping you'll want to consider bugs and mud. Camping in the winter is not advisable, as many campgrounds close after October and don't reopen until May or so. Note that camping on the side of the road is prohibited in Massachusetts.

Resources

Cape Cod Times (*capecodtimes.com*) The local newspaper, with news, movie listings and events around the Cape and islands.

Boston Magazine (*bostonmagazine.com*) Lists events, music venues and shows, theatre performances and articles covering the Boston scene.

04

MASSACHUSETTS

Cape Cod & the Islands

BEST FOR FOOD & DRINK

Slurp oysters and devour classic pastries in Wellfleet.

DURATION	DISTANCE	GREAT FOR
5–7 days	128 miles / 206km	Families & nature

BEST TIME TO GO	Enjoy fine weather but avoid the crowds in May, June or September.

Hydrangea, Heritage Museums & Gardens

As the sun sets and the sky darkens, you slide your car into place alongside dozens of others facing the massive screen. Roll down the window, feel the salty breeze and recline your seat. After an exhilarating day at the beach, it's time to sit back and enjoy a double feature at the drive-in. Sound like something out of a 1950s fantasy? It's summer on Cape Cod.

Link Your Trip

01 Coastal New England

From Hyannis, take I-195 to New Bedford to intersect with this trip through maritime New England.

09 Rhode Island: East Bay

A longer trip on I-195 will zip you to Providence to take in the pleasures of picturesque Rhode Island.

01 SANDWICH

Cape Cod's oldest town (founded in 1637) makes a perfect first impression as you cross over the canal from the mainland. In the village center, white-steepled churches, period homes and a working grist mill surround a picturesque swan pond.

Fun for kids and adults alike, the nearby 100-acre **Heritage Museums & Gardens** (heritage museumsandgardens.org) sports a vintage-automobile collection, an authentic 1908 carousel and unusual folk-art collections. Too tame? Within the complex, an adventure park houses ziplines, rope bridges and aerial trails.

WHY THIS IS A CLASSIC TRIP

Isabel Albiston, Writer

Coastlines like Cape Cod are worth taking time over, stopping on a whim when a beach is just too beautiful to drive past. Jump out of the car to hike a trail or splash in the sea when the sun comes out. Snap photos that could never capture the screeching seagulls, crashing waves, and gasps of salty air inhaled between mouthfuls of seafood.

Before leaving town, take a stroll across the **Sandwich Boardwalk** (parking is $15 in summer), which extends 1350 scenic feet across an expansive marsh to **Town Neck Beach**. From MA 6A, head north onto Jarves St, go left at Factory St and right onto Boardwalk Rd.

THE DRIVE
Heading east on MA 6A, also known as Old King's Hwy, wind your way past cranberry bogs, wetlands and Shaker-shingle cottages. In Barnstable, take a right on MA 132 and head to the more commercial southern side of the Cape. For a faster but less scenic version of this trip, take the Mid-Cape Hwy (US 6) instead of 6A.

02 HYANNIS
Most people traveling through Hyannis are here to catch a ferry to Nantucket or Martha's Vineyard (just like you). Fortunately, the village port has a few sights to keep you entertained while you wait for your boat – or even longer.

Take a walk through the **HyArts District** (hyartsdistrict. com), which includes the **Guyer Barn** (artsbarnstable.com) community art space and neighboring studios, the colorful artist shanties near the ferry docks, and the art-strewn **Walkway to the Sea**.

Politics aficionados will know that Hyannis has been the summer home of the Kennedy clan for generations. Back in the day, JFK spent his summers here – times that are beautifully documented with photographs and video at the **John F Kennedy Hyannis Museum** (jfkhyannismuseum. org). There's also a JFK Memorial at the family-friendly **Veterans Beach**, about a half-mile south of the Hy-Line Cruise dock.

THE DRIVE
Leave your car in Hyannis and take a one-hour catamaran trip or a cheaper two-hour ferry trip to Nantucket. Don't miss the picturesque Brant Point Lighthouse as the ferry pulls into Nantucket harbor.

03 NANTUCKET
Nantucket is New England at its most rose-covered, cobblestoned, picture-postcard perfect. The island's main population center, Nantucket Town, was once home port to the world's largest whaling fleet. Now a National Historic

Landmark, the town boasts leafy streets lined with gracious period homes and public buildings. For the finest stroll, walk up cobbled **Main Street**, just past the Pacific National Bank (c 1818), where the grandest whaling-era mansions are lined up in a row.

While strolling the streets, pay a visit to the excellent **Nantucket Whaling Museum** (nha.org), which occupies a former spermaceti (whale oil) candle factory. The evocative exhibits relive Nantucket's 19th-century heyday as the whaling center of the world.

Close to town, there's a pair of family-friendly beaches to cool off at. For wilder, less-frequented strands, you'll need to cycle or hop on a bus to **Surfside** or **Nobadeer Beach**, 3 to 4 miles south of town.

🚗 THE DRIVE

Ferry back to Hyannis Port to pick up your car. From South St, turn north on Lewis Bay Rd/Camp St, and then turn right on Yarmouth Rd. Continue north for 3 miles, then turn right on MA 6A and continue into Yarmouth Port.

↱ Detour

Martha's Vineyard
Start: **02** Hyannis or **03** Nantucket
Your island destination is Oak Bluffs, the Vineyard's mecca for summer fun. Originally a retreat for a revivalist church group, it's now a retreat for beach-bound, ice-cream-eating party people.

In the mid-19th century, the members of the Methodist Camp Meeting Association (CMA) enjoyed a day at the beach as much as a good gospel service. They first camped out in tents, then built some 300 wooden cottages, each adorned with whimsical filigree trim. From bustling Circuit Ave, slip down the alley to discover the

Campgrounds, a world of gingerbread houses adorned with Candyland colors. For a peek inside one, visit the **Cottage Museum** (mvcma.org), which contains exhibits on CMA history. The brightly painted cottages surround emerald-green **Trinity Park** and its open-air **Tabernacle** (1879), where the lucky descendants of the campers still gather for community singalongs and concerts.

Further north on Circuit Ave, you can take a nostalgic ride on the **Flying Horses Carousel** (mvpreservation. org), a National Historic Landmark that has been captivating kids of all ages since 1876. It's the country's oldest continuously operating merry-go-round, where the antique horses have manes of real horse hair.

Beginning just south of the Steamship Authority's ferry terminal, a narrow strip of sandy **beach** runs unbroken for several miles. There is also a scenic **bike trail** (with plenty of places to rent) connecting Oak Bluffs with other parts of the Vineyard.

From Hyannis, **Hy-Line Cruises** (hylinecruises.com) operates a high-speed passenger ferry to Oak Bluffs several times daily from May to October. It also has a ferry link between Nantucket and Oak Bluffs.

04 YARMOUTH PORT

Nearly 50 historic sea captains' homes are lined up along MA 6A in Yarmouth Port, in a stretch known as **Captains' Mile**. Most of them are private homes; however, the Historical Society of Old Yarmouth maintains the 1840 **Captain Bangs Hallett House** (hsoy.org). For more historic sites in Yarmouth Port, pick up the free self-guided *Captains' Mile* walking-tour booklet or download a PDF online (yarmouthcapecod. com/captains-mile-walking-tour).

Alternatively, stroll or walk 1 mile up Center St to **Gray's Beach**, also known as Bass Hole. A terrific quarter-mile-long boardwalk extends over a tidal marsh and creek, offering a unique vantage point for viewing all sorts of sea life.

🚗 THE DRIVE

Continue east on MA 6A through the classy village of Dennis and on to Brewster. This section of road (between Barnstable and Brewster) is lined with old homes that have been converted into antique shops. Take the time to stop and browse, and come home with treasures ranging from nautical kitsch to art-deco cool.

05 BREWSTER

Brewster's best-known landmark is the **Brewster Store** (brewsterstore.com), an old-fashioned country store that has been in operation since 1866. Penny candy is still sold alongside the local newspaper. Upstairs, you'll discover a stash of museum-quality memorabilia as old as the building.

When the tide goes out on Cape Cod Bay, the bayside beach becomes a giant sandbar, offering opportunities to commune with crabs, clams and gulls, and to take in brilliant sunsets. Best access to the tidal flats is via the **Point of Rocks** or **Ellis Landing Beaches** (parking is $20 in summer). Pick up a parking sticker and check the tide charts at the town hall.

🚗 THE DRIVE

Head east on MA 6A out of Brewster, then hop on US 6, lined with roadside motels and clam shacks. It's a quick trip through Orleans and Eastham to your next destination.

Right: Nantucket Whaling Museum

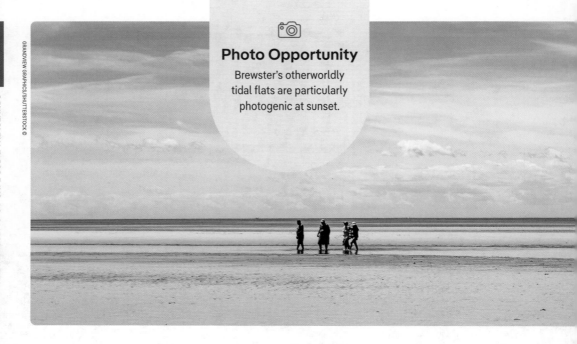

GRANDVIEW GRAPHICS/SHUTTERSTOCK ©

📷

Photo Opportunity

Brewster's otherworldly tidal flats are particularly photogenic at sunset.

06 CAPE COD NATIONAL SEASHORE

Extending some 40 miles around the curve of the Outer Cape, the Cape Cod National Seashore is a treasure trove of unspoiled beaches, dunes, salt marshes, nature trails and forests. Start your explorations at the **Salt Pond Visitor Center** (nps.gov/caco), which offers a wonderful view of the namesake salt pond. Numerous walking and cycling trails begin right at the visitor center; this is also the place to purchase a parking permit if you intend to spend time at any of the National Seashore beaches.

After this brief introduction, take Nauset Rd and Doane Rd to the picturesque **Coast Guard Beach** for swimming and body-surfing. Afterward, drive along the aptly named Ocean View Dr to **Nauset Light** (nausetlight. org), which has been shining on the Cape since 1877 (and gracing the packets of Cape Cod potato chips for over 30 years).

THE DRIVE

Take Nauset Rd back to the Mid-Cape Hwy and continue north to Main St in Wellfleet. For a scenic detour, turn right off the highway onto Le Count Hollow Rd, then left on Ocean View Dr. From here, Long Pond Rd will cross the highway and deposit you on Main St in Wellfleet center.

07 WELLFLEET

Wellfleet is one of Cape Cod's unsung gems, offering some unspoiled beaches, a charming historic center and plenty of opportunities to slurp glorious oysters.

By day, browse the galleries that are sprinkled around town. (The Wellfleet Art Galleries Association map has descriptive listings.) Or spy on the birdlife at Mass Audubon's 1100-acre **Well-fleet Bay Wildlife Sanctuary** (massau dubon.org), where trails cross tidal creeks, salt marshes and sandy beaches.

At night, park your car at the 1950s-era **Wellfleet Drive-In** (wellfleetcinemas.com), where everything except the feature flick is true to the era. Grab a bite to eat at the old-fashioned snack bar, hook the mono speaker over the car window and settle in for a double feature.

For a more raucous night, head to **Cahoon Hallow Beach**, where the Cape's coolest summertime hang-out is housed in the former lifeguard station, now

Tidal flats (p44), Brewster

known as the **Beachcomber** (thebeachcomber.com).

THE DRIVE
US 6 continues north through Truro, passing Truro Vineyards and Pilgrim Heights. On the right, the picturesque East Harbor is backed by pristine parabolic dunes; on the left, wind-blown beach shacks front Provincetown Harbor. Alternatively, take the slower-going Shore Rd (MA 6A), which branches off in North Truro and eventually becomes Commercial St in Provincetown.

08 PROVINCETOWN
Provincetown is far out. We're not just talking geographically (though it does occupy the outermost point on Cape Cod); we're also talking about the flamboyant street scenes, brilliant art galleries and unbridled nightlife. Once an outpost for fringe writers and artists, Provincetown has morphed into the hottest gay and lesbian destination in the Northeast. Even if you're only in town for a day, you'll want to spend part of it admiring the art and watching the local life as you stroll along Commercial St.

Provincetown is also the perfect launching point for whale-watching, since it's the closest port to **Stellwagen Bank National Marine Sanctuary**, the summer feeding ground for humpback whales. **Dolphin Fleet Whale Watch** (whale-watch.com) offers up to 10 tours daily, each lasting three to four hours.

LGBTIQ+ Provincetown

While other cities have their gay districts, in Provincetown the entire town is the gay district.

A-House
ahouse.com
P-town's gay scene got its start here and it's still the leading bar in town.

Boatslip Beach Club
boatslipresort.com
Hosts wildly popular tea dances each afternoon.

Crown & Anchor
onlyatthecrown.com
A popular complex that attracts lesbians and gay men. Hosts lots of shows and events.

05

MASSACHUSETTS

Pilgrim Trail

DURATION	DISTANCE	GREAT FOR
4–5 days	147 miles / 237km	Families & history

BEST TIME TO GO	Most sites are open from April to November.

Pilgrim Monument, Provincetown

Your car is a time machine, transporting you back 400 years. The region's living museums allow you to experience firsthand what life was like for the colonists as they settled in the New World. Explore the sites and structures – churches and trading posts, homesteads and grist mills – that are still standing from those early days.

Link Your Trip

01 Coastal New England

See more of maritime Massachusetts and Connecticut.

25 Maritime Maine

For a round of lighthouse photos and lobster feasts, take I-95 to Kittery.

01 PROVINCETOWN

Most people don't know that months before the 'official' landing on Plymouth Rock, the Pilgrims arrived at the tip of Cape Cod. Despite the protected harbor and good fishing, they were unable to find a reliable source of fresh water, so they headed off to Plymouth. But not before signing the Mayflower Compact, which is considered the first governing document of the Plymouth Colony. The **Pilgrim Monument** (pilgrim-monument.org) commemorates the signing of the compact, as do a few exhibits at the on-site **Provincetown Museum**. Climb 252ft

THE DRIVE

Hop on US 6 heading west over the Sagamore Bridge. Stay on MA 3 or branch off to MA 3A, which hugs the coast for the 14 miles north to Plymouth.

Detour

Bourne

Start: 02 **Sandwich**

Bourne is not as picturesque as nearby Sandwich, but it is historically significant, thanks to its strategic location at the northeastern corner of Buzzards Bay, halfway between the Manomet and Scusset Rivers. Here, in 1627, the Pilgrims founded the Aptucxet Trading Post, which allowed easy access to the Dutch settlements to the south. The trading center would eventually lead to the construction of the Cape Cod Canal, which was built so traders could avoid the Cape's hazardous eastern shore.

Nowadays, the **Aptucxet Trading Post Museum** (bournehistorical society.org) is an eclectic little museum, built on what is believed to be the oldest remains of a Pilgrim building ever found. Although the simple, unpainted clapboard structure standing today is a replica built on the original foundation, it's still possible to imagine Pilgrims, Wampanoag and Dutch people coming here to barter goods, seeds, tools and food.

To reach the Aptucxet Trading Post, take MA 6A out of Sandwich and continue on Sandwich Rd for 7 miles along the Cape Cod Canal. Once in Bourne, turn right on Perry Rd and take the first left on Aptucxet Rd.

03 PLYMOUTH

Plymouth is 'America's Home Town,' where the Pilgrims first settled in the

---

(116 steps) to the top of the tall tower for magnificent views of Provincetown Harbor and the National Seashore.

In addition to its historic interest, Provincetown is a cauldron of contemporary creativity, which you can see for yourself on a walk along artsy Commercial St.

THE DRIVE

Head out of Provincetown on US 6, passing picturesque East Harbor and windblown beach shacks. You'll also pass Pilgrim Heights, where the settlers found fresh water, and First Encounter Beach, site of the first violent clash with the native population. From Orleans, continue west on US 6 or take slower, more scenic MA 6A,

which shows off the Cape's historic villages.

02 SANDWICH

With the waterwheel at the old mill, the white clapboard houses and the swans on the pond, the center of Sandwich is as pretty as a Cape Cod town can be. The restored 17th-century **Dexter Grist Mill** on the edge of Shawme Pond has centuries-old gears that still grind cornmeal. Nearby, **Hoxie House** is the oldest house on Cape Cod. The 1640 salt box–style structure has been faithfully restored, complete with antiques and brick hearth, giving a good sense of early-settler home life.

winter of 1620. An innocuous, weathered ball of granite – the famous **Plymouth Rock** – marks the spot where they (might have) stepped ashore in this foreign land, while **Mayflower II** (plimoth.org/what-see-do/mayflower-ii) is a replica of the small ship in which they made the fateful voyage. Many museums and historic sites in the surrounding streets recall the Pilgrims' struggles, sacrifices and triumphs.

The best is **Plimoth Patuxet Museums** (plimoth.org), a historically accurate re-creation of the Pilgrims' settlement. Everything in the 1627 English Village – costumes, implements,

Photo Opportunity

The Dexter Grist Mill in Sandwich is a beautiful spot.

vocabulary, artistry, recipes and crops – has been painstakingly researched and remade. Costumed interpreters, acting in character, explain the details of daily life and answer your questions as you watch them work and play. The on-site **Wampanoag Homesite** replicates the life of a Native American com-

munity in the same area during that time. Unlike the English Village, the homesite is staffed by indigenous people speaking from a modern perspective.

THE DRIVE
Take MA 3 north for about 25 miles. In Quincy, take the Burgin Pkwy 2 miles north into the center.

04 QUINCY
Quincy was first settled in 1625 by a handful of raucous colonists who could not stand the strict and stoic ways in Plymouth. History has it that this group went so far as to drink beer, dance around a maypole and engage in other festive Old English customs, which enraged

Adams National Historic Park, Quincy

the Pilgrims down the road. Nathaniel Hawthorne immortalized this history in his fictional account, *'The Maypole of Merrimount'*. Eventually, Myles Standish arrived from Plymouth to restore order to the wayward colony.

What earns this town the nickname 'The City of Presidents' is that it is the birthplace of John Adams and John Quincy Adams. The collection of houses where the Adams family lived now composes the **Adams National Historic Park** (nps.gov/adam). Besides the homes, you can also see where the presidents and their wives are interred in the crypt of the **United First Parish Church** (ufpc.org).

THE DRIVE
Take Newport Ave north out of town and merge onto I-93 heading north. Continue on the Central Artery straight through (and under) Boston, experiencing firsthand the benefits of the infamous Big Dig. Take exit 26 onto Storrow Dr for downtown Boston.

05 BOSTON
Ten years after the Pilgrims settled in Plymouth, they were followed by a group of Puritans – also fleeing the repressive Church of England – who founded the Massachusetts Bay Colony about 40 miles up the coast. The Puritans' first seat of government was on the north shore of the Charles River, where excavations have uncovered the foundations of Governor John Winthrop's home, known as the **Great House**. Winthrop is buried alongside other early settlers in the **King's Chapel Burying Ground** (kings-chapel.org).

Not too many physical structures remain from these earliest days of Boston's settlement. The city's oldest dwelling (1680) is **Paul Revere House** (paulreverehouse.org) where the celebrated patriot lived. The oldest church (1723) is **Old North Church**, where two lanterns were hung on the eve of the American Revolution. To see these and other sites from Boston's revolutionary history, follow the **Freedom Trail** (thefreedomtrail.org), which connects the most prominent historic landmarks. For a contemporary perspective, stroll around the city's green spaces and shopping places.

THE DRIVE
As you exit Boston to the north, take US 93 to US 95/MA 128. At the fork, stay on MA 128. Take exit 25A to MA 114, and follow the signs to Salem center. Alternatively, for a scenic seaside route, take MA 1A all the way up the coast through Swampscott and Marblehead.

06 SALEM
Founded by English fisherfolk in 1626, Salem was part of the Massachusetts Bay Colony. **Salem Pioneer Village** (pioneervillagesalem.org) is an outdoor, interactive museum that gives visitors an idea of what daily life was like for settlers.

Salem is most famous – or infamous – as the site of the witch trials in 1692, when 19 people were hanged as a result of witch-hunt hysteria. Don't miss the **Witch Trials Memorial**, a simple but dramatic monument that honors the innocent victims. To understand more about how this hysteria snowballed, visit the **Witch House** (thewitchhouse.org). This was the home of Jonathan Corwin, a local magistrate who investigated witchcraft claims.

The town has dozens of other related sites, as well as a month-long Halloween extravaganza in October. But there's a lot more to Salem than bed knobs and broomsticks. Take a walk and discover the town's many historical charms.

06

MASSACHUSETTS

Around Cape Ann

BEST FOR OUTDOORS

Parker River Wildlife Refuge offers excellent hiking, swimming, kayaking and canoeing.

DURATION	DISTANCE	GREAT FOR
2–3 days	54 miles / 87km	Families, nature, food & wine

BEST TIME TO GO	The water is warmest from July to September.

Monarch butterfly, Parker River Wildlife Refuge

Somebody – a New Englander, no doubt – once said that 'the humble clam...reaches its quintessence when coated and fried.' The big-bellied bivalve – lightly battered and deeply fried – supposedly originated in Essex, Massachusetts, so Cape Ann is an ideal place to sample the specialty. This North Shore route takes you from clam shack to clam shack, with breaks for beachcombing, bird-watching, gallery hopping and plenty of picture taking.

Link Your Trip

01 Coastal New England

Continue south from Gloucester and follow the coastline all the way through Connecticut.

25 Maritime Maine

From Newburyport, drive 26 miles north on I-95 to Kittery to experience the coastal culture of Maine.

01 **NEWBURYPORT**
Situated at the mouth of the Merrimack River, the town of Newburyport prospered as a shipping port and silversmith center during the late 18th century. Not too much has changed in the last 200 years, as Newburyport's brick buildings and graceful churches still show off the Federal style that was popular back then.

Today the center of town is a model of historic preservation and gentrification. Admire the public art as you take a stroll along the **Matthews**

plant and animal reside in its many ecological habitats, which include beaches, sand dunes, salt pans, salt marshes, freshwater impoundments and maritime forests. Several miles of foot trails allow access to the inland area, with observation towers and platforms punctuating the trails at prime bird-watching spots. Stop at the **visitor center** (fws.gov/refuge/parker_river) for information and exhibits about the refuge.

 THE DRIVE
Depart the island on the Plum Island Turnpike. After 2 miles, turn left on Ocean Ave, then left on High Rd (MA 1A). Continue south through picturesque farmland, stopping at farm stands along the way. Go through the tiny town of Newbury and picturesque Rowley, with the famous Sunday-morning Todd Farm Flea Market. Continue south into Ipswich.

03 **IPSWICH**
Ipswich is one of those New England towns that are pretty today because they were poor in the past. It had no harbor and no source of water-power for factories, so commercial and industrial development went elsewhere. As a result, Ipswich's 17th-century houses were not torn down to build grander residences. Nowadays, there are 58 existent First Period homes, including the 1677 **Whipple House** (ipswichmuseum.org), which is open to the public. For more historic homes, pick up a map from the **Ipswich Museum** (ipswichmuseum.org).

 THE DRIVE
Head out of town on S Main St (MA 133) and turn left on Argilla Rd. Drive for about 4 miles through

---

Memorial Boardwalk, which runs along the Merrimack and ends at the granite **Custom House Maritime Museum** (customhousemaritime museum. org). From here, you can browse in the boutiques along State St or admire the art galleries on Water St.

 THE DRIVE
Go east on Water St, which follows the coastline out of town. It becomes the Plum Island Turnpike before passing the eponymous airport and the Parker River Visitor Center. Cross the river onto Plum Island and turn right on Sunset Dr to reach the wildlife refuge.

02 **PLUM ISLAND**
A barrier island off the coast of Massachusetts, Plum Island has 9 miles of wide, sandy beaches surrounded by acres of wildlife sanctuary. These are among the most pristine beaches on the North Shore, especially if you head to the furthest points on the island. **Sandy Point** (mass.gov/dcr), on the southern tip, is a state park that's popular for swimming, sunning and tide pooling.

Parker River Wildlife Refuge (fws.gov/refuge/parker_river) is the 4662-acre sanctuary that occupies the southern three-quarters of Plum Island. More than 800 species of bird,

NAYADARA/SHUTTERSTOCK ©

Rockport Harbor

beautiful woods and marshland. The entrance to the Great House is on the left, while the beach is straight ahead.

04 CRANE ESTATE
One of the longest, widest, sandiest beaches in the region is **Crane Beach** (thetrustees.org), which has 4 miles of fine-sand barrier beach on Ipswich Bay. The beach is set in the midst of the Crane Wildlife Refuge, so the entire surrounding area is wildly beautiful. Five miles of trails traverse the dunes.

Above the beach, on Castle Hill, sits the 1920s **estate** (thetrustees.org) of Chicago plumbing-fixture magnate Richard T Crane. The 59-room Stuart-style Great House is sometimes open for tours. The lovely landscaped grounds, which are open daily, contain several miles of walking trails.

THE DRIVE
Depart by way of Argilla Rd, but turn left on Northgate Rd, which will take you back to MA 133. Turn left and continue 2.6 miles east into Essex.

05 ESSEX
The meandering Essex River shares its name with this tiny town, home to some 3500 souls. The town's proud maritime history is on dis-play at the **Essex Shipbuilding Museum** (essexshipbuilding. org). Most of the collection of photos, tools and ship models came from local basements and attics, allowing Essex to truly preserve its history. The collection is housed in the town's 1835 schoolhouse (check out the **Old Burying Ground** behind it). The historical society also operates a museum shipyard, a section of waterfront property where shipbuilding activities have taken place for hundreds of years.

Despite centuries of maritime history, nowadays the town is more famous for its ample antique shops and succulent clams. With plenty of picnic tables overlooking the namesake estuary, there is no better lunch stop.

THE DRIVE
Continue east on MA 133, then merge onto MA 128 heading north. At the traffic circle, take the third exit to Washington St (MA 127), which circles Cape Ann. Heading up the cape's western side, the winding road follows the Annisquam River, with a long bridge over the inlet at Goose Cove. Rounding the tip of the cape, you'll pass through tiny Lanesville and Pigeon Cove before arriving in Rockport.

06 **ROCKPORT**
Rockport is named for its 19th-century role as a shipping center for granite cut from local quarries. The stone is still ubiquitous: monuments, building foundations, pavements and piers remain as a testament to Rockport's past.

That's about all that's left of this industrial history, however. A century ago, Winslow Homer, Childe Hassam, Fitz Henry Lane and other acclaimed artists arrived, inspired by the hearty fisherfolk who wrested a hard-won but satisfying living from the sea. Today Rockport's main revenue source is the tourists who come to look at the artists. (The artists have long since given up looking for hearty

Photo Opportunity

The red fishing shack at Rockport Harbor is called Motif No 1 for its artistic appeal.

fisherfolk because their descendants are all running B&Bs.)

The town hub is Dock Sq, recognizable by an oft-painted red fishing shack, decorated with colorful buoys. From here, **Bearskin Neck**, lined with galleries, lobster shacks and souvenir shops, juts into the harbor.

THE DRIVE
Leave Rockport on South St (MA 127A), heading south past Delmater Sanctuary. Now Thatcher St, the road passes the lovely Good Harbor Beach, which is a fine spot for a cool-off. Merge onto Main St as you enter Gloucester center.

Detour
Rocky Neck Art Colony
Start: 06 Rockport
The narrow peninsula of Rocky Neck, jutting into Gloucester Harbor, offers inspiring views of the ocean and the harbor. Between

WWI and WWII, artists began renting the local fisherfolk's seaside shacks, which they used as studios. Today these same shanties, considerably gentrified, constitute the **Rocky Neck Art Colony** (rocky neckartcolony.org), home to dozens of studios and galleries. In addition to the **Salted Cod Arthouse and Winebar**, about a dozen galleries and studios are open to visitors. There's also a couple of restaurants.

From MA 127A (at the junction with MA 128), turn left onto E Main St and right onto Rocky Neck Ave.

07 **GLOUCESTER**
Gritty Gloucester offers a remarkable contrast to the rest of Cape Ann. The working waterfront is dominated by marinas and shipyards, with a backdrop of fish-processing plants. This hardworking town has its own unexpected charm, which is particularly visible in the brick buildings along Main St. Nearby, the tiny **Cape Ann Museum** (capeannmuseum.org) is a gem – particularly for its impressive collection of paintings by Gloucester native Fitz Henry Lane. Exhibits also showcase the region's granite-quarrying industry and – of course – its maritime history.

07

MASSACHUSETTS

Berkshire Back Roads

DURATION	DISTANCE	GREAT FOR
2–3 days	31 miles / 50km	Nature, history & families

BEST TIME TO GO	Cultural events are in full swing from mid-June to September; fall foliage is best in October.

Mount, Lenox

Pack a picnic of farm-fresh fruit and local cheese, spread your blanket on the lush green lawns, and settle in for an evening of world-class music under the stars. Or world-class dance. Or Shakespeare. Or experimental theater. Indeed, for every day you spend hiking the hills and photographing the scenery, you can spend an evening taking in a cultural masterwork.

Link Your Trip

02 Fall Foliage Tour

Expand your leaf-peeping to the other New England states.

08 Mohawk Trail

For more beautiful Berkshire scenery and artistic offerings, drive north on US 7 to Williamstown.

01 LENOX

Prized for its bucolic peace, this gracious town was a summer retreat for wealthy families with surnames like Carnegie, Vanderbilt and Westinghouse. Lenox is the cultural heart of the Berkshires, and its illustrious past remains tangibly present today.

In the 19th century, writers such as Nathaniel Hawthorne and Edith Wharton set up shop here. Wharton's fabulous mansion, **Mount** (edithwharton. org), shows off a magnificent interior and formal gardens, demonstrating the principles that she describes in her book *The Decoration of Houses*.

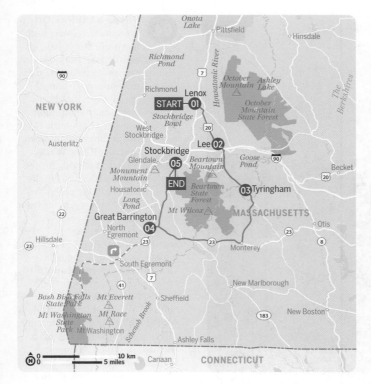

the outdoor Simon Stage, which has an amazing backdrop of the Berkshire hills.

🚙 THE DRIVE

Continue east on US 20, crossing under the turnpike. Turn right on MA 102, then make an immediate left on Tyringham Rd. Hugging the Housatonic River, this scenic road passes some pretty homesteads and woodsy hillsides before entering Tyringham as Main St.

03 TYRINGHAM

Once the home of a Shaker community (1792–1874), this tiny village enjoys a gorgeous setting in the midst of the Tyringham Valley. To get some perspective on the pastoral splendor, take a 2-mile hike over the knobs of **Tyringham Cobble** (thetrustees.org), which offers wildflower-strewn hillsides and spectacular views.

You don't have to get out of your car to see the village's most famous attraction: the **Tyringham Gingerbread House** (santarella gardens.com), an architectural fantasy designed by sculptor Henry Hudson Kitson. This fairy-tale thatched-roofed cottage is readily visible from the road, though the interior is not open to the public.

🚙 THE DRIVE

Depart Tyringham on Main St. Turn right on Monterey Rd, passing the inviting Monterey Town Beach. Look for the old-fashioned General Store in Monterey, then head west on MA 23. Pass Beartown State Forest and Butternut Mountain as you enter Great Barrington. Continue on State Rd, cross the bridge over the Housatonic River and turn left onto Main St.

About a mile west of Lenox center, **Tanglewood** (bso.org/tanglewood) is the summer home of the esteemed Boston Symphony Orchestra. From June to September, these beautifully manicured grounds host concerts of pop and rock, chamber music, folk, jazz and blues, in addition to the symphony. Traditionally, the July 4 extravaganza features Massachusetts native James Taylor.

🚙 THE DRIVE

Head out of Lenox on Walker St (MA 183), passing the historic Ventfort Hall, an impressive Jacobean Revival mansion that was a Morgan family home. One mile southeast of the center, turn right onto US 20 and drive 3 miles south,

passing pretty Laurel Lake. Cross the bridge over the Housatonic River as you enter Lee.

02 LEE

Welcome to the Berkshires' towniest town, at once cute and gritty. The main street runs through the center, curving to cross some railroad tracks. On it you'll find a hardware store, a bar and a few places to eat, including a proper diner featured in a famous Norman Rockwell painting. The biggest draw to Lee is **Jacob's Pillow**, the prestigious summertime dance festival that takes place in neighboring Becket. Free Inside/Out performances are held on

JOE BENNING/SHUTTERSTOCK ©

Tanglewood Music Festival

SUMMER FESTIVALS

Aston Magna (astonmagna.org)

Listen to Bach, Brahms and Buxtehude and other early classical music in Great Barrington during June and July.

Shakespeare & Company (shakespeare.org)

Shakespearean plays are performed outdoors in a bucolic context in Lenox in July and August.

Berkshire Theatre Festival (berkshiretheatre.org)

Stop by for experimental summer theater in an old playhouse in Stockbridge from late July through October.

Jacob's Pillow (jacobspillow.org)

The best dance troupes of most cities can't top the stupefying and ground-breaking dance of Jacob's Pillow, which runs from mid-June through August near Lee.

Tanglewood Music Festival (tanglewood.org)

For many, the Berkshires' most famous festival and its outstanding orchestral music are reason enough to return to Lenox each summer.

04 **GREAT BARRINGTON**
Woolworths, diners and hardware stores have given way to galleries, boutiques and 'locavore' restaurants on Main St, Great Barrington, once named the 'best small town in America' by the Smithsonian Institution. The picturesque Housatonic River flows through the center of town, with the parallel **River Walk** (gbriverwalk.org) offering a perfect perch from which to admire it. Access the walking path from Main St (behind Rite-Aid) or from Bridge St.

After a few hours' rest in small-town America, you might hanker for a hike in the hills. Head to **Monument Mountain** (thetrustees.org), 5 miles north. In 1850 Nathaniel Hawthorne climbed this mountain with Oliver Wendell Holmes and Herman Melville, thus sealing a lifelong friendship. You can follow their footsteps on a hike to the 1642ft summit of Squaw Peak. From the top you'll get fabulous views all the way to Mt Greylock in the northwestern corner of the state and to the Catskills in New York.

THE DRIVE
Head north out of town on Main St and turn right on State St to cross the Housatonic River. Drive north on US 7, passing the pretty Fountain Pond on the right and Monument Mountain on the left. Turn left on MA 102, which is Main St, Stockbridge.

Detour
Bash Bish Falls
Start: **04** **Great Barrington**
In the southwesternmost corner of the state, near the New York state line, is Bash Bish Falls (mass.gov/locations/bash-bish-falls-state-park), the largest waterfall in

Massachusetts. The water feeding the falls runs down a series of gorges before the torrent is sliced in two by a massive boulder perched directly above a pool. There it drops as a photogenic double waterfall. These 60ft-high falls are a popular spot for landscape painters to set up their easels.

To get here from Great Barrington, take MA 23 southwest to South Egremont. Turn right onto MA 41 south and then take the immediate right onto Mt Washington Rd (which becomes East St) and continue for 7.5 miles. Turn right onto Cross Rd, then right onto West St and continue 1 mile. Turn left onto Falls Rd and follow that for 1.5 miles.

There are two trailheads. The first is for a short, steep trail that descends 300ft over the course of a quarter-mile. For a more leisurely,

Photo Opportunity

Compare your photo of Main St, Stockbridge, to the Rockwell painting.

level hike, continue another mile over the New York state line. This 0.75-mile trail takes about 20 minutes in each direction.

 STOCKBRIDGE
Main St, Stockbridge, is so postcard-perfect it looks like something out of a Norman Rockwell painting. In fact, it was depicted in the painting *Stockbridge Main Street at Christmas*. Stockbridge people

and places inspired many of Rockwell's illustrations, as the artist lived here for 25 years. The **Norman Rockwell Museum** (nrm.org) displays the world's largest collection of Rockwell's original art, including the beloved *Four Freedoms* and a complete collection of *Saturday Evening Post* covers.

Norman Rockwell is the main draw, but Stockbridge was also home to Daniel Chester French in an earlier era. Sculptor of *Abraham Lincoln* at the Lincoln Memorial and *The Minuteman* in Concord, French spent his summers at **Chesterwood** (chesterwood.org), a 122-acre estate. His house and studio are substantially as they were when he lived here, with nearly 500 pieces of sculpture, finished and unfinished, in the studio.

Norman Rockwell Museum, Stockbridge

08

MASSACHUSETTS

Mohawk Trail

BEST FOR SCENERY

The 19 miles from stops three to five offer hair-raising turns and astonishing views.

DURATION	DISTANCE	GREAT FOR
2–3 days	46 miles / 74km	History & nature

BEST TIME TO GO	Enjoy clear views and open access to sites from June to October.

Bridge of Flowers

The road winds ever upward. Suddenly, around a bend, there's a clearing in the forest and the landscape sprawls out in a colorful tapestry, yielding views across the valley and into neighboring states. Welcome to the Western Summit of the Mohawk Trail, a 63-mile stretch of scenic byway, showing off raging rivers, idyllic farms and forest-covered mountains. Drivers, beware: it's practically impossible to keep your eyes on the road.

Link Your Trip

07 Berkshire Back Roads

From Williamstown, drive south on US 7 to hook up with this loop around the Massachusetts mountains.

21 Connecticut River Byway

Drive north or south from Deerfield to explore the mighty New England waterway.

01 DEERFIELD

Start your tour in **Historic Deerfield Village** (historic-deerfield.org), an enchanting farming settlement that has escaped the ravages of time. Old Main St now presents a noble prospect: a dozen houses dating from the 1700s and 1800s, well preserved and open to the public. The homes have been restored and furnished according to actual historical records, reflecting different periods in the village's history.

One block east of Old Main St, **Memorial Hall Museum** (americancenturies.mass.edu) contains

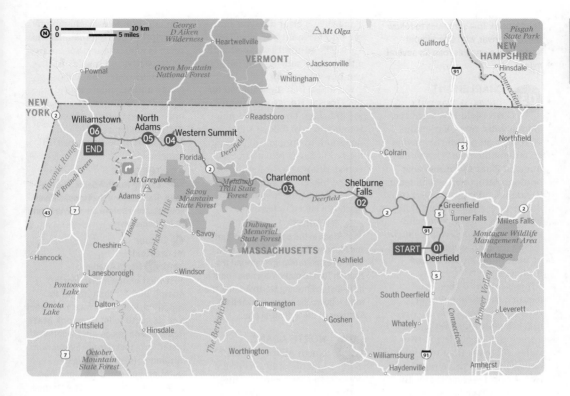

lots of original artifacts from local homes, including the storied Indian House Door. This farming family's front door was hacked through during the infamous 1704 raid, when some 50 villagers were killed by French and Native American attackers.

THE DRIVE
From Historic Deerfield Village, drive north on MA 10 (US 5) for 3 miles and turn left to head west on MA 2A. At the traffic circle, take the second exit onto the Mohawk Trail (MA 2). Turn left on Bridge St to continue into Shelburne Falls.

02 SHELBURNE FALLS
The main drag in this artisan community is only three blocks long — a tiny but charming stretch of turn-of-the-20th-century buildings, housing art galleries and coffee shops alongside a barber shop, a general store and an old-fashioned pharmacy. Forming the background are the forested mountains, the Deerfield River and a pair of picturesque bridges across it – one made of iron, the other covered in flowers.

Gardeners and volunteers have been maintaining the **Bridge of Flowers** (bridgeofflowersmass.org) since 1929. From April to October, more than 500 varieties of flowering plant, shrub and vine flaunt their colors on the 400ft-long span.

Two blocks south, the swirling of water around rocks in the Deerfield River has created an impressive collection of **glacial potholes** – near-perfect circular craters in the river bed. There are more than 50 potholes on display, including the world's largest, which has a 39ft diameter.

THE DRIVE
At the end of Bridge St, cross the metal bridge and turn right on State St, which runs parallel to the Deerfield River, and turn left on MA 2.

The Mohawk Trail continues to follow the raging river, with Charlemont spread out along this road for several miles.

03 CHARLEMONT

Tucked between the Deerfield River and the Hoosac hills, tiny Charlemont is worth a stop if you're craving an adrenaline rush. This is the home of **Zoar Outdoor** (zoar outdoor.com), offering canoeing, kayaking and white-water rafting on the river rapids for all skill levels, including trips for children as young as seven. Come in spring for high-water adventure or in autumn for fall-foliage brilliance.

If you prefer to keep your feet dry, the same operator runs zipline tours that let you unleash your inner Tarzan on a treetop glide above the river valley. All in all, the three-hour outing includes three rappels, two sky bridges and 11 zips that get progressively longer. The hardest part is stepping off the first platform – the rest is pure exhilaration!

THE DRIVE
Leaving Charlemont, you'll pass the *Hail to the Sunrise* statue, honoring the Five Indian Nations of the Mohawk Trail. The next stretch is the highlight of the route, as it cuts across the eponymous state forest. Continue climbing through the town of Florida, punctuated by three lookouts: the unmarked Eastern Summit, the Whitcomb Summit (the highest along the trail) and the Western Summit.

04 WESTERN SUMMIT

Also known as Perry's Peak, the Western Summit (2100ft) shows off amazing views of the surrounding Hoosac

Range. On a clear day, you can see into Vermont and even New York. The summit is topped with a ticky-tacky tourist shop, so you can buy some fudge.

You'll also find the trailhead for the **Hoosac Range** just east of the gift shop. This scenic 6-mile round-trip hike follows the ridge-line south to Spruce Hill summit, located in Savoy Mountain State Forest. Allow at least four hours for the hike; if you're pressed for time, the 1.5-mile loop to Sunset Rock is a shorter alternative.

THE DRIVE
Back in the car, you'll find that the Mohawk Trail descends quickly, with an exhilarating spin around the Hairpin Turn to make your heart beat a little faster. Entering North Adams, the road follows the Hoosac River past vestiges of the industrial era.

05 NORTH ADAMS

North Adams' beautiful and bleak 19th-century downtown seems out of sync with the rest of the Berkshires. And nestled into this industrial-era assemblage is a contemporary art museum of staggering proportions.

MASS MoCA (massmoca. org) sprawls over 13 acres of downtown North Adams. After the Sprague Electric Company packed up in 1985, more than $31 million was spent to modernize the property into the country's biggest art gallery, which now encompasses 222,000 sq ft and over 25 buildings, including art-construction areas, performance centers and 19 galleries. One gallery is the size of a football field, giving installation artists the opportunity to take things into a whole new dimension.

In addition to ever-changing, description-defying installations, there is a fascinating Sol LeWitt retrospective, on display until 2033. Little ones can always create and speculate in Kidspace, while the on-site theater space hosts music festivals, dance parties, poetry recitals and every kind of performance art imaginable.

THE DRIVE
Exiting North Adams, the Mohawk Trail crosses the Hoosac River several times before becoming Main St, Williamstown.

Detour
Mt Greylock
Start: 05 North Adams
Just west of downtown North Adams, look for the turn-off to Notch Rd, which will take you about 5 miles south to **Mt Greylock State Reservation** (mass.gov/locations/ mount-greylock-state-reservation). In summer (mid-May to mid-October) you can drive up; otherwise, park your car at the entrance and hike 5 miles to the summit, where you will be rewarded with a 360-degree vista, taking in five states and hundreds of miles.

At 3491ft, Mt Greylock is the state's highest peak. In the 19th century, Greylock was a favorite destination for New England's nature-loving writers, including Nathaniel Hawthorne and Henry David Thoreau. Herman Melville even dedicated a novel to 'Greylock's Most Excellent Majesty.' Nowadays, it is ceremoniously topped with the 92ft-high War Memorial Tower, which you can climb (making the mountain effectively 3583ft). From May to October, you can also eat and sleep at the magnificently sited Bascom Lodge.

Photo Opportunity

Snap a photo of the vast three-state vista from the Western Summit.

Mt Greylock

WILLIAMSTOWN

06 Tiny Williamstown is nestled in the heart of the Purple Valley, so named because the surrounding mountains often seem shrouded in a lavender veil at dusk. It is the quintessential college town, dominated by the marble-and-brick buildings of elite Williams College.

In addition to welcoming green spaces and academic architecture, Williamstown is home to a pair of exceptional art museums. The **Clark Art Institute** (clarkart.edu) is a gem, with wonderful paintings by French impressionists and their American contemporaries, all set amid 140 gorgeous acres of expansive lawns.

Down the road, the **Williams College Museum of Art** (art museum.williams.edu) has an impressive cache of its own. The American Collection includes substantial works by notables such as Edward Hopper, Winslow Homer and Grant Wood, to name only a few. The photography collection is also noteworthy, with images by Man Ray and Alfred Stieglitz.

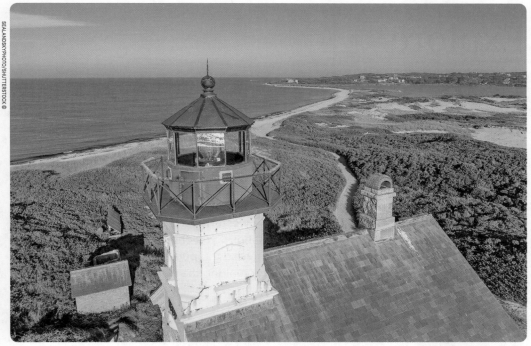

North Lighthouse (p74), Block Island

Connecticut & Rhode Island

Explore

Connecticut & Rhode Island

Connecticut and Rhode Island are often overlooked by visitors who want the drama of the higher mountains and wilderness of Maine, New Hampshire and Vermont, but these smaller states have rolling hills, wineries, mill towns, rushing rivers, surfing spots and miles of spectacular coastline. In the western parts of Connecticut you'll find exciting parks and a surprising bit of wildlands if you choose to look for it. Rhode Island, the country's tiniest state, packs a good road trip punch and is a great place for those looking to stop and sample the seafood along the way.

Providence, RI

Providence's TF Green International Airport is a good alternative to Boston's Logan International. Providence is a convenient arrival point, especially if you're planning on linking many of the northerly trips together into one big loop. The bustling city has a beautiful riverfront area and lots to see and do, as well as hotels of all types and stripes, ranging from cheap motels to boutique B&Bs.

Newport, RI

Ritzy Newport is one of New England's original tourist destinations. It became famous in the 1900s as a summer getaway for industry magnates in coal, oil and steel, though they often only stayed for a few weeks. As a kind of keeping-up-with-the-Joneses game, these tycoons built enormous mansions, opulent to excess, much in the same way that many billionaires have yachts with swimming pools and helicopter pads today. These mansions are now museums, and touring them is a popular Newport activity. Nearby white-sand beaches make for great surfing and sunbathing, and the waters here are much warmer than those off the coast of Maine and New Hampshire.

Hartford, CT

Connecticut's capital city isn't known as a grand architectural destination, though it does have a historic capitol building. Its authentic Italian district, known as Little Italy, will delight and surprise, and the city has a spectacular fireworks display on the 4th of July. You'll find it has many of the benefits of a big city without feeling too overwhelming.

WHEN TO GO

Connecticut and Rhode Island are on the southern edge of the New England jigsaw puzzle, meaning spring comes earlier and it stays warm longer in fall. Leaf peepers will need to add a week, maybe even two, to their trip dates. Hikers wanting to hit the trails can do so much earlier after winter thaws.

New Haven, CT

New Haven is known for its Ivy League university (that would be Yale) and for a delightful waterside food-truck collection of mostly Latin American cuisines. Craving a good *torta* (sandwich) or *pollo empanizada* (breaded chicken) platter? Add Exit 46 on I-95 to your maps app. Thanks to the student influx, New Haven also has a rich variety of other dining options and plenty of places to lay your head, from cheap chains all the way up to stately historic hotels and B&Bs.

Norfolk, CT

Tiny Norfolk, not to be confused with much larger Norwalk (on the Connecticut coast) or the identically named town in nearby Massachusetts, is a delightful rural mix of Tudor and Victorian buildings, train tracks, bridge-covered rivers, conifer forests and quiet inland charm. Staying here will likely mean

a B&B as there are no motels. Dining options are also limited, but if you're looking to unplug and enjoy nature for a while, Norwalk is an excellent hub from which to explore western Connecticut.

TRANSPORTATION

If you're flying here, opt for TF Green in Rhode Island or Bradley International near Hartford. Alternatively, if you're only touring Connecticut, New Haven might make sense. It's also possible to arrive at these coastal cities by train on the Acela line. New Haven has commuter train and bus connections to New York City.

 WHAT'S ON

Newport Jazz Festival

The famous jazz event takes place every July, drawing top-name musicians and thousands of fans. Greats who've performed include Louis Armstrong, Dizzy Gillespie, Aretha Franklin, Dave Brubeck, Wynton Marsalis and others.

Woodstock Fair

The town that 'changed everything' in the summer of 1969 still hosts an impressive county fair, with agriculture exhibits, rides, games and events. It's held on Labor Day weekend (first weekend in September).

 WHERE TO STAY

This region runs the gamut of options for overnight stays, from cozy B&Bs in wine regions to campsites near the water to log cabin shelters for hikers in the woods. Reserve well in advance if you're planning on visiting from mid-fall onward (October into November), as the region floods with vacationers hoping to take selfies among the brilliant colors. Peak times in summer, such as the July 4 weekend, can also be full, so don't be afraid to plan ahead.

Resources

Discover Newport (*discovernewport.org*) Newport's official tourism website. Especially helpful for choosing where to eat and stay in peak season when availability is limited.

Yale Events Calendar (*calendar.yale.edu*) Has an assortment of events and activities available to students and the public.

09

CONNECTICUT & RHODE ISLAND

Rhode Island: East Bay

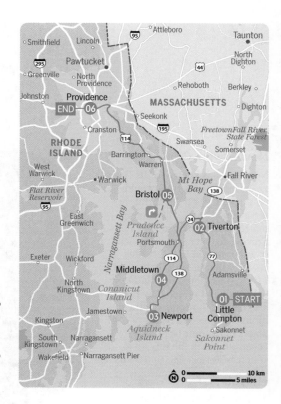

DURATION	DISTANCE	GREAT FOR
3–4 days	52 miles / 84km	Families, history & nature

BEST TIME TO GO	May to October for good weather and farm food.

Rhode Island's jagged East Bay tells the American story in microcosm. Start in Little Compton with the grave of Elizabeth Pabodie (1623–1717), the first European settler born in New England. Then meander through historic Tiverton and Bristol, where slave dealers and merchants grew rich. Prosperous as they were, their modest homes barely hold a candle to the mansions, museums and libraries of Newport's capitalist kings and Providence's intelligentsia.

Link Your Trip

05 Pilgrim Trail

Continue the historical journey in Plymouth with the Massachusetts Pilgrim Trail.

10 Rhode Island: Coastal Culture

Explore Rhode Island's coastal culture, heading southwest along I-95 from Providence.

01 LITTLE COMPTON

No doubt tiring of the big-city bustle of 17th-century Portsmouth, early settler Samuel Wilbor crossed the Sakonnet River to Little Compton. His plain family home, **Wilbor House** (littlecompton.org), built in 1690, still stands on a manicured lawn behind a traditional five-bar gate and tells the story of eight generations of Wilbors who lived here.

The rest of Little Compton, from the hand-hewn clapboard houses to the white-steepled **United Congregational Church**, overlooking the **Old**

BEST FOR HISTORY

Find modern America's beginnings in Little Compton.

United Congregational Church, Little Compton

Commons Burial Ground, is one of the oldest and most quaint villages in all of New England. Elizabeth Pabodie, daughter of Mayflower pilgrims Priscilla and John Alden and the first settler born in New England, is buried here.

Lovely, ocean-facing **Goosewing Beach** is the only good public beach. Parking costs $10 at **South Shore Beach**, from where you can walk across a small tidal inlet.

THE DRIVE
Head north along RI 77 at a leisurely pace, enjoying the peaceful country scenery of rambling stone walls and clapboard farmhouses. As you approach Tiverton, look out to your left and you'll occasionally get glimpses out to the water, which is particularly pretty in the late afternoon.

02 TIVERTON
En route to Tiverton's historic Four Corners, stop in at **Carolyn's Sakonnet Vineyard** (sakonnetwine.com) for free daily wine tastings and guided tours. This will set you up nicely for the gourmet treats that await in Tiverton: **Gray's Ice Cream** (graysicecream.com), where over 40 flavors are made on-site daily, and waterfront dining at the fabulous **Boat House** (boathousetiverton.com).

Tiverton has a clutch of local artists as well as chic boutiques hawking classy, original wares.

THE DRIVE
Head north up Main St, leaving Tiverton and its green fields behind you, and merge onto the westbound RI 138/ RI 24 S, which leads you directly into Newport.

03 NEWPORT
Established by religious moderates fleeing persecution from Massachusetts Puritans, the 'new port' flourished to become the fourth-richest city in the newly independent colony. Downtown, the Colonial-era architecture is beautifully

preserved along with notable landmarks, such as Washington Sq's **Colony House**, where Rhode Island's declaration of independence was read in May 1776.

Just off the square, the gaslights of the White Horse Tavern, America's oldest tavern, still burn, and on Touro St, America's first synagogue, **Touro Synagogue** (tourosynagogue.org), still stands. Tour the past on a guided **Newport Historical Society Walking Tour** (newporthistory tours.org).

Fascinating as Newport's early history is, it struggles to compete with the town's latter-day success, when wealthy industrialists made Newport their playground and

built summer houses along lantern-lined Bellevue Ave. Modeled on Italianate palazzos, French châteaux and Elizabethan manor houses, and decorated with valuable furnishings and artworks, the stately homes are now collectively referred to as the **Newport Mansions**. Tour the most outstanding with the **Preservation Society of Newport County** (newportmansions.org).

THE DRIVE

Leave Newport by way of 10-mile Ocean Dr, which starts just south of Fort Adams and curls around the southern shore, past the grand mansions, and up Bellevue Ave before intersecting with Memorial Blvd. Turn right here for a straight shot into Middletown.

LOCAL KNOWLEDGE

Polo in Portsmouth

Drab though the urban environs of Portsmouth may seem, in-the-know locals rate Portsmouth as a family-friendly destination – not least because the polo matches hosted at Glen Farm make for a great family day out. Home to the **Newport Polo Club** (nptpolo. com), the 700-acre 'farm' was assembled by New York businessman Henry Taylor, who sought to create a gentleman's country seat in the grand English tradition. In summer, the farm is host to the club's polo matches (check the website for dates), which are a perfect way to enjoy the property and get an authentic taste of Newport high life.

The Breakers, Newport

WANGKUN JIA/SHUTTERSTOCK ©

04 MIDDLETOWN

Flo's (flosclamshacks. com) jaunty red-and-white clam shack and her competition, **Anthony's Seafood** (anthonysseafood.net), would be enough reason to visit Middletown, which now merges seamlessly with Newport. But the best fried clams in town taste better after a day on **Second Beach** (middletownri.gov/101/Beaches-Recreation), the largest and most beautiful beach on Aquidneck Island. Curving around Sachuest Bay, it is backed by the 450-acre **Norman Bird Sanctuary** (normanbird sanctuary.org), which teems with migrating birds. All this driving might inspire you to check out the stunning collection of antique, luxury, hot-rod and muscle cars at the shiny new **Newport Car Museum** (newportcarmuseum.org), located just north of Middletown, in Portsmouth.

THE DRIVE
Leave Aquidneck Island via East Main Rd, which takes you north through the suburbs of Middletown and Portsmouth. After 6.5 miles, pick up the RI 114 and cross the bay via the scenic Mt Hope suspension bridge. From here it's a short 3-mile drive into Bristol.

05 BRISTOL

One-fifth of all slaves transported to America were brought in Bristol ships and by the 18th century the town was one of the country's major commercial ports. The world-class **Herreshoff Marine Museum** (herreshoff.org) showcases some of America's finest yachts, including eight that were built for the America's Cup.

Local resident Augustus Van

Photo Opportunity

Capture the mansions and sheer cliffs along the Cliff Walk.

Wickle bought a 72ft Herreshoff yacht for his wife Bessie in 1895, but having nowhere suitable to moor it, he then had to build **Blithewold Mansion** (blithewold.org). The arts-and-crafts mansion sits in a peerless position on Narragansett Bay and is particularly lovely in spring, when daffodils line the shore. Other local magnates included slave trader General George DeWolf, who built **Linden Place** (lindenplace.org), famous as a film location for *The Great Gatsby*.

Bristol's **Colt State Park** (riparks.ri.gov) is Rhode Island's most scenic park, with its entire western border fronting Narragansett Bay, fringed by 4 miles of cycling trails and shaded picnic tables.

THE DRIVE
From Bristol it's a straight drive north along RI 114, through the suburbs of Warren and Barrington, to Providence. After 17 miles, merge onto I-195 W, which takes you the remaining 18 miles into the center of town.

Detour
Prudence Island
Start: 05 Bristol

Idyllic **Prudence Island** (prudence bayislandtransport.com) sits in the middle of Narragansett Bay, an easy 25-minute ferry ride from Bristol. Originally used for farming and later as a summer vacation spot for fami-

---

lies from Providence and New York, who traveled here on the Fall River Line Steamer, the island now has only 88 inhabitants. There are some fine Victorian and beaux-arts houses near Stone Wharf, a lighthouse and a small store, but otherwise it's wild and unspoiled. Perfect for mountain biking (BYO bike), barbecues, fishing and paddling.

06 PROVIDENCE

Providence, the first town of religious liberal Roger Williams' new Rhode Island and Providence Plantation colony, was established so that 'no man should be molested for his conscience sake.' A self-guided stroll along **Benefit Street** or, better still, a **Rhode Island Historical Society** (rihs.org) walking tour, reveals the city's rich architectural legacy. Here alone are scores of Colonial, Federal and Revival houses. Amid them you'll find William Strickland's 1838 **Providence Athenaeum** (providence athenaeum.org), inside which plaster busts of Greek gods and philosophers preside over a collection that dates from 1753.

Atop the hill sits **Brown University** (brown.edu), with its Gothic and beaux-arts buildings arranged around the College Green. Nearby is the **John Brown House Museum** (rihs. org/museums/john-brown-house), which should be considered a must-see for American history and architecture buffs.

End the tour with a nod toward the bronze statue of *Independent Man*, which graces the pearly white dome of the impressive **Rhode Island State House** (sos. ri.gov).

10

CONNECTICUT & RHODE ISLAND

Rhode Island: Coastal Culture

BEST FOR OUTDOORS

Block Island's 25 miles of trails weave through wildflowers and past nesting birds.

DURATION	DISTANCE	GREAT FOR
4 days	111 miles / 179km	Nature & families

BEST TIME TO GO	June to September for sun, sand and surfing.

Rhode Island School of Design

Rhode Island might only take an hour to drive across but it packs 400 miles of coastline into its tiny boundaries. Much of this takes the form of white-sand beaches, arguably the finest places for ocean swimming in the northeast. There are also islands to explore, sea cliffs to stroll along and isolated lighthouses where you can frame perfect sunset shots.

Link Your Trip

09 Rhode Island: East Bay

Head east down RI 114 for a trip back in time to the earliest days of the colony.

12 Connecticut Wine Trail

From Westerly, drive west to Stonington on US 1 for a gourmet tour of Connecticut's vineyards and farms.

01 **PROVIDENCE**
Rhode Island's capital presents visitors with some fine urban strolling, from Brown University's campus on 18th-century College Hill to the city's **Riverwalk** and the historic downtown along Weybosset St. Along the way, visit the **Rhode Island School of Design** (risd.edu), the top art school in the USA and home to the **RISD Museum of Art** (risdmuseum.org), with its collection of Roman and Etruscan artifacts, medieval and Renaissance works, and 19th-century French paintings. RISD maintains several other fine galleries: **Sol Koffler** (info.risd.edu/sol-koffler-gallery) serves as the main exhibition space for

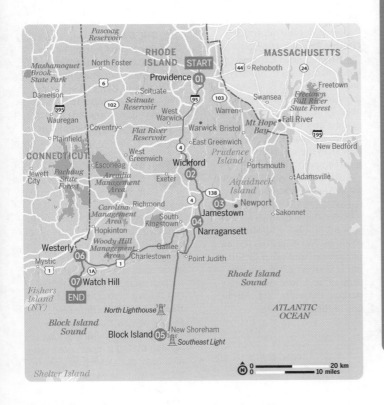

graduate students, while **risd|works** (risdworks.com) offers some of their work for sale.

If you're in town on the third Thursday of the month, you can catch **Gallery Night** (gallery night.org), when 23 galleries and museums open their doors for free viewings.

THE DRIVE
Leave Providence via Memorial Blvd and pick up the I-95 S. Meander through the suburbs for 1.5 miles and veer left onto RI 4 S toward North Kingstown. Exit at 7A–7B onto RI 403 east toward Quonset and after a couple of miles turn onto US 1 for Wickford.

02 WICKFORD
Bypassed by the era of steamboats and train travel, Wickford's Main St and Pleasant St languished sleepily through the Industrial Revolution and are still lined with 18th-century Colonial and Federal homes, which lead down to the harbor where fishers cast their lines off the pier. Rent kayaks from the **Kayak Centre** (kayakcentre.com) for a paddle around the bay.

Then visit the **Old Narragansett Church** (stpaulswickford. org). It dates from 1707 and retains its box pews and upstairs gallery where plantation slaves were allowed to worship. The local artist Gilbert Scott

(1755–1828), who painted the portrait of George Washington that graces the one-dollar bill, was baptized here in the silver baptismal font.

THE DRIVE
It is a short 4-mile drive along RI 1A S from Wickford to Conanicut Island. Once you're through the Wickford suburbs, take the RI 138 ramp over the Jamestown Bridge, which affords expansive views of the bay. Once on the island, turn right down North Rd to Jamestown past the old smock windmill.

03 JAMESTOWN
More rural than its prosperous neighbor, Newport, Jamestown's first inhabitants were Quaker farmers,

shepherds and pirates. Captain Kidd spent considerable time here and is said to have buried his treasure hereabouts.

These days, the real treasure in Jamestown is the peace and quiet. The waterfront is undeveloped and you can walk along **Conanicus Avenue** and perch on a bench overlooking the harbor or enjoy eclectic Modern American fare on the gorgeous patio at Simpatico The **Jamestown Newport Ferry** (jamestownnewportferry. com) sails to Newport with stops at Fort Adams and Rose Island. It is the best deal going for a harbor tour.

At the southernmost tip of Conanicut Island is **Beavertail State Park** (riparks.ri.gov/parks/beavertail-state-park), where you can enjoy one of the best vistas – and sunsets – in the Ocean State. Many vacationers bring lawn chairs, barbecues and picnics, and spend all day enjoying the walking trails and cliff-top views. At the point, picturesque 1749 **Beavertail Light** (beavertaillight.org), one of the oldest along the Atlantic coast, still signals ships into Narragansett Bay.

THE DRIVE
Leaving Conanicut Island, head south along the scenic route RI 1A, along which you'll enjoy woodsy roads around Saunderstown and glimpses of the bay as you skirt the shoreline south of Narragansett Pier.

04 NARRAGANSETT
Scarborough State Beach (riparks.ri.gov/beaches/scarborough-north-state-beach), just south of Narragansett Pier, is one of the state's biggest beaches and is considered by many to be the best.

A few miles further south is **Galilee**, the departure point for the **Block Island Express** (go blockisland.com) to Block Island. Sometimes called Point Judith in ferry schedules, Galilee is a workaday fishing town. Arrive in time and eat at dockside **Champlin's Seafood** (champlins.com), where they haul the fish right out of the bay onto your plate.

Further south still, the **Roger W Wheeler State Beach** (riparks.ri.gov/beaches/roger-w-wheeler-state-beach) is a good spot for families with small children. Not only does it have a playground and other facilities, but it also has a very gradual drop-off and little surf. All-day parking in Galilee costs $10 in any of the several lots.

Fantastic Umbrella Factory

A collection of 19th-century farm buildings and unkempt gardens, the Fantastic Umbrella Factory (fantasticumbrellafactory.com), a former commune, got its start as one of Rhode Island's strangest stores in 1968. You can find almost anything in a series of shacks filled with gift items, flowers, toys, handmade jewelry and hemp clothing. Exotic birds and farm animals walk all over the place, much to the delight of children.

THE DRIVE
Car-and-passenger ferries and fast catamarans run from Galilee State Pier, Point Judith, to Old Harbor, Block Island, daily in off-season (October to May). In the busy summer season (June to September) boats depart almost hourly.

05 BLOCK ISLAND
From the deck of the ferry you'll see a cluster of mansard roofs and gingerbread houses rising picturesquely from **Old Harbor**, Block Island's main center of activity.

Beyond here, the island's attractions are simple. Stretching for several miles to the north of Old Harbor is the 3-mile **State Beach** (blockislandinfo.com/plan-your-visit/maps/beaches-and-parks-map), which is long enough to find a quiet spot even on a busy day. Otherwise, bike or hike around the island's rolling farmland, pausing to admire the island's lighthouses: **Southeast Light**, set dramatically atop 200ft red clay cliffs, and **North Lighthouse**, which stands at the end of a long sandy lane lined with beach roses. In spring and fall, when migratory species fly south along the Atlantic Flyway, bird-watching opportunities abound and if you're traveling with kids or just like a good treasure hunt yourself, take part in the unique **Glass Float Project** (glassfloatproject.com).

Hire bikes from **Island Moped and Bike Rentals** (bimopeds.com).

THE DRIVE
Take the ferry back to Galilee and follow the signs to the main interstate RI 1. This 20-mile stretch of highway to Westerly is pleasant

enough, lined with thick woods and plenty of opportunities to detour to various beaches.

06 WESTERLY

Westerly sits on Rhode Island's western border, sharing the banks of the Pawcatuck River with Connecticut. In the 19th century it was a town of some wealth, thanks to its high-grade granite quarries. That heyday is long gone, although local **Misquamicut State Beach** (riparks.com/Locations/LocationMisquamicut.html) still draws weekending crowds who favor its scenic situation on Winnapaug Pond. Nearby is the old-fashioned amusement resort of **Atlantic Beach Park** (atlanticbeachpark.com), which offers miniature golf, wave rides, batting cages and the like.

Photo Opportunity

The Southeast Light atop red clay cliffs.

THE DRIVE

It's a short and scenic 2-mile drive south down RI 1A from the center of Westerly to the heady heights of mansion-clad Watch Hill. Along the way, enjoy views over Little Narragansett Bay across landscaped lawns and gardens.

07 WATCH HILL

The wealthy summer colony of Watch Hill, with its huge Queen Anne summerhouses, occupies a spit of land at the southwestern tip of Rhode Island.

Visitors spend their time at **East Beach**, which stretches for several miles from Watch Hill lighthouse all the way to Misquamicut. (The public access to the beach is on Bluff Ave near Larkin Rd.) For children, an ice-cream cone and a twirl on the **Merry-go-Round** (merrygoroundbeach.com) provide immediate gratification. The antique carousel dates from 1883 and its horses, suspended on chains, really do appear to 'fly' when the carousel spins.

For a leisurely beach walk, the half-mile stroll to the **Napatree Point Conservation Area** (thewatchhillconservancy.org/napatree.html) is unbeatable with the Atlantic on one side and yacht-studded Little Narragansett Bay on the other.

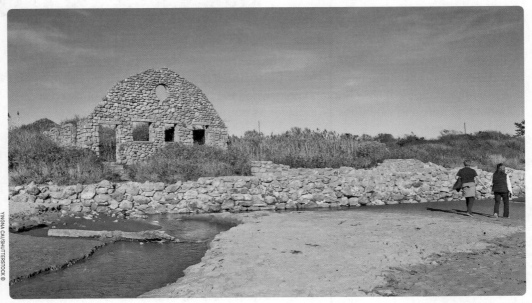

YINONA CAI/SHUTTERSTOCK ©

Scarborough State Beach

11

CONNECTICUT & RHODE ISLAND

Quiet Corner

BEST FOR FOODIES

Fresh apples and berries from Woodstock Orchards.

Revolutionary War Office, Lebanon

DURATION	DISTANCE	GREAT FOR
3 days	72 miles / 116km	Families, history & nature

BEST TIME TO GO	June to October for historic home openings.

The Quiet Corner has the distinction of nurturing state hero Nathan Hale, the patriot-spy from Coventry whose only regret was that he had 'but one life to lose for his country,' and state heroine, abolitionist and Canterbury school teacher Prudence Crandall. Take this trip for a glimpse of New England past, when Washington plotted revolution on Lebanon's Green, and where today, local farms continue to welcome visitors with small-town friendliness.

Link Your Trip

12 Connecticut Wine Trail

Meander south down CT 2 to the Jonathan Edwards Winery in North Stonington and join the Connecticut Wine Trail.

13 Lower River Valley

From hills and meadows to the banks of the Connecticut River, pick up the National Scenic Byway at Springfield and travel north along its course.

01 **COVENTRY**
Begin where it all began, at the **Nathan Hale Homestead** (ctlandmarks.org) on the edge of the **Nathan Hale State Forest**. Nathan, whose five brothers also served in the Revolutionary War, was already in the Continental Army when his father built this rather fine red clapboard farmhouse in 1776. Inside, period furnishings re-create the domestic life of the early colony, along with a display of memorabilia of the schoolteacher turned patriot who was eventually pegged as a spy by the British and hanged at the age of 21. There are also tours of the heirloom gardens, guided walks around

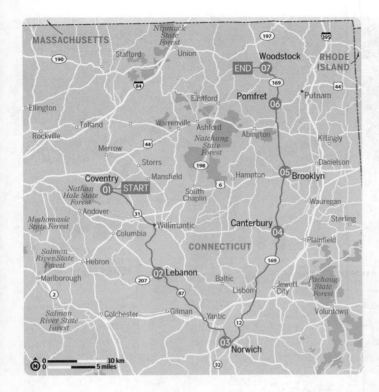

Next door, the strange little Palladian clapboard is actually the **Wadsworth Stable**, where Washington's horse overnighted. A little beyond that is the two-room **Revolutionary War Office** (lebanonct.gov), where Washington met with Trumbull and the Comte de Rochambeau to coordinate military strategy.

THE DRIVE
Pick up CT 87 and head south along its leafy route, straight into Norwich. It's a short 11-mile drive.

03 NORWICH
Money from the Quiet Corner's mills flowed into Norwich, accounting for the handsome Victorian houses set around the **Norwichtown Green**, the gorgeous Second Empire **City Hall** and the unique Romanesque Revival **Slater Memorial Museum** (slatermuseum. org), designed by Stephen Earle in 1886.

The museum was commissioned by William Slater, an educated and well-traveled man who aspired to make the great art of the classical and Renaissance periods accessible to Norwich's citizens. With this in mind, he commissioned the 227 plaster casts that fill the museum's beaux-arts interior on his grand tour in 1894–95. Ranging from the Parthenon Marbles to Michelangelo's *Pieta*, the casts were created via a now-illegal process from molds of the original. Visit the exhibit of Slater's grand tour before heading into the museum, which still forms part of the Norwich Free Academy.

Just about a mile away, a crucial cog in the town's industrial history and Native American legend, **Yantic Falls**, awaits your visit.

the 450-acre estate, Colonial cooking demonstrations and fall lantern tours.

THE DRIVE
Sweep round Lake Wangumbaug, past the Nathan Hale Cemetery and onto CT 31, which soon merges with CT 32 southwards. Loop through industrial Willimantic, once home to the American Thread Company and known as 'Thread City,' and stop for barbecued ribs or a brew at 'The Willi' if you're hungry. Cross the bridge, adorned with its giant bullfrogs sitting atop concrete spools of thread, and pick up CT 289 south to Lebanon.

02 LEBANON
The best way to get acquainted with Lebanon's mile-long historic **Green** is to take a stroll around it on the walking path. On the eastern side, the butter-yellow **Jonathan Trumbull Jr House** was home to Washington's military secretary, who hosted the great general in front of its eight fireplaces in March 1781. On the southwestern side of the Green you'll find **Governor Jonathan Trumbull House** (govtrumbullhousedar. org), the home of Trumbull's father, governor of Connecticut and the only Colonial governor to defy the Crown and support the War of Independence.

Prudence Crandall House Museum

THE DRIVE
From the Norwichtown Green, head down Washington St and Broadway, past grand Victorian mansions and the architecturally noteworthy City Hall, before picking up N Main St and heading out of town in a northeasterly direction to pick up the National Scenic Byway CT 169. Once en route, the scenery quickly becomes picturesque following low stone walls into deeply rural Canterbury.

04 CANTERBURY
Tiny Canterbury was at the forefront of the abolitionist cause some 30 years before the Civil War, thanks to Baptist schoolmistress Prudence Crandall. The **Prudence Crandall House Museum** (portal.ct.gov/ecd-prudencecrandall museum) was the site of an academy that Crandall opened in 1831.

When Crandall later accepted Sarah Harris, the daughter of a free African American farmer, among her students in the fall of 1832, many prominent townspeople withdrew their daughters from the school in protest. Rather than give in, Crandall changed her admissions policy and offered schooling to the free African American community. By April 1833, some 20 girls from Boston, Providence, New York and Philadelphia had enrolled. This caused an angry backlash; the school was vandalized, its well poisoned and, in July, Prudence was arrested. When the case against her was finally dismissed on September 9, 1834, the school was set on fire and Prudence reluctantly closed its doors.

THE DRIVE
Leaving Canterbury's clapboard homesteads behind you, continue north on CT 169 to Brooklyn. To your right, sweeping views across paddocks and the distant

valley open up and the country road is lined with farmyards and historic Dutch barns.

05 BROOKLYN

By the time you hit Brooklyn, you're in the heart of the Quiet Corner, where admiring the scenery and stopping in at local farms and ice-cream stalls is the main activity.

First stop is the **Creamery Brook Bison Farm** (creamery brookbison.squarespace.com), where you can take the equivalent of a Quiet Corner safari among the bison herd before stocking up at the farm shop: phone ahead so staff know you're coming. Next, hit the **Bafflin Sanctuary** (ctaudubon.org/sanctuarybafflin/) on the way into Pomfret for hiking and birding along the rolling hills.

THE DRIVE

On your way out of Brooklyn, you'll pass the access road to the Golden Lamb Buttery (sadly closed, but the sign is still there) on your left. Continue along CT 169, beneath the leafy canopy that creates the impression of driving through a verdant green tunnel. You'll pass fruit orchards on your right, which belong to Lapsley Orchard farm, where you can PYO in season.

Photo Opportunity

Trumbull's house on Lebanon's village Green.

06 POMFRET

With its expansive Colonial homes and hearty restaurants, Pomfret is considered the heart of the Quiet Corner, and is where many visitors choose to base themselves. 'The Bean' will amaze you with its filling grub and superb acoustic jams.

Farming lives on in the vineyards, nurseries and orchards that surround Pomfret, while legends live on in **Mashamoquet State Park** (ct.gov). Here, local hero Israel Putnum, who led the troops at Bunker Hill in Boston, is said to have crawled into the den of a she-wolf that was ravaging local sheep, and shot it.

To follow in his footsteps, take the trail past the campground to Wolf Den. You can then continue on a 5-mile loop through thick woodland. Take a swimming costume along if you fancy bathing in the shallow pond.

THE DRIVE

The final stretch of CT 169 from Pomfret to Woodstock continues past farmland and the Roseland Lake, up through the modern buildings and grassy playing fields of South Woodstock, before arriving in Woodstock proper.

07 WOODSTOCK

Roseland Cottage (historicnewengland.org) is proof that wealthy Americans had fancy summer homes even in the mid-1800s. Beautifully preserved, this lovely Gothic Revival house sports pointed arches, crockets and stained-glass windows.

The garden is also a historic treasure, laid out according to the 1850 plan with some 4000 blooms bordered by formal boxwood parterres. Other follies include an aviary, a summerhouse, an icehouse and a vintage bowling alley.

After a stroll around the garden, head down to **Woodstock Orchards** for a glass of fresh cider and to stock up on apples and berries before heading home. If you're in town around Labor Day, be sure to check out the enormous **Woodstock Fair** (woodstockfair.com).

12

CONNECTICUT & RHODE ISLAND

BEST FOR
OUTDOORS

Picnicking at
the Jonathan
Edwards
Winery.

Connecticut Wine Trail

DURATION	DISTANCE	GREAT FOR
5 days	132 miles / 212km	History, food & wine

BEST TIME TO GO	August to October for the grape harvest.

Greenwich Avenue

Starting on Connecticut's moneyed Gold Coast, this tour wends its way between vineyards to encompass the compact downtown of Greenwich, with its high-end shops and notable museums; Philip Johnson's radical mid-century modern Glass House in New Canaan; and New Haven's neo-Gothic turrets. At its northern reaches Stonington's 19th-century sea captains' homes cluster amid maritime vineyards, which produce some of the state's finest drops.

Link Your Trip

01 Coastal New England

From Stonington, continue north along I-95 across the Jamestown Bridge to Newport for more salty coastal scenery.

11 Quiet Corner

Continue north along scenic CT 169 to Canterbury for a laid-back tour of the Quiet Corner.

01 **GREENWICH**

In the early days, Greenwich was home to farmers and fishers who shipped oysters and potatoes to nearby New York. But with the advent of passenger trains and the first cashed-up commuters, the town became a haven for Manhattanites in search of country exclusivity. Along **Greenwich Avenue**, high-end boutiques and gourmet restaurants line the route where the town's trolley once traveled.

One of Greenwich's wealthiest 19th-century inhabitants was Robert Moffat Bruce, a textile tycoon

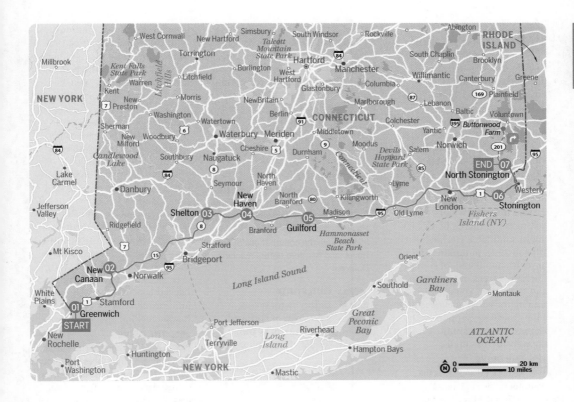

who lived in what is now the **Bruce Museum** (brucemuseum.org). Now a variety of galleries house a natural science collection and a permanent display of impressionist works by the Cos Cob art colony, as well as hosting more than a dozen art exhibits a year.

🚗 **THE DRIVE**
Head northeast along I-95, paralleling US 1, the old Boston–New York post road, until you come to the steel-and-glass towers of metropolitan Stamford. Then take exit 9 onto CT 106 and head inland through the suburbs to New Canaan.

02 NEW CANAAN
The only Gold Coast town without a shoreline, New Canaan is characterized by large clapboard houses, grand Georgian mansions and, unusually, one of the most famous modern houses in the world: the 1949 **Philip Johnson Glass House** (theglasshouse.org). This icon of mid-century modern architecture, set in a dappled wood on 47 acres, was the home of late Pritzker Prize–winner Philip Johnson, and his art collector partner, David Whitney.

Almost totally transparent, the house offers stunning views of the autumnal countryside and Johnson's intriguing collection of contemporary art. Guided tours must be reserved; visitors assemble at the visitor center across the street from the New Canaan train station. In addition to the house, the tour includes a look at Da Monsta, the concrete-and-Styrofoam gatehouse to the property.

🚗 **THE DRIVE**
Leave bucolic New Canaan via CT 123 S and after 2 miles merge with the CT 15. Head north toward New Haven, skirting the suburbs of Norwalk, Westport and Trumbull, then take exit 8 onto CT 8 toward Waterbury. After 6 miles you'll arrive in Shelton.

SHELTON

03 Nestled in the White Hills of Shelton you'll find the 150-year-old, 400-acre **Jones Family Farm** (jonesfamilyfarms.com), home of one of the premier wineries in the state. Jones Winery is known for using its own grapes and those from local vineyards. The vineyard's founder and resident winemaker, Jamie Jones, is now the sixth generational family member to operate the farm.

Aside from the winery and tasting room there's berry picking in summer, a Heritage Farm Hike in June, pumpkins and hayrides in fall and, of course, Christmas trees in November and December. You can also sign up for cooking classes and wine-education suppers at the Harvest Kitchen studio. Check the website for details.

THE DRIVE
Rejoin CT 8 and cross the Housatonic River before taking exit 15 onto CT 34. After less than a mile, take the ramp onto CT 15 N, which weaves through New Haven's exclusive golf greens for 4 miles. Then take exit 59 onto CT 69 S, which takes you right into the center of New Haven.

NEW HAVEN

04 New Haven is home to America's third-oldest university, Yale, and its leafy green is bordered by graceful Colonial buildings, statehouses and churches. The 1816 **Trinity Church** resembles England's Gothic York Minster, while the Georgian-style, 1812 **Center Church on the Green** is a fine example of New England Palladian. But nowhere is the city's history more palpable than at **Yale University** (yale.edu).

Pick up a free map of the campus from **Yale University Visitor Center** (visitorcenter.yale. edu) and take a stroll around the stately buildings, where alumni such as Presidents William H Taft, George HW Bush and Bill Clinton once studied.

In more recent years, New Haven has also built a reputation for itself as an arts mecca.

THE DRIVE
The 14-mile drive east from New Haven to Guilford is easy but uneventful. The highlight is crossing the New Haven harbor bridge before rejoining I-95 through the conurbations of East Haven and Branford before reaching Guilford.

GUILFORD

05 In the historic seaside town of Guilford, **Bishop's Orchards Winery** (bishopsorchards.com) has been

Finding Those Wineries

It's worth bearing in mind that most wineries are tucked away down country roads, and finding your way can often be a challenge. A useful resource is the **Connecticut Wine Trail** (ctwine.com) brochure, which covers all the wineries in the state along with detailed driving directions. Ambitious vinophiles can get their 'passport' stamped at each vineyard and be eligible for prizes.

serving shoreline communities with fresh produce since 1871. Much more than just a winery, Bishop's is also a pick-your-own farm, where berries, peaches, pears, apples and pumpkins can be picked from June through October. The rich variety of produce means the **Bishop's market** (open year-round) is one of the best in the area. If you have kids, they'll get a kick out of the llamas, alpacas and grazing goats.

The coastline around Guilford is wonderful, but much of it is built up. However, the nearby **Hammonasset Beach State Park** (ct.gov) provides a 1100-acre oasis, with a 2-mile pine-backed beach, boardwalk trails and excellent facilities for camping, picnicking and swimming.

THE DRIVE
Leave I-95 and pick up the old post road, US 1. This takes you through genteel Madison to the marshy doorstep of Hammonasset Beach State Park. Stop for a stroll or a picnic, then continue on US 1 for another 6 miles before rejoining I-95 for the remaining 28 miles to Stonington.

STONINGTON

06 Stonington is one of the most appealing towns on the Connecticut coast. Compactly laid out on a peninsula, the town offers complete streetscapes of 18th- and 19th-century houses, many of which were once sea captains' homes.

The main thoroughfare, **Water Street**, features shops selling antiques and Quimper porcelain, colorfully painted dinnerware handmade in France since the 17th century. At the southern end is the 'point,' with a park, a lighthouse and a tiny beach.

Situated on Stonington's south-facing slopes, **Stonington Vineyards** (stoningtonvineyards.com) produces some of the state's finest table wines, thanks to its glacial soils and maritime climate not unlike that of Bordeaux in France. As a result, you can expect creamy chardonnays and award-winning cabernet franc. It may also be worth your while to wet your whistle at the recommended **Saltwater Farm Vineyard** (saltwaterfarmvineyard.com), on the way out of town on Rte 1.

THE DRIVE
Exit Stonington on US 1, which takes you through some very pretty rural countryside lightly dotted with handsome country homes. At Westerly, turn northward on US 2 for a further 5 miles, before turning right on Main St and heading into North Stonington.

⊙ Photo Opportunity
Philip Johnson's glass cube amid the trees.

07 NORTH STONINGTON
Heading northward away from the coast, you arrive at one of the most picturesque and scenically situated vineyards on the tour, the **Jonathan Edwards Winery** (jedwardswinery.com) in North Stonington. Housed in a lovingly renovated dairy barn on a hilltop overlooking the Atlantic, it is the perfect spot for a late-afternoon BYO picnic and wine tasting.

In winter, oenophiles warm themselves around the stone fireplace in the wood-paneled tasting room, while the knowledgeable and enthusiastic staff talk through a variety of wines, both from the Connecticut coast and the Edwards vineyards in Napa, CA.

➤ Detour
Buttonwood Farm
Start: 07 **North Stonington**
Beginning as early as mid-July, an astonishing number of interactive corn mazes begin cropping up on farms throughout New England. Travel north up CT 201 and you can get lost in the themed maze at **Buttonwood Farm** (buttonwoodfarmicecream.com), pick pumpkins from their patches, take hayrides and finish up with some of the farm's delicious homemade ice cream. In October, the maze is also open for nighttime adventures – if you dare!

RITU MANOJ JETHANI/SHUTTERSTOCK ©

Saltwater Farm Vineyard, Stonington

13

CONNECTICUT & RHODE ISLAND

Lower River Valley

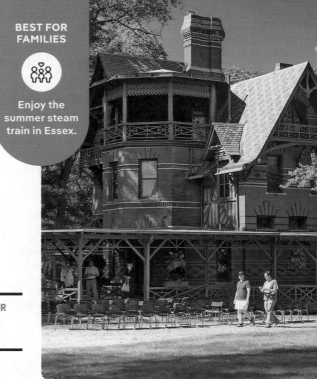

DURATION	DISTANCE	GREAT FOR
4 days	60 miles / 97km	History & families

BEST TIME TO GO	September to February for cruising and eagle-spotting.

Mark Twain House, Hartford

Once the engine of 19th-century commerce, the Connecticut River – New England's longest waterway – now enchants visitors with its historic towns, artist colonies, nature conservancies and gracious country inns. River cruises and steam train rides allow for authentic glimpses into provincial Connecticut life. Even Hartford, the state capital, is rediscovering the river these days with new parks and walkways landscaped along its banks.

Link Your Trip

12 Connecticut Wine Trail

Travel west to Guilford along I-95 for a taste of Connecticut's cabernet sauvignon and New Haven culture.

14 Litchfield Hills Loop

Head into the hills on US 44 for bucolic rural views, market towns and gourmet eats.

01 HARTFORD

Despite the exodus of the insurance companies that earned Hartford its reputation as the 'filing cabinet of America,' those passing through will be surprised at how much the city has to offer. The standout **Wadsworth Atheneum** (thewadsworth.org) houses 40,000 pieces of art in a castlelike Gothic Revival building. These include some by Hartford native Frederic Church, alongside 19th-century impressionist works and a small but outstanding collection of surrealist art.

Other notable sites include **Mark Twain House** (marktwainhouse.org), where novelist Samuel

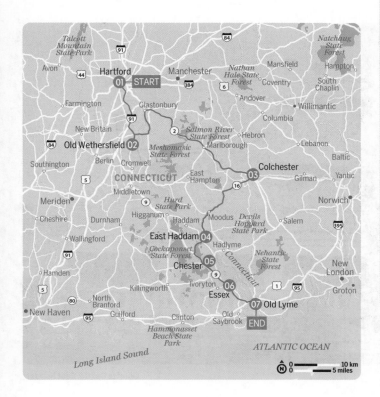

TOP TIP:

Chester–Hadlyme Ferry

In summer you can cross the Connecticut River on the **Chester–Hadlyme Ferry** (ctvisit.com/listings/chesterhadlyme-ferry). The five-minute river crossing on the *Selden III* is the second-oldest ferry service in America, beginning in 1769. The ferry ride affords great views of Gillette Castle and is a fun way to link up with the Essex Steam Train, which runs between Chester and Essex.

Langhorne Clemens (1835–1910) spent 17 years of his life writing the *Adventures of Tom Sawyer* and *Huckleberry Finn*. Architect Edward Tuckerman Potter embellished the house with turrets and gables, and some of the interiors were styled by Louis Comfort Tiffany. Next door to the Twain house is **Harriet Beecher-Stowe Center** (harriet beecherstowe.org). Built in 1871, the house reflects Stowe's ideas about decorating and domestic efficiency, which she expressed in her bestseller *American Woman's Home*. Stowe is most famous for her antislavery book, *Uncle Tom's Cabin*.

THE DRIVE
Exit Hartford along Capitol Ave and Hudson, and merge onto the Colin Whitehead Hwy. Join I-91 S for a short 3.5-mile drive through Hartford's suburbs before taking exit 26 for Old Wethersfield.

02 OLD WETHERSFIELD
A quick jaunt down I-91 will bring you to the historic district of Old Wethersfield. Despite sitting in the larger Hartford suburbs, Old Wethersfield is a living monument to the past, perfectly preserved for more than 375 years. Wander around and you'll find hundreds of historic homes, as well as a number of interesting museums.

The best way to get your bearings, however, is to start at the **Wethersfield Museum** (wethers fieldhistory.org).

THE DRIVE
Accommodations in Hartford and Old Wethersfield tend to be underwhelming, expensive and business oriented. It's far better to push on across the river, via CT 3 N. The pretty, historic town of Glastonbury has some great B&B options. From there, continue along CT 2 toward Colchester.

03 COLCHESTER
Rural Colchester, with its grazing fields and serried ranks of vines, is a certified Community Wildlife Habitat and

RITU MANOJ JETHANI/SHUTTERSTOCK ©

Gillette Castle, East Haddam

listed on the National Register of Historic Places. However, the real reason to come to Colchester is so you can visit **Cato Corner Farm** (catocornerfarm.com), where mother-and-son cheese-makers Elizabeth and Mark craft dozens of aged farmhouse cheeses with raw milk from their herd of Jersey cows. Many of the cheeses, such as the Dairyere (a firm washed-rind cheese), are prizewinners.

Near the cheese shop is the notable **Priam Vineyards** (priamvineyards.com), a 24-acre, solar-powered, sustainable vineyard growing French and American varieties, such as cabernet sauvignon, riesling, merlot, Cayuga and St Croix. In summer, visitors can take self-guided tours of the vineyards, picnic amid the vines and even enjoy live music concerts.

🚗 **THE DRIVE**
Leaving the interstate, turn southwest along Middletown Rd (CT 16) through farmland and alongside Babcock Pond until you reach CT 149, where you turn left and head directly south back toward the river. This part of the drive passes pleasantly through rural communities and historic towns along tree-lined roads.

04 EAST HADDAM
Looming on one of the Seven Sisters hills just above East Haddam is **Gillette Castle** (ctparks.com), a turreted mansion made of fieldstone. Built in 1919 by eccentric actor William Gillette, who made his fortune in the role of Sherlock Holmes, the folly is modeled on the medieval castles of Germany's Rhineland and the views from its terraces are spectacular. The surrounding 125 acres are a designated state park and open year-round but the interior is only open for tours from late May through September (and on special holiday weekends in November and December).

With residents such as Gillette and banker William Goodspeed, East Haddam became a regular stopover on the summer circuit for New Yorkers, who traveled up on Goodspeed's steamship.

To entertain them, he built the **Goodspeed Opera House** (goodspeed.org) in 1876. It's now dedicated to preserving and developing American musicals, and you can still enjoy your intermission drinks on the balcony overhanging the river.

THE DRIVE
From East Haddam, cross the Connecticut River via the steel swing bridge and meander southeast through rural countryside for about 5 miles before merging with I-9 S toward Old Saybrook. After 1.5 miles, take exit 6 for Chester.

05 CHESTER

Cupped in the valley of Pattaconk Brook, Chester is one of the most charming river towns along the Connecticut River. Its quaint Main St is lined with good restaurants and thriving galleries and workshops, and most visitors come to simply browse the antique shops and indulge in some fine dining.

The town's brewpub, **Little House Brewing Co** (littlehouse brewing.com), offers a respite from road stress, but if you're seeking caffeination, drop in to have a coffee at local provender **Simon's Marketplace** (simons marketplace.net) and pick up some tasty deli treats.

THE DRIVE
Rejoin I-9 for the short 6-mile hop to Essex.

Photo Opportunity

William Gillette's ruined Gothic folly.

---

06 ESSEX

Handsome, tree-lined Essex, established in 1635, features well-preserved Federal-period homes, legacies of rum and tobacco fortunes made in the 19th century. Today the town prides itself on the oldest-known continuously operating waterfront in the country. That and the **Connecticut River Museum** (ctrivermuseum.org), next to the Steamboat Dock, where exhibits recount the area's history, including a replica of the world's first submarine, the *American Turtle*, built by Yale student David Bushnell in 1776.

The best way to experience the river is to take the **Essex Steam Train & Riverboat Ride** (essexsteamtrain.com), which transports you to Deep River on a steam train and then runs you up to the Goodspeed Opera House at East Haddam in a riverboat. The train trip takes about an hour; with the riverboat ride, the excursion takes 2½ hours. In February look out for

---

eagle-watching cruises (ctvisit.com/articles/tours-soar-eagle-watching-connecticut) as bald eagles migrate.

THE DRIVE
For the final leg of the trip, rejoin I-9 for an uneventful drive south. Just the other side of the highway, Ivoryton offers some good accommodations options. Leave I-9 at exit 70 onto CT 156 E, which will loop round onto Shore Rd. Then follow the signs into Old Lyme.

07 OLD LYME

Since the early 20th century, Old Lyme has been the center of the Lyme Art Colony, which embraced and cultivated the nascent American impressionist movement. Numerous artists, including William Chadwick, Childe Hassam, Willard Metcalfe and Henry Ward Ranger, came here to paint, staying in the mansion of local art patron Florence Griswold.

Her house, which her artist friends decorated with murals (often in lieu of paying rent), is now the **Florence Griswold Museum** (florencegriswold museum.org) and contains a fine selection of both impressionist and Barbizon paintings. The estate consists of her Georgian-style house, the Krieble Gallery, the Chadwick studio and Griswold's beloved gardens.

14

Litchfield
Hills Loop

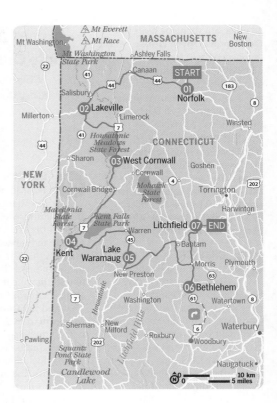

DURATION	DISTANCE	GREAT FOR
5 days	77 miles / 123km	Families, history & nature

BEST TIME TO GO	August to October for harvest bounty.

With scenery to match the Green Mountains of Vermont, pre-Colonial villages worthy of any movie set, and the finest food, culture and music in Connecticut, the Litchfield Hills attract a sophisticated crowd of weekending Manhattanites. But its hardwood forests, dappled river valleys, covered bridges, waterfalls, lakes and abundant fall fairs also offer endless possibilities for intrepid walkers, anglers, antiquers and history buffs.

Link Your Trip

02 Fall Foliage Tour

Head north on CT 7 for leaf-peeping, walking and ziplining in Massachusetts, Vermont and New Hampshire.

13 Lower River Valley

From Woodbury, take CT 84 for Mark Twain's hometown of Hartford and a leisurely drive down the Connecticut River Valley.

01 NORFOLK

Norfolk's bucolic scenery and cool summers have long attracted prosperous New Yorkers. They built many of the town's fine mansions, its well-endowed Romanesque Revival library and its arts-and-crafts-style town hall, now the **Infinity Music Hall & Bistro** (infinityhall.com).

Most opulent of all was **Whitehall**, the summer estate of Ellen and Carl Battell Stoeckel, passionate (and moneyed) music-lovers who established the **Norfolk Chamber Music Festival** (music.yale.edu/

BEST FOR FOODIES

Dine in style in Litchfield and Bantam.

10'-11"

ONE LANE BRIDGE

Covered bridge, West Cornwall

norfolk). These extravagant affairs – the couple thought nothing of recruiting a 70-piece New York philharmonic orchestra and paying for a special train to transport it to their festival – were among the most popular summer events in New England. On her death in 1939, Ellen Stoeckel bequeathed the redwood 'Music Shed' to Yale University Summer School of Music, ensuring the tradition continues.

THE DRIVE
Head west along the main, forest-lined route US 44 for Lakeville's twin town of Salisbury. From here it's a short, 1-mile drive along historic Main St to Lakeville's town center.

02 LAKEVILLE
The rolling farmland in this quiet and remote corner of the Litchfield Hills is home to millionaires and movie luminaries such as Meryl Streep. The Rockefellers favored the famous Hotchkiss preparatory school, and in Lakeville, Paul Newman raced the **Lime Rock Race Track** (limerock.com), which he thought was the most beautiful racing track in America. Today the seven-turn, 1.5-mile circuit hosts vintage and historic automobile races, along with regular stock-car races.

Otherwise, head to the peaks of **Bear Mountain** or **Lion's Head** for eye-popping panoramas. Part of the Appalachian National Scenic Trail (appalachiantrail.com), you'll find the trailheads leading off Rte 41.

THE DRIVE
Exit Lakeville south on Sharon Rd before picking up the CT 112 E past the Lime Rock Race Track. From here, the drive swoops south through rolling farmland, dotted with big red-and-white barns and stables. After 5 miles, turn south on US 7 into West Cornwall.

03 WEST CORNWALL
The village of West Cornwall is just one of six Cornwall villages in Connecticut, but it is the most famous thanks to its picturesque **covered bridge**. The bridge was known

as the 'Kissing Bridge,' because horse-drawn carriages were able to slow down to a steady trot inside, thus allowing their passengers a brief bit of alone time.

Otherwise, the area attracts nature-lovers and birders who come to hike, fish and boat on the Housatonic River. In winter, nearby **Mohawk Mountain Ski Area** (mohawkmtn.com) is the largest ski resort in the state, with 24 slopes and trails.

THE DRIVE
The 14-mile drive south along US 7 to Kent from West Cornwall is the most scenic stretch of the trip, especially in fall, when the thickly forested hillsides are ablaze. The road runs parallel to the Appalachian Trail and Housatonic River for most of the way, offering lots of opportunities to stop and stretch your legs along the river.

Photo Opportunity

Cornwall's picturesque covered bridge over the Housatonic.

04 KENT
The area around Kent presents some of the loveliest rural scenery in the hills. At **Kent Falls State Park**, a waterfall tumbles 250ft over the rocky hillside. Hike the easy trail to the top, or just settle into a sunny picnic spot. Nearby, the **Sloane-Stanley Museum** (portal.ct.gov) houses a barn full of early American tools, collected by artist and author Eric Sloane, who painted the cloud-filled sky

mural at the Smithsonian Air and Space Museum in Washington, DC. In autumn, the adjacent **Connecticut Antique Machinery Museum** (camamuseum. org) is a fun, mostly outdoor child-friendly attraction with all manner of steam-powered locomotives. One inventive sculptor has turned his yard into a public art space called **Sculpturedale** (deniscurtisssculptor.com).

Worth a detour before heading east out of town is a drive further south to Bulls Bridge, the area's other drivable covered bridge.

THE DRIVE
Take the CT 341 eastward out of Kent, climbing up out of the valley through more forested hills. After 10 miles, turn south toward Warren along CT 45. After a further 1.6 miles, Lake Waramaug will peek between the trees on your left.

LOCAL KNOWLEDGE

Waterbirds

The **Livingston Ripley Waterfowl Conservancy** (ripleyconservancy.org), home to former director of Yale's Peabody Museum and later a Smithsonian bigwig, S Dillon Ripley, hosts a collection of more species of waterbird (from around the world) than nearly any facility in the US. There's also a resident falconer and some spooky birds of prey, and even African cranes cavort around the expansive property.

Hopkins Vineyard, Lake Waramaug

LAKE WARAMAUG

05 Of the dozens of lakes and ponds in the Litchfield Hills, Lake Waramaug stands out. As you make your way around the northern shore of the lake on North Shore Rd, you'll come to the **Hopkins Vineyard** (hopkinsvineyard. com). The wines here are made mostly from French American hybrids and the low-oak chardonnay frequently wins awards. The vineyard offers wine flights from the bar and the view is worth the trip, particularly when the foliage changes in the fall. Be sure to arrive well before closing time, and call ahead during the low season.

THE DRIVE
Leaving Lake Waramaug along North and East Shore Rd, turn left onto US 202 toward Bantam. At Lake Bantam, take CT 209 and 109 around the western and southern edges of the lake and after 3.5 miles turn right onto CT 61 S into Bethlehem.

BETHLEHEM

06 Bethlehem is Connecticut's 'Christmas Town' and every year thousands of visitors come for the **Christmas Fair** (christmastownfestival.com) and to have their Christmas mail hand-stamped in the village post office.

The town's religious history extends to the founding of the first theological seminary in America by local resident Reverend Joseph Bellamy. His home, the **Bellamy-Ferriday House & Garden** (ctlandmarks. org), a 1750s clapboard mansion, is open to the public and is a treasure trove of delftware, Asian art and period furnishings. Equally exquisite is the garden, the design of latter-day owner Caroline Ferriday, who designed it to resemble an Aubusson Persian carpet. Its geometrical box hedges are in-filled with frothing peonies, lilacs and heirloom roses.

THE DRIVE
The final drive north to Litchfield passes through more bucolic scenery, dotted with country farmhouses and past the shores of Lake Bantam. Head north out of Bethlehem along CT 61, past the Bellamy-Ferriday House & Garden, then connect to CT 63 via Old Litchfield Rd, for a straight run into town.

Detour
Woodbury
Start: **06** Bethlehem
At the southern border of the Litchfield Hills, Woodbury is justifiably famous as the 'antiques capital' of Connecticut, boasting over 30 dealerships and 20 stores along historic Main St. **Woodbury Antiques Dealers Association** (antiqueswoodbury.com) publishes an online guide.

LITCHFIELD

07 The centerpiece of the region is Connecticut's best-preserved late-18th-century town. Founded in 1719, Litchfield prospered as a main thoroughfare between New York and Boston. The town itself converges on a long oval green, and is surrounded by swaths of protected land. In late July or early August the **Litchfield Jazz Festival** (litchfieldjazzfest. com), in nearby Goshen, draws a thousands-strong crowd.

Walk down **North Street** and **South Street** (with a free walking tour sheet from the information kiosk) and admire the great mansions. Washington slept at the **Sheldon Tavern** on North St on his way to confer with General Rochambeau. Down the street, **Bull House** was home to Ludlow Bull, the American Egyptologist who participated in the discovery of Tutankhamen's gold-filled tomb. On South St, New Jersey judge Tapping Reeve founded America's first law school, the **Litchfield Law School** (litchfield historicalsociety.org), in 1775. Admission to the small **Litchfield History Museum** is free.

Camel's Hump, Huntington (p111)

Vermont

Explore
Vermont

Vermont, the only one of New England's six states that is entirely without an Atlantic coastline, is nonetheless a highlight of any trip here. Come for gorgeous university towns, beautiful mountain peaks, lush river valleys, old mills, wildlife and, in the fall, brilliant maple trees. It's also one of the best spots to find the liquid gold known as maple syrup, which is collected in the spring when the sap runs and is then boiled down to a syrup in vats. The drives here will leave you sated in the way that a perfect meal leaves you full.

Montpelier

Vermont's capital is also the state's largest city, so you can stock up on supplies, find a tool to repair your tent with, and stay in a hotel or motel that's perfectly suited to your needs. But more than all the logistics, spending a night or two in Montpelier will let you soak up the culture of Vermont and get a sense of what makes its people tick. Get your hair cut at a barbershop, find a great cup of coffee or chat with the sommelier about wine over dinner. You'll also find that this is one of the region's most picturesque big cities, with lots of tall church steeples, barn-red buildings and a gorgeous gold-domed statehouse.

Burlington

On the placid eastern shores of Lake Champlain is Burlington, a storied Vermont city that has beautiful parks, quiet avenues, stunning fall foliage and a waterfront beach and real estate. Some would argue that it's the state's prettiest city, though with so much natural beauty here such a statement can be hard to quantify. Unmissable are sunsets over the lake, the stunning Billings Library (a gorgeous red sandstone structure) and dozens of excellent restaurants. If you're combining several drives into a big loop around the state, or even mixing in a bit of Maine and New Hampshire, you'll be well served to pencil in a night or two to spend here.

Stowe

One of the most iconic ski resorts in New England, Stowe floods with skiers and snowboarders from the moment there's enough powder

WHEN TO GO

There's no bad time to visit Vermont, so toss the bags in the trunk, fill the tank and go. You'll find the leaves are at their prettiest in the fall, but spring – with its sap greens, yellows and palette of verdant forest colors – is nearly as pretty. Bring bug repellent, though.

(sometimes in the fall) to the sad reckoning that the season has ended in the spring. Winter drivers looking for fun, excitement and company will find the bars packed and other venues full, with both daytime and evening activities planned for those of all ages. In summer it's quieter, but as the tourism board says, it's a 'four season' destination. Take that with a grain of salt, but there's no debating that Ben & Jerry's Ice Cream headquarters is open year-round.

Brattleboro

On Vermont's southern border, Brattleboro is a worthy bookend for a loop through the state or good as a stopover point for those driving up from western Massachusetts. It has a decent arts scene in addition to pretty views along the Connecticut River.

TRANSPORTATION

Those wanting to fly into the state should choose a carrier that serves Patrick Leahy Burlington International Airport. Logan International in Boston is the closest large airport, and from there it's about a 3½-hour drive to Burlington. Rutland is a more central option.

 WHERE TO STAY

If a rustic log-cabin stay doesn't sound delightful, consider an overnight at the Trapp Family Lodge (p101), a 96-room Swiss-style chalet overlooking Stowe that was built by the von Trapp family after their *Sound of Music* escape to the US. Budget travelers will be glad to know that 'boondocking' (camping where space allows along rivers, roadsides or clearings) is allowed through many parts of the Green Mountains. You'll also find the state has plenty of high-end lodgings, ranging from fancy ski chalets to ritzy or historic B&Bs. Whatever your budget, Vermont has what you're looking for.

👍 **WHAT'S ON**

Stowe Winter Carnival

This multiday event in January includes ice-carving competitions, sleigh rides, snow golf (yeah, you heard that right) and lots of other winter-themed merriment.

Vermont Cheese Festival

In July head to Shelburne, where you can partake in its cheese festival, with tastings, pairings, cooking demos and cheese-making workshops.

Bennington Battle Day

Commemorate August 16, when Bennington played a key part in the Revolutionary War.

Resources

Burlington Free Press
(*burlingtonfreepress.com*)
This major Vermont newspaper has all the state's current events, emergencies and other listings.

Brattleboro Reformer
(*reformer.com*)
Another news source focusing on the Brattleboro area, with state news, local movie listings and other read-worthy tidbits.

15

VERMONT

Vermont's Spine: Route 100

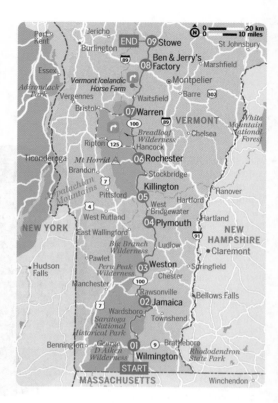

DURATION	DISTANCE	GREAT FOR
3–4 days	130 miles / 209km	Food & drink, history & families

BEST TIME TO GO	May to October for snow-free roads and sun-filled days.

Spanning the state from bottom to top, Vermont's revered Route 100 winds past the Northeast's most legendary ski resorts and through some of New England's prettiest scenery, with the verdant Green Mountains always close at hand. This drive takes you on a slow meander through the state, though you might speed up in anticipation of the Ben & Jerry's Factory tour beckoning on the final stretch of road.

Link Your Trip

16 Cider Season Sampler

From Killington, head west on US 4 to enjoy fall's delicious delights.

19 Southern Vermont Loop

In Weston, branch off onto this circle tour of southern Vermont.

01 WILMINGTON

Chartered in 1751, Wilmington is the winter and summer gateway to Mt Snow, one of New England's best ski resorts and an excellent summertime mountain-biking and golfing spot. There are no main sights per se, but the **Historic District** on W Main St is a prime example of 18th- and 19th-century architecture and is chock-full of restaurants and boutiques; the bulk of the village is on the National Register of Historic Places. This is an excellent base where you can stay overnight and grab a bite before your journey up north.

BEST FOR FAMILIES

Poking around the Weston country store and taking a Ben & Jerry's Factory tour.

Wilmington

 THE DRIVE
Ski country (look for Mt Snow on your left) gives way to sleepy hamlets as you drive 26 miles north on VT 100 to the village of Jamaica.

02 JAMAICA
A prime dose of rural Vermont, with a country store and several antique shops, this artsy community tucked into the evergreen forest is also home to **Jamaica State Park** (vtstateparks.com/jamaica.html), the best place in Vermont for riverside camping. The annual **Whitewater Weekend** held here in late September draws kayaking enthusiasts from all over New England to pit their skills against the rampaging West River. There's good swimming right in the heart of the campground, and walkers can also head 3 miles upstream along a 19th-century railway bed to **Hamilton Falls**, a 50ft ribbon of water cascading into a natural swimming hole.

 THE DRIVE
Continue north 17 miles on VT 100 to Weston.

03 WESTON
Picturesque Weston is home to the **Vermont Country Store** (vermont countrystore.com), founded in 1946 and still going strong under the Orton family's ownership, four generations later. It's a time warp from a simpler era, when goods were made to last and quirky products with appeal had a home. The eclectic mix filling the shelves today ranges from the genuinely useful (cozy old-fashioned flannel nighties) to the nostalgic (vintage tiddly-winks and the classic 1960s board-game Mystery Date) to the downright weird (electronic yodeling pickles, anyone?). For a midtrip pick-me-up, prowl through their vast array of traditional penny-candy jars and enjoy free tastes of Vermont cheeses, cookies and other temptations.

 THE DRIVE
Continue north on VT 100.

WHY THIS IS A CLASSIC TRIP

Gregor Clark, Writer

After 20-plus years living in Vermont, I'm still smitten with VT 100. No other route so fully captures Vermont's four-season beauty, from the Green Mountains' fall colors to the Mad River's ski areas and sculpted-rock swimming holes; from the lonely moose country near Granville to the cozy village feel of Weston. For an unforgettable add-on, climb VT 108 from Stowe through Smugglers Notch at trip's end.

At Plymouth Union, veer off to the right onto VT 100A for about a mile until you reach Plymouth Center. The total drive is 22 miles.

 04 **PLYMOUTH**
Gazing across the high pastures of Plymouth, you feel a bit like Rip Van Winkle – only it's the past you've woken up to. President Calvin Coolidge's boyhood home looks much as it did a century ago, with houses, barns, a church, a one-room schoolhouse and a general store gracefully arrayed among old maples on a bucolic hillside. At Plymouth's heart is the preserved **President Calvin Coolidge State Historic Site** (historicsites. vermont.gov/calvin-coolidge). The village's streets are sleepy today, but the museum tells a tale of an earlier America filled with elbow

grease and perseverance. Tools for blacksmithing, woodworking, butter making and hand laundering are indicative of the hard work and grit it took to wrest a living from Vermont's stony pastures. As a boy, Calvin hayed with his grandfather and kept the woodbox filled.

Cofounded by Coolidge's father, **Plymouth Cheese** (plymouth cheese.com) still produces a classic farmhouse cheddar known as granular curd cheese. Its distinctively sharp tang and grainy texture are reminiscent of the wheel cheese traditionally found at general stores throughout Vermont. Panels downstairs tell the history of local cheese-making, while a museum upstairs displays cheese-making equipment from another era.

 THE DRIVE
Drive back along VT 100A and turn right to return to VT 100 N. The drive is 13 miles.

05 **KILLINGTON**
The largest ski resort in the east, Killington spans seven mountains, highlighted by 4241ft **Killington Peak**, the second highest in Vermont. It operates the largest snow-making system in North America and its numerous outdoor activities – from skiing and snowboarding in winter to mountain biking and hiking in summer – are all centrally located on the mountain. **Killington Resort** (killington. com), the East Coast's answer to Vail, runs the efficient **K1-Express Gondola**, which in winter transports up to 3000 skiers per hour in heated cars along a 2.5-mile cable – it's the highest lift in Vermont. In summer and fall it whisks you to impeccable vantage

points above the mountains: leaf-peeping atop the cascading rainbow of copper, red and gold in foliage season is truly magical.

 THE DRIVE
Enter the idyllic valley of the White River as you drive 24 miles north on VT 100 to Rochester.

 06 **ROCHESTER**
This unassuming blink-and-you'll-miss-it town, with a vast village green lined by well-maintained, historic New England homes, is worth a stop to experience rural Vermont life minus the masses of tourists in other towns along VT 100.

Stop in at **Sandy's Books & Bakery** (sandysbooksand bakery.com), a cafe, bookstore and popular local hang-out. With homemade everything – granola, bagels, whole-wheat bread – Sandy's serves up mean dishes such as spinach-and-egg-filled biscuits, spanakopita, salads and soups. Tables are scattered between bookshelves, so it's a great spot for a java break and a browse of the new and used books (or the locally made Vermont soap). We dare you to resist the cookies.

 THE DRIVE
Continue north on VT 100. Roughly 10 miles past Rochester, a pullout on the left provides views to Moss Glen Falls. A mile or so later, the small ponds of Granville Gulf comprise one of the state's most accessible moose-watching spots. About 5 miles further north, turn right onto Covered Bridge Rd and cross the bridge into Warren village.

Detour
Middlebury & Lincoln Gaps
Start: **06** Rochester
The 'gap roads' that run east–west over the Green Mountains offer some

Right: Killington Peak

of the most picturesque views in Vermont. Ready to explore? Four miles north of Rochester, in Hancock, scenic VT 125 splits west off VT 100 and climbs over **Middlebury Gap**. Stops to look out for as you make the 15-mile crossing from Hancock to East Middlebury include beautiful **Texas Falls** (3 miles from Hancock), Middlebury Gap (6 miles) and the **Robert Frost Interpretive Trail**, an easygoing loop trail enlivened by plaques featuring Frost's poetry (10 miles). For a scenic loop back to the main route, continue west on VT 125 to East Middlebury, then take VT 116 north. Soon after crossing through the pretty village of **Bristol**, turn right on Lincoln Gap Rd and follow it 14 miles east to rejoin the main route at Warren. The return trip also offers some nice stops. As you turn onto Lincoln Gap Rd, look for the parked cars at **Bartlett Falls**, where the New Haven River's raging waters cascade into one of Vermont's most pristine swimming holes. Later, after a crazy-steep climb (partly unpaved) to **Lincoln Gap**, stop at the 2428ft summit for lovely views and some nice trails, including the 5-mile round trip to the 4000ft summit of Mt Abraham.

07 WARREN

This sweet village is the southern gateway into Vermont's picturesque Mad River Valley. The river is popular with swimmers and kayakers, while the surrounding mountains are a mecca for skiers, who flock to the slopes at nearby **Sugarbush** (sugarbush.com) and **Mad River Glen** (madriverglen.com).

Stop in at the **Warren Store** in the village center, an animated community hang-out with wavy 19th-century wood floors, a deli serving gourmet sandwiches and

Photo Opportunity

The 360-degree views from the K1-Express Gondola above Killington.

pastries, and a front porch ideal for sipping coffee while poring over the *New York Times*. The store upstairs sells an eclectic mix of jewelry, toys, Vermont casual clothing and knickknacks, while the sundeck below overlooks a pretty swimming hole framed by sculpted granite rocks.

THE DRIVE

Continue north 20 miles on VT 100 through pretty farm country to Waterbury, then follow signs for Stowe, crossing the overpass over I-89 to reach Ben & Jerry's.

Detour

Vermont Icelandic Horse Farm
Start: 07 Warren
Icelandic horses are one of the oldest, and some say most versatile, breeds in the world. They're also friendly and unbelievably affectionate creatures, and are fairly easy to ride even for novices – they tend to stop and think (rather than panic) if something frightens them. The **Vermont Icelandic Horse Farm** (icelandichorses.com), 3 miles west of VT 100 (where the tarmac ends and becomes a dirt road), takes folks on one- to three-hour or full-day jaunts year-round; it also offers two- to five-day inn-to-inn treks (some riding experience required). The farm also runs **Mad River Inn** (madriverinn.com), a pleasant inn a short trot away. Head 9 miles north of Warren on VT 100 and follow the signs to the horse farm.

08 BEN & JERRY'S FACTORY

No trip to Vermont would be complete without a visit to **Ben & Jerry's Factory** (benjerry.com/about-us/factory-tours), the biggest production center for America's most famous ice cream. Sure, the manufacturing process is interesting, but a visit here also explains how school pals Ben and Jerry went from a $5 ice-cream-making correspondence course to a global enterprise, and offers a glimpse of the fun, in-your-face culture that made these frozen-dessert pioneers so successful. You're treated to a (very) small free taste at the end – for larger doses head to the on-site scoop shop.

Quaintly perched on a knoll overlooking the parking lot, the Ben & Jerry's Flavor Graveyard's neat rows of headstones pay silent tribute to flavors that flopped, like Makin' Whoopie Pie and Dastardly Mash. Each memorial is lovingly inscribed with the flavor's brief life span on the grocery store of this earth and a tribute poem. Rest in peace, Holy Cannoli (1997–98)! Adieu, Miss Jelena's Sweet Potato Pie (1992–93)!

THE DRIVE

Wipe that ice-cream smile off your face and replace it with an ear-to-ear grin as you continue 9 miles up VT 100 to the legendary ski village of Stowe.

09 STOWE

In a cozy valley where the West Branch River flows into the Little River and mountains rise to the sky in all directions, the quintessential Vermont village of Stowe (founded in 1794) bustles quietly.

Nestled in the **Green Mountain National Forest**, the highest point in Vermont, Mt Mansfield (4393ft) towers in the background, juxtaposed against the pencil-thin steeple of Stowe's Community Church, creating the classic Vermont picture-postcard scene.

With more than 200 miles of cross-country ski trails, some of the finest mountain biking and downhill skiing in the east and world-class hiking, this is a natural mecca for adrenaline junkies and active families. If shopping and cafe-hopping are more your style, the village center also makes a delightful spot for a leisurely stroll. In addition to winter snow sports, **Stowe Mountain Resort** (stowe.com) opens from spring through to fall with gondola sky rides, an alpine slide and a scenic auto toll road that zigzags to the top of Mt Mansfield.

If *The Sound of Music* is one of your favorite things, the hilltop **Trapp Family Lodge** (trapp family.com) boasts sprawling views and oodles of activities, such as hiking, horse-drawn sleigh and carriage rides, lodge tours detailing the family history (often led by a member of the Trapp family), summer concerts on their meadow and some frothy goodness at the nearby **Von Trapp Bierhall** (vontrapp brewing. com/bierhall.htm).

Robert Frost's Vermont

In 1920 poet Robert Frost (1874–1963) moved from New Hampshire to Vermont seeking 'a better place to farm and especially grow apples.' For almost four decades, Frost lived in the Green Mountain State, growing apples and writing much of his poetry in a log cabin in **Ripton**, a beautiful hamlet set in the Green Mountains 12 miles west of VT 100, where he kept a summer home. Today, tiny Ripton and the surrounding area in the Green Mountain National Forest have been officially designated **Robert Frost Country**.

Flavor Graveyard, Ben & Jerry's Factory

16

VERMONT

Cider Season Sampler

BEST FOR FOODIES

Award-winning cheddar and crisp apples from Shelburne Farms, or divine meals with a waterfall view at Simon Pearce.

DURATION	DISTANCE	GREAT FOR
3–4 days	229 miles / 369km	Families, food & drink

BEST TIME TO GO	August to October – apple-picking is at its prime.

Billings Farm & Museum, Woodstock

When most people think 'Vermont food and drink,' beer or maple syrup come to mind. But these days, vineyards, makers of craft cider and locavore restaurants are also sprouting up around the state. Chefs, farmers and communities have begun working together in mutually supportive ways, revitalizing local culture as they build on Vermont's deep agricultural roots. Fall, with its blaze of colors, is the best time to embrace the bounty.

Link Your Trip

15 Vermont's Spine: Route 100

Connect to VT 100 from Cambridge via mountain-hugging VT 108 through Smugglers Notch.

18 Lake Champlain Byway

In Shelburne you can connect with this scenic journey up through Vermont's Champlain Islands.

01 QUECHEE

Vermont's tongue-in-cheek answer to the Grand Canyon, the **Quechee Gorge** is a 163ft-deep scar that cuts about 3000ft along the Ottauquechee River. View it from the bridge or work off those pancake breakfasts with a hike to the bottom – the 15-minute descent through pine forest is beautiful, following a trail on the south side of US 4.

In downtown Quechee Village, make a beeline for **Simon Pearce Glass** (simonpearce.com), in the old woolen mill cantilevered out over the Ottauquechee River. Pearce, an Irish glassblower, immigrated to Quechee in 1981, drawn by a vision of running his

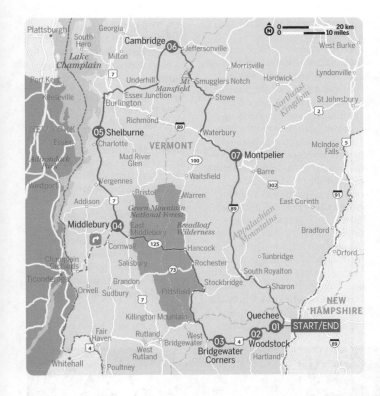

the beautifully conserved fields and forests surrounding Mt Tom. The centerpiece is a 19th-century mansion once owned by early American conservationist George Perkins Marsh and members of the Rockefeller family. Combined tickets with the Billings Farm & Museum are available.

THE DRIVE
Drive west on US 4 for 8 miles to Bridgewater Corners, following the curve of the Ottauquechee a few miles upstream.

03 BRIDGEWATER CORNERS
Just off the road on the left, **Long Trail Brewing Company** (longtrail.com) is one of Vermont's leading producers of craft beer. On a sunny day, it's delightful to sit in its riverside beer garden, modeled after Munich's Hofbrauhaus. Inside is a cozy beer hall that's great for sampling brews. Check out the self-guided brewery tour on the 2nd floor – panels on the small observation platform explain the beer-making process unfolding on the floor below.

THE DRIVE
Take US 4 for 12 miles west through Killington, then head north 23 miles on VT 100 to Hancock. From here, scenic VT 125 snakes 20 miles west over the Green Mountains into Middlebury.

04 MIDDLEBURY
Middlebury's original claim to fame was its prestigious liberal-arts college, founded here in 1800. The pretty campus, dotted with buildings constructed of local marble and gray limestone, makes for a pleasant stroll, as does the pedestrian bridge along the base

entire operation self-sufficiently with hydropower. Four decades later, he's built a small empire. His flagship Quechee store displays pottery and glassware and offers glassblowing demonstrations daily.

THE DRIVE
Follow US 4 west for 7 miles to Woodstock.

02 WOODSTOCK
Chartered in 1761, Woodstock has been the highly dignified seat of scenic Windsor County since 1766. The townspeople built grand Federal and Greek Revival homes surrounding the oval village green, and four of Woodstock's churches can claim

bells cast by Paul Revere. Senator Jacob Collamer, a friend of Abraham Lincoln's, once observed, 'The good people of Woodstock have less incentive than others to yearn for heaven.'

Billings Farm & Museum (billingsfarm.org) employs a mix of 19th- and 20th-century methods. Visitor activities are seasonal, from horse and sleigh rides and afternoon milking of cows to demonstrations of strawberry shortcake made in a cast-iron stove.

At the adjacent **Marsh-Billings-Rockefeller National Historical Park** (nps.gov/mabi), a 20-mile network of carriage paths and trails wind through

Vermont Fresh Network

Fresh local food is never far away in the Green Mountain State, thanks to the Vermont Fresh Network (vermontfresh. net), a partnership between the state's restaurants and farmers. Restaurants commit to supporting local producers by buying direct from the farm, while 'farmers dinners' throughout the year allow diners to meet the people who put the food on their table.

For a full list of participating restaurants and upcoming events, see their website.

of Otter Creek Falls in the heart of town.

Surrounded by fertile farm and orchard land, Middlebury is also a leader in Vermont's locavore movement and a major producer of craft beer and cider. On Wednesdays and Saturdays in summer, head down to the Marble Works, near the falls, to revel in the cornucopia of organic produce at the twice-weekly **farmers market**. Just under 2 miles north, you can stop at **Woodchuck Cidery** (woodchuck.com/ ciderhouse), Vermont's largest producer of hard cider, for tastes ($3 gets you any four flavors from their dozen-plus lineup). If wine tasting is more your thing, continue 2 miles north on US 7 to New Haven's **Lincoln Peak Vineyard** (lincolnpeakvineyard.com), one of the finest wineries in the state.

THE DRIVE
Head north 27 miles on US 7 into Shelburne, then take Harbor Rd 1.6 miles northwest to Shelburne Farms.

Detour
Champlain Orchards
Start: 04 Middlebury
Wide-open farm country cascades toward Lake Champlain as you detour 16 miles southwest from Middlebury along VT 30 and VT 74 to **Champlain Orchards** (champlain orchards.com). Here you can pick two dozen varieties of apples – including many New England heirloom varieties – or watch the pressing and bottling of ultrafresh cider. The orchard is famous for its free 'while-you-pick' acoustic concerts and an annual October harvest celebration.

T PHOTOGRAPHY/SHUTTERSTOCK ©

Champlain Orchards

05 SHELBURNE

In 1886 William Seward Webb and Lila Vanderbilt Webb built a little place for themselves on Lake Champlain. The 1400-acre farm, designed by landscape architect Frederick Law Olmsted (who also designed New York City's Central Park), was both a country house for the Webbs and a working farm. These days, the century-old estate and National Historic Landmark exists as **Shelburne Farms**, a working farm and environmental education center.

Tours in a truck-pulled open wagon are a barrel of fun: you can admire the buildings (inspired by European Romanticism), observe cheese-making and learn about maple syrup and mustard production. Hikers can meander the walking trails and kids love the animals in the children's farmyard. In mid-September, drop by and celebrate autumn traditions at the annual **Harvest Festival**, featuring hay rides, a hay-bale maze, music and antique farm machines.

🚗 THE DRIVE

Head north on US 7 through Burlington. Hop on VT 15, then VT 128 and VT 104 to Cambridge. The drive is 35 miles.

Photo Opportunity

Shelburne Farms orchards in the late-afternoon light.

06 CAMBRIDGE

Tucked into the stunningly beautiful Lamoille River valley at the foot of Mt Mansfield, **Boyden Valley Winery** (boydenvalley.com) is one of Vermont's leading producers of dessert wines. Savor the views and check out the award-winning Gold Leaf, a Vermont-inspired concoction that uses maple syrup straight from the farm combined with local apples.

🚗 THE DRIVE

For spectacular mountain scenery, take VT 108 south through Smugglers Notch to Stowe, then pick up VT 100 south to Waterbury and hop on I-89 east to Montpelier. The drive is 42 miles.

07 MONTPELIER

With 9000 residents, Montpelier is America's smallest capital city and the only one without a McDonald's.

Adjacent to the gold-domed **State House** (statehouse.vermont.gov; tours must be arranged in advance), whose front doors are guarded by a massive statue of American Revolutionary hero Ethan Allen, is **Vermont History Museum** (vermonthistory.org/museum). Its award-winning 'Freedom and Unity' (the state motto) exhibit shows 400 years of Vermont history. From your first steps into an Abenaki wigwam, you're asked to consider the true meaning of this phrase. Controversies aren't brushed under the rug: a short film presents the early-20th-century debate over women's suffrage alongside footage from the 1999 statehouse hearings where citizens voiced support for or opposition to civil unions. In a very Vermontish way, you're invited to ponder issues on your own regardless of any party line. The panoply of voices and imaginative presentation keep this exhibit fun and lively.

🚗 THE DRIVE

From Montpelier, a straight 54-mile shot down I-89 returns you to your starting point at Quechee.

17

VERMONT

Northeast Kingdom to Camel's Hump

BEST FOR OUTDOORS

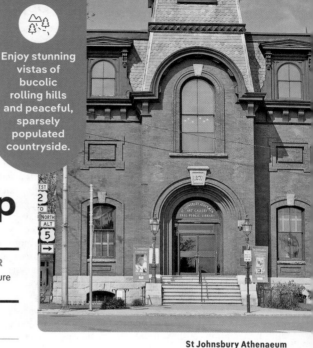

Enjoy stunning vistas of bucolic rolling hills and peaceful, sparsely populated countryside.

DURATION	DISTANCE	GREAT FOR
3–4 days	169 miles / 272km	History & nature

BEST TIME TO GO	May to October for warmish weather and snow-free roads.

St Johnsbury Athenaeum

Some say this is the real Vermont: historic villages frozen in time, narrow mountain passes and expanses of farmland stretching out to lush, maple-covered mountains. A word of warning: this trip is full of curves, lesser-known attractions and dirt roads without phone service. Translation? This trip is perfect for spontaneous explorers ready to embrace Vermont's quirky spirit of off-the-radar back-road adventure.

Link Your Trip

16 Cider Season Sampler

After Craftsbury Common, join the Cider Season Sampler trip in Cambridge for a taste of Vermont's harvest season.

18 Lake Champlain Byway

After hitting Richmond, hop on I-89 north to Burlington for a trip along pristine islands and jagged shorelines.

01 **PEACHAM**

Surrounded by a dreamy landscape of high pastures and stone walls, Peacham is one of Vermont's quintessential historic villages. Originally a stop on the Bayley–Hazen Military Rd – intended to help Americans launch a sneak attack on the British during the Revolutionary War – Peacham today retains a sleepy, lost-in-time quality. Take a self-guided **walking tour** using the free brochure from the town library, or browse the antiques and handicrafts at the **Peacham Corner Guild** (peachamcornerguild.com).

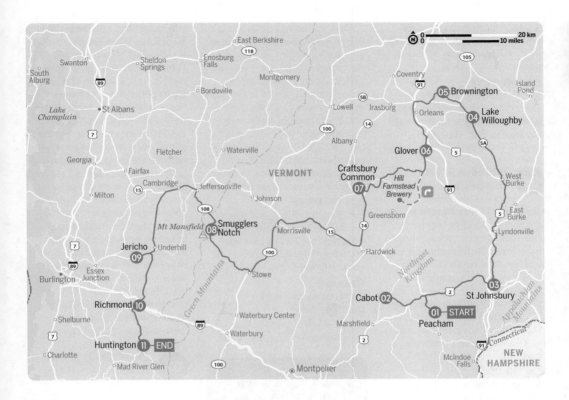

THE DRIVE
Head northwest over the mountains on unpaved Mack Mountain Rd; 7 miles out, a quick drive west on US 2 brings you to Danville Hill Rd, which plunges steeply down to Cabot. The drive is 11 miles.

02 CABOT
Despite its nationwide distribution network, **Cabot Creamery** (cabotcheese.coop) remains basically true to its roots as a New England dairy cooperative. A video tour of the creamery gives you a look at the cheese-making process (not to mention high-tech machinery painted like Holstein cows), after which you can pig out to your heart's content in the sample room.

THE DRIVE
Backtrack 3.5 miles up Danville Hill Rd, then follow US 2 east for 14 miles into St Johnsbury.

03 ST JOHNSBURY
Home to America's oldest art gallery (founded in 1871) still preserved in its original layout, the **St Johnsbury Athenaeum** (stjathenaeum.org) is built around its crown jewel, Albert Bierstadt's 10ft-by-15ft painting *Domes of the Yosemite*. The rest of the collection consists of works by such Hudson River School painters as Asher B Durand, Worthington Whittredge and Jasper Cropsey.

THE DRIVE
Take exit 23 off I-91 north in Lyndonville, then continue north on US 5 and VT 5A to Lake Willoughby, 27 miles away.

04 LAKE WILLOUGHBY
Sandwiched between Mt Hor and Mt Pisgah, whose cliffs plummet more than 1000ft to the waters below, this stunningly beautiful glacial lake resembles a landlocked fjord. To appreciate the dramatic scenery, head for the good swimming beach at the lake's northern tip, or climb to one of the surrounding summits. The **South Trail** to Mt Pisgah (3.4 miles, three-hour round trip) and the easier **Herbert Hawkes Trail** to Mt

Hor (1.9 miles, 1½-hour round trip) both begin just south of the great cleft along Lake Willoughby's southern shore.

🚗 THE DRIVE
Head briefly north of the lake on VT 5A, then turn left onto Schoolhouse Rd, continuing west into Brownington. The drive is 7 miles.

05 BROWNINGTON
Brownington's well preserved but little-visited **Old Stone House Museum** (oldstonehousemuseum.org; book your tour to enter) is just one of many lovely 19th-century buildings reposing under the shade of equally ancient maple trees. The museum pays tribute to educational trailblazer Alexander Twilight, the USA's first African American college graduate, who built Brownington's boarding school and ran it for decades.

🚗 THE DRIVE
Take VT 58 west, I-91 south and VT 16 south to Glover (13 miles), then turn left onto VT 122 and look for the Bread & Puppet Museum on your left within less than 1 mile.

06 GLOVER
A rusting school bus parked across from a barn with painted letters proclaiming 'Cheap Art Store' is your sign that you've stumbled upon the **Bread & Puppet Museum** (breadandpuppet.org/museum). Since 1974, the internationally renowned Bread & Puppet Theater has been staging politically charged, avant-garde satirical spectacles starring gigantic papier-mâché puppets (some up to 20ft tall) borne through the fields on the company's hilltop farm.

When no show is going on (the troupe tours nationally and internationally outside summer), visit the museum in the cavernous old barn and admire freakishly impressive angels, devils, horses and other fantastic creatures from past performances, hauntingly crammed over two stories. Oh, and about that name? The troupe bakes bread and shares it with the audience at each performance to create a sense of community.

🚗 THE DRIVE
Return to Glover and take VT 16 south for 2 miles, then head 13 miles west on Shadow Lake Rd, E Craftsbury Rd and S Craftsbury Rd into Craftsbury Common.

↪ Detour
Hill Farmstead Brewery
Start: 06 Glover
You know you're getting close when the asphalt disappears and

Covered Bridges of Montgomery

A 20-mile drive north from Johnson via VT 100C and VT 118 takes you to the covered-bridge capital of Vermont. In an idyllic valley at the confluence of multiple watersheds, the twin villages of Montgomery and Montgomery Center share seven spans crisscrossing the local rivers. Especially beautiful – though challenging to find – is remote **Creamery Bridge** just off Hill West Rd, which straddles a waterfall with a swimming hole at its base.

you haven't had a phone signal for 30 minutes. Down two dirt roads in the middle of nowhere, **Hill Farmstead Brewery** (hillfarmstead.com) is, well, a farm on a hill, with a garage that holds a brewery that has repeatedly been voted best in the world. Production is limited to 150,000 gallons per year, and the output rarely leaves the state, yet Hill Farmstead has a cult following for its small-batch brews. Produced by Shaun Hill, who's known for his creative concoctions and uncompromising adherence to quality, many of the beers have names based on the Hill family: Damon, a bourbon-barrel-aged Russian Imperial Stout, is the namesake of Shaun's childhood dog; the hoppy IPA, Edward, is named after Shaun's grandfather. Bitter, malty, spicy – friendly staff will guide you to your favorite at the adjacent taproom.

07 CRAFTSBURY COMMON
Welcome to Craftsbury Common, where you'll find one of Vermont's most impressive village greens. White clapboard buildings surround a rectangular lawn that hasn't changed one iota since the mid-19th century. Nearby, the community-owned **Craftsbury General Store** has a well-stocked deli and a nice array of Vermont-made products, while the **Craftsbury Outdoor Center** (craftsbury.com) offers year-round outdoor activities (skiing, biking, running, kayaking, canoeing and stand-up paddleboarding) on its 80 miles of trails and Big Hosmer Pond.

🚗 THE DRIVE
Take VT 14 south past Hardwick, then follow VT 15 west to Morrisville, looking on your left for the

Right: Montgomery covered bridge

LOCAL KNOWLEDGE

Kingdom Trails

In 1997 a group of dedicated locals linked together 200-plus miles of single and double tracks and dirt roads to form the Northeast Kingdom's astounding, award-winning Kingdom Trails network (kingdomtrails. org). Passing through century-old farms and soft forest floors dusted with pine needles, it offers one of New England's best mountain-biking experiences. In winter, the trails are ideal for cross-country skiing, snowshoeing and fat biking. Buy passes at the Kingdom Trails Welcome Center on VT 114 in East Burke, 5 miles east of I-91.

Fisher Covered Railroad Bridge, one of America's last covered railroad bridges. At Morrisville, turn south to Stowe on VT 100, then climb 9 miles up VT 108 to Smugglers Notch. The drive is 36 miles.

08 SMUGGLERS NOTCH

Tucked beneath Mt Mansfield (Vermont's highest peak; 4393ft), Smugglers Notch is Vermont's narrowest and most visually stunning paved mountain pass. As you crest the notch, the painted center line disappears in deference to a fairy-tale landscape of encroaching cliffs and boulders that squeeze the roadway down to a scant lane and a half. It's the trailhead for numerous (uphill!) hikes, including the scenic 1.2-mile scramble through the boulders to pretty **Sterling Pond**.

THE DRIVE

Descend through pretty mountain scenery along VT 108 to Jeffersonville, where you'll take VT 15 west for 24 miles to Jericho.

09 JERICHO

Jericho's photogenic **Old Red Mill** (jericho historicalsociety.org/the-old-red-mill.html) sits astride the Browns River gorge. Inside the mill, a nice display of Vermont crafts shares space with a free museum showcasing the captivating microphotography of native son 'Snowflake' Bentley,

Photo Opportunity

Snap the papier-mâché creatures at the Bread & Puppet Museum.

Huntington

who provided groundbreaking evidence that no two snowflakes are identical. Out back, the **Browns River Trail** traverses a soft carpet of evergreen needles to a little sandy beach with big boulders and a deep pool for swimming.

 THE DRIVE
Return 2 miles east on VT 15, then take Browns Trace Rd 8 miles south through Jericho Center into Richmond.

 RICHMOND
Straddling the shores of the Winooski River, this pleasant village is worth a stop for its early-19th-century **Old Round Church** (richmondvt history.org/old-round-church), one of Vermont's most noteworthy structures. The graceful 16-sided edifice, used by multiple congregations over the years, is as elegant inside as outside.

 THE DRIVE
The main road (Huntington Rd) curves west just beyond the Old Round Church, then turns south toward Huntington, 7 miles away. In July and August, consider a brief detour off-route to Owl's Head Blueberry Farm, a scenic spot to pick your own berries.

 HUNTINGTON
Huntington's gorgeous valley is presided over by Vermont's most distinctively shaped peak, **Camel's Hump** (known to early French explorers as 'Le Lion Couchant' for its resemblance to a sleeping lion). It remains one of the state's wildest spots – the only significant Vermont peak not developed for skiing – and the summit is a hiker's dream: from Huntington Center, head east 3 miles, dead-ending at the trailhead for the 6-mile **Burrows to Forest City loop**. After climbing through forest, the final ascent skirts rock faces above the tree line, affording magnificent views.

18

VERMONT

Lake Champlain Byway

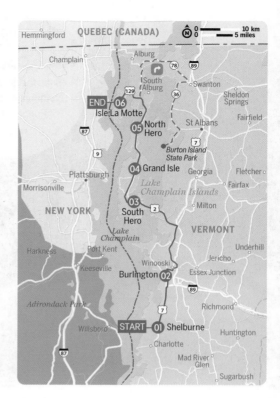

DURATION	DISTANCE	GREAT FOR
1–2 days	53 miles / 85km	Nature, food & drinks

BEST TIME TO GO	June to October for long, summery days and leaf-peeping opportunities.

Between the Green Mountains and the Adirondacks, beautiful Lake Champlain is the defining feature of northwest Vermont's landscape. Survey the lake from the historical museum in Shelburne and the waterfront in Burlington, then set off to the Champlain Islands, a 27-mile ribbon of largely undeveloped isles where simpler pleasures prevail: boating, apple-picking, wine toasting, or rambling along sleepy farm roads and interisland causeways.

Link Your Trip

02 Fall Foliage Tour

In Burlington, branch off to discover New England's blazing fall colors.

16 Cider Season Sampler

In Shelburne, hook up to the fall food-and-drink-filled loop.

01 SHELBURNE

Feast your eyes on the impressive array of 17th- to 20th-century American artifacts – folk art, textiles, toys, tools, carriages and furniture – spread over the 45-acre grounds and gardens at **Shelburne Museum** (shelburnemuseum.org). This remarkable place is set up as a mock village, with 150,000 objects housed in 39 buildings. Highlights include a full-size covered bridge, a classic round barn, an 1871 lighthouse, a one-room schoolhouse, a train station with a locomotive, and a working blacksmith's forge.

BEST FOR FOODIES

Sample the state's most famous beer export and indulge in Burlington's vibrant restaurant scene.

Lake Champlain, Burlington

The collection's sheer size lets you tailor your visit. Families are drawn to the carousel, the Owl Cottage children's center and the *Ticonderoga* steamship, while aficionados of quilts or, say, duck decoys can spend hours investigating their personal passion. Indeed, the buildings themselves are exhibits. Many were moved here from other parts of New England to ensure their preservation.

 THE DRIVE
Head north on US 7 for 4 miles until you reach South Burlington. Continue north on US 7 for 4 miles to Burlington.

02 BURLINGTON
Perched above glistening Lake Champlain, Vermont's largest city would be small in most other states. Yet Burlington's diminutive size is one of its charms, with an easily walkable downtown and a gorgeous, accessible lakefront. With the University of Vermont (UVM) swelling the city (by 13,000 students) and a vibrant cultural and social life, Burlington has a spirited, youthful character. And when it comes to nightlife, this is Vermont's epicenter.

Just before you reach the city center, a chocolate stop is in order. The aroma of rich melted cocoa is intoxicating as you enter the gift shop next to the glass wall overlooking the small factory at **Lake Champlain Chocolates** (lakechamplain chocolates.com). Take the tour to get the history of the chocolatier and ample samples to taste-test the gooey goodness. Oh, and this shop is the only one with factory-seconds shelves containing stacks of chocolate at a discount. It tastes the same as the pretty stuff but for cosmetic reasons can't be sold at the regular price. The cafe serves coffee drinks and its own luscious ice cream.

THE DRIVE
Cast off for the Champlain Islands, cruising 10 miles north of Burlington on I-89 to exit 17, then

west on US 2 for 9 miles. After Sand Bar State Park – a great picnic and swimming spot – cross the causeway and look for the photo-perfect parking island halfway across.

03 **SOUTH HERO**
Settle into the slower pace of island life at **Allenholm Farm** (diginvt.com/places/detail/allenholm-farm), just outside the town of South Hero; grab a creemee (that's Vermont-speak for soft-serve ice cream) or pick a few apples for the road ahead. About 3 miles west is **Snow Farm Vineyard** (snowfarm.com), Vermont's first vineyard, which boasts a sweet tasting room tucked away down

Photo Opportunity

Water's edge on Isle La Motte.

a dirt road (look for the signs off US 2). Sample its award-winning whites or have a sip of ice wine in the rustic barn (three tastes are free), or drop by on Thursday summer evenings at 6:30pm for the free **concert series** on the lawn next to the vines – you can expect anything from jazz to folk to rock.

 THE DRIVE
Continue north on US 2 for 8 miles.

04 **GRAND ISLE**
The **Hyde Log Cabin** (www.gihsvt.org), the oldest (1783) log cabin in Vermont and one of the oldest in the USA, is worth a short stop to see how settlers lived in the 18th century and to examine traditional household artifacts from Vermont.

 THE DRIVE
Continue north on US 2 for another 8 miles.

05 **NORTH HERO**
Boaters for miles around cast anchor at popular

St Anne's Shrine, Isle La Motte

Champlain's Lovable Lake Monster

Dinosaur relic or Ice Age proto-whale? Tree trunk? Really, really big fish? Lake Champlain's legendary lake monster – nicknamed 'Champ' – has long fascinated local residents. Known to the Abenaki as Tatoskok, Champ was even sighted by French explorer Samuel de Champlain back in the early 17th century. Indulge your curiosity at the Champ display in Burlington's **Echo Leahy Center for Lake Champlain** (echovermont.org). For a more dependable sighting, attend a Vermont Lake Monsters baseball game, where a lovable green-costumed Champ mascot dances on the dugout roof between innings.

general store **Hero's Welcome** (heroswelcome.com). The store's amusing wall display of 'World Time Zones' – four clocks showing identical hours for Lake Champlain's North Hero, South Hero, Grand Isle and Isle La Motte – reflects the prevailing island-centric attitude. Pick up a souvenir, grab a sandwich or coffee and snap some pics on the outdoor terrace overlooking the boat landing.

THE DRIVE
From US 2, head west 4 miles on VT 129 to historic Isle La Motte.

Detour
Burton Island State Park

Start: 06 **North Hero Island**
For a deeper immersion in Lake Champlain's natural beauty, spend a night or two camping at **Burton Island State Park** (vtstateparks. com/burton.html), in the middle of the lake. Between Memorial Day and Labor Day, the *Island Runner* ferry (10 minutes) shuttles campers and their gear across a narrow channel from the mainland near St Albans to this pristine, traffic-free island with over two dozen lakefront lean-tos and campsites. Park facilities include boat rentals, a nature center with daily kids' activities and a store selling breakfast, lunch and groceries; the sign outside ('No shoes, no shirt, no problem!') epitomizes the island's laid-back vibe.

It's an easy 45-minute loop around the lake from North Hero to the ferry dock at **Kill Kare State Park** (vtstateparks.com/killkare). Head 10 miles north on US 2 and then 10 miles east on VT 78 to get to Swanton; from there drive 10 miles south on VT 36 and turn right onto Hathaway Point Rd for the final 2.5 miles.

06 ISLE LA MOTTE
Pristine Isle La Motte is one of the most historic of the Champlain Islands. Signs along its western shore signal its traditional importance as a cross-roads for Native Americans and commemorate French explorer Samuel de Champlain's landing here in 1609.

Tool around the loop road hugging the coast, stopping at **St Anne's Shrine** (saintannesshrine. org) on the site of Fort St Anne, Vermont's oldest settlement. (Though it is welcoming to all, this is a religious place, so be respectful of those who come to pray.) The site features a striking granite statue of Samuel de Champlain, and its waterfront has spectacular views and a large picnic area.

Isle La Motte is also home to the 20-acre **Fisk Quarry Preserve** (ilmpt.org), the world's largest fossil reef, 4 miles south of St Anne's Shrine. Half a million years old, the reef once provided limestone for Radio City Music Hall and Washington's National Gallery. Interpretive trails explain the history of the quarry.

19

VERMONT

Southern Vermont Loop

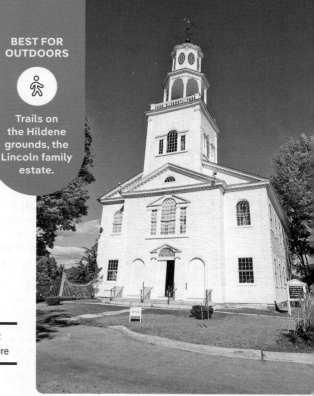

Old First Church, Bennington

DURATION	DISTANCE	GREAT FOR
2–3 days	131 miles / 211km	History & nature

BEST TIME TO GO	May to October for great weather and autumnal colors.

Tidy white churches and inns surround village greens throughout historic southern Vermont, a region that's home to several towns that predate the American Revolution. This scenic loop takes in all the region's highlights: history-rich Bennington, the picture-postcard villages of Grafton and Weston, upscale Manchester, the imposing peak of Mt Equinox, the old stone home of Robert Frost and the opulent mansion of Abraham Lincoln's descendants.

Link Your Trip

08 Mohawk Trail

Explore New England's oldest scenic highway in Massachusetts. From Bennington, drive 13 miles south on US 7 to Williamstown.

21 Connecticut River Byway

Follow the river and visit college towns in New Hampshire. From Brattleboro drive 23 miles north on I-91 to Walpole.

01 BRATTLEBORO

Perched at the confluence of the Connecticut and West Rivers, Brattleboro is a little gem packed with independent shops, eateries and cultural venues such as the **Latchis Theater** (latchis. com) and the **Brattleboro Museum & Art Center** (brattleboromuseum.org), housed in the town's 1915 former train station. An energetic mix of aging hippies and the latest crop of pierced and tattooed hipsters fuels the town's sophisticated eclecticism, keeping the downtown scene percolating and skewing its politics decidedly leftward.

defenses during this battle, the colonies might well have been split. The obelisk, built between 1887 and 1891, offers impressive views – an elevator whisks you two-thirds of the way up the 306ft tower.

THE DRIVE
Head out of town along scenic VT 7A and drive 4 miles north to the Robert Frost Stone House Museum. As the road winds along the valley, the southernmost section of the Green Mountains emerges on your left.

03 SHAFTSBURY
When he moved his family to Shaftsbury, Robert Frost was 46 years old and at the height of his career. The **Robert Frost Stone House Museum** (bennington.edu/robert-frost-stone-house-museum) opens a window into the life of the poet, with one entire room dedicated to his most famous work, 'Stopping by Woods on a Snowy Evening,' which he penned here in the 1920s.

THE DRIVE
Drive 5 miles north along scenic VT 7A to Shaftsbury itself, then continue 6 miles further through bucolic farmland and wooded hollows to Arlington.

04 ARLINGTON
Arlington's tiny maple-syrup shop (the sweet stuff is made on-site) houses the **Norman Rockwell Exhibition** (sugarshackvt.com), an homage to the artist, who lived in Arlington from 1939 to 1953. A section of the shop displays 500 of Rockwell's *Saturday Evening Post* covers and shows a short film about his life. (Exhibition

THE DRIVE
Take VT 9 west along the Molly Stark Scenic Byway for 40 miles to Bennington. After an ear-popping climb, 5 miles past the turnoff for the town of Marlboro, you'll come to the Hogback Mountain overlook; make sure to stop and admire the three-state views over Massachusetts, New Hampshire and Vermont.

02 BENNINGTON
Bennington is divided into three sections: workaday town (Bennington proper), college town (North Bennington) and **Old Bennington**, which is where you'll find the main sights. The charming hilltop Colonial site is studded with 80 Georgian and Federal houses and the **Old First Church** (oldfirstchurch benn.org), built in 1806 in Palladian style. Its churchyard holds the remains of five Vermont governors, numerous soldiers of the American Revolution and poet Robert Frost (1874–1963), one of the best-known and best-loved American poets of the 20th century.

Up the hill to the north, the **Bennington Battle Monument** (benningtonbattlemonument.com) commemorates the crucial Battle of Bennington, fought during the American Revolution. Had Colonel Seth Warner and the local 'Green Mountain Boys' not helped weaken British

hours vary; call to confirm.)

THE DRIVE
Continue for 8 miles north along scenic VT 7A, passing the base of imposing Mt Equinox as you approach Hildene, on the southern outskirts of Manchester. The area is an excellent place for an overnight stay – oodles of B&Bs and hotels congregate in Manchester proper and along VT 7A as you approach town.

05 HILDENE
Abraham Lincoln's wife, Mary Todd Lincoln (1818–82), and their son, Robert Todd Lincoln (1843–1926), came here during the Civil War; as an adult Robert built **Hildene** (hildene.org), a 24-room Georgian Revival mansion. Robert enjoyed the house until his death in 1926, and his great-granddaughter lived here until her death in 1975. Soon after, it was converted into a museum filled with Lincoln family personal effects and furnishings, including the hat Abraham Lincoln probably wore when he delivered the Gettysburg Address, and a brass cast of his hands, the right one swollen from shaking hands while campaigning for the presidency.

The surrounding grounds feature 8 miles of **walking trails**, an exquisite flower garden designed to resemble a stained-glass Romanesque cathedral window and a solar-powered barn where you can watch Hildene goat's cheese being produced.

THE DRIVE
Continue north on VT 7A for 2 miles to central Manchester.

06 MANCHESTER
Manchester has been a fashionable resort town for almost two centuries. These days, the draws are the nearby skiing and hiking, the relaxed New England town vibe and the upscale outlet shopping (Manchester contains more than 100 shops, from Armani to Marimekko).

Two families put the place on the map – the Lincolns and the Orvises. Franklin Orvis (1824–1900) established the Equinox House Hotel; his brother, Charles, founded the Orvis Company, makers of fly-fishing equipment with a worldwide following. Orvis Company products are showcased in the **American Museum of Fly Fishing** (amff. org), with fly collections and rods used by Ernest Hemingway, Bing Crosby and several US presidents.

Hikers can hit the trail for the dramatic climb to the summit of Mt Equinox (3848ft), which looms large just south of town. The five-hour hike (2918ft elevation gain) will reward you with exhilarating views; look for the trailhead behind the Equinox Hotel.

THE DRIVE
Follow VT 11 northeast for 15 miles toward Londonderry, then take VT 100 another 5 miles north into Weston.

 Detour
Merck Forest
Start: 06 **Manchester**
Encompassing more than 2700 acres of high-country farmland, meadow and forest, **Merck Forest & Farmland Center** (merckforest. org) is a blissful place to experience Vermont's natural beauty and agricultural heritage. The park's centerpiece is a working organic farm with animals, vegetable gardens, renewable energy installations and a sugar house where you can watch maple syrup being produced during sugaring season (generally mid-March to early April). It's hidden away on a gorgeous hilltop only 25 minutes from Manchester – but a world apart from the village hustle and bustle.

The center offers a wide range of hikes, environmental education programs and events such as sheepdog trials. It also rents out cabins and tent sites, which are spread around the property. Sales of produce and syrup, coupled with voluntary contributions, help sustain the nonprofit foundation at its heart.

To get here from Manchester, take VT 30 northwest 8 miles to East Rupert, then head 2 miles south on VT 315, looking for signs on your left at the top of the hill.

07 WESTON
Crowds flock to Weston for three main reasons: to browse the shelves at the Vermont Country Store, to attend the renowned summer theater festival at Vermont's oldest professional theater, the **Weston Playhouse** (weston theater.org), or simply to bask in the glow of one of Vermont's most picturesque villages. From the gazebo at the center of Weston's circular town green, the views upstream to the town's waterfall and 19th-century mill are the stuff of tourist legend.

THE DRIVE
Head 12 miles east on Weston–Andover Rd and VT 11 through the gorgeous stone village of Chester, then turn south on VT 35 and continue 7 miles south to Grafton.

08 GRAFTON

One of Vermont's prettiest villages, Grafton exudes a peaceful grace reminiscent of a bygone century. It's not that way by accident. In the 1960s the private Windham Foundation established a preservation program for the entire village, burying all electrical and telephone lines and restoring historic buildings and covered bridges. The town's most picturesque building is the **Grafton Inn** at the center of town. Stop for a bite at the formal New England dining room or the casual tavern in the carriage house out back.

Photo Opportunity

The quintessential New England beauty of Grafton's clapboard homes, covered bridges and venerable old brick inn.

South of town, the **Grafton Trails & Outdoor Center** (graftoninnvermont.com/southern-vt-trails-outdoors) offers year-round recreation on its network of mountain-biking, hiking and cross-country ski trails, along with canoeing, swimming, snow-tubing and adventure camps for kids. Along the same road you'll also find the **Grafton Village Cheese Company** (graftonvillagecheese. com), whose mouthwatering and nose-tingling cheddars regularly win awards at international cheese festivals.

THE DRIVE

Continue 27 miles south along Grafton–Townshend Rd, VT 35 and VT 30 into Brattleboro, taking time to stop and admire the Georgian and Greek Revival architecture in postcard-worthy Newfane.

Grafton

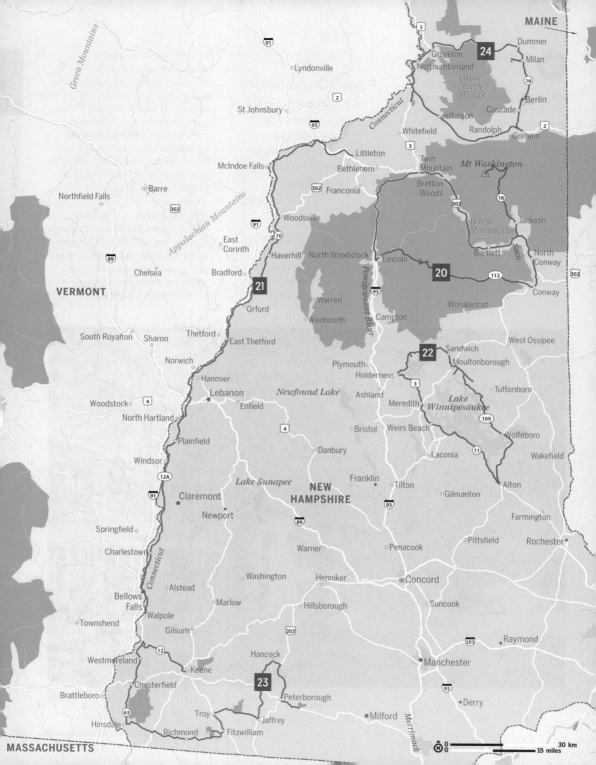

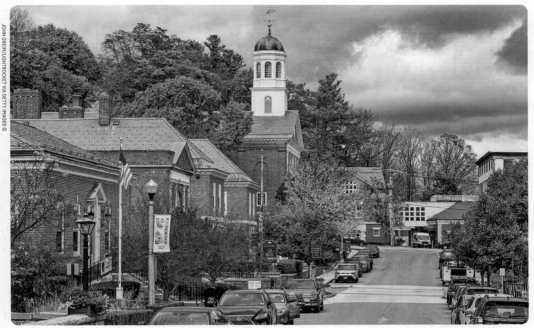

Peterborough (p139)

New Hampshire

20 White Mountains Loop

Drive or hike to waterfalls, gorges and summits in the shadow of Mt Washington in New Hampshire's prettiest parks. **p124**

21 Connecticut River Byway

Follow New England's great scenic river to find farms, view mastodon fossils, and peruse candy counters and an irresistible chocolate shop. **p128**

22 Lake Winnipesaukee

This family-friendly lakeside loop features laughing loons, great hiking trails, abundant wildlife and birding with a dollop of ice-cream parlors! **p132**

23 Monadnock Villages

Discover the trails and artsy villages of the Mt Monadnock region. And while you're at it, climb the state's most-hiked peak. **p138**

24 Woodland Heritage Trail

Explore northern New Hampshire's theme parks, rivers, forests and logging history. **p142**

Explore
New Hampshire

The Granite State has plenty of charms to see and its drives are some of the region's most spectacular. Follow rushing rivers, detour to Mt Washington, the White Mountain's highest summit and also the spot of the coldest recorded temperature on earth, or take scenic train rides and meander past lakes and swamps that are filled with wildlife and birds. The various towns and cities are delightful interruptions, giving you the full gamut of things to see, do, taste and enjoy. New Hampshire is a natural playground: so get out and play!

Conway

With its White Mountains proximity and the gorgeous scenic Conway Railroad, this little town packs an oversized punch. You'll have a wealth of options to choose from in terms of lodging, great restaurants, breweries and tasty coffee shops. The Kancamagus Hwy, one of the state's premier leaf-peeping drives, ends (or begins) here. Those wanting to add the 'This Car Climbed Mt Washington' bumper sticker will only have to drive about an hour. This is a hip, happening town as well as being a good spot for families.

Claremont

Picturesque Claremont offers visitors both historical value and adrenaline-filled excitement. Places like the famous Claremont Opera House, an iconic building still in use today, combine with nearby hikes, biking trails and river-rafting opportunities to make Claremont a popular stopover. You'll find it's quaint – even quiet – but there's enough here to sate the realm of whatever it is you're looking for, be it a nice B&B or a tasty dinner with the family.

Keene

A great stop for Mt Monadnock hikers, Keene is a south-central settlement that's close to the Massachusetts border. Cut in half by the Ashuelot River, this is yet another beautiful New England town – but unlike some of its more famous brethren, Keene is relatively off the map (not that it wants to be). The town's pumpkin festival was a big draw until it moved to Laconia in 2015, but Keene is still a nice pit stop for any of the southern

WHEN TO GO

New Hampshire's a delight year-round, but drivers will find the roads are a tad more slippery in the winter when some of the passes and peaks, like Mount Washington, are closed for the season. If summits are in your travel plans, come in the summer, spring or fall.

New Hampshire drives. It's also a university town, meaning it's a bit more artsy and has a bit more diversity than some of its neighbors.

Gorham

Those who plan on summiting Mt Washington before continuing their drive should overnight in Gorham, a small but delightful tourist town in the northeastern part of the state. Unlike Conway, Gorham is only 30 minutes from the state's tallest peak. Not to be confused with the other Gorham (Maine), New Hampshire's Gorham sits on the banks of the Androscoggin River and is pretty quiet. You'll find some motels and family-run cabins, but nothing grand or resorty. While there's no skiing in the town proper, Wildcat Mountain and Breton Woods are within a 30 minute drive. The back roads here are gorgeous, and you'll have a good chance of spotting deer, moose, bald eagles and perhaps even a black bear if you're lucky.

TRANSPORTATION

New Hampshire is so close to Boston's Logan International that most people fly in there. From Logan, express buses can get you to several points in southern NH in a mere 90 to 120 minutes. However, most people find renting a vehicle at the airport is more convenient and costs about the same.

 WHAT'S ON

Mt Washington

This incredible mountain is a must-do for many road-trippers. Be sure to check weather reports, as it's often closed fall through spring due to perilous conditions. Make sure your brakes are in top shape. You'll need them.

Laconia Pumpkin Festival

Every fall Laconia puts on a pumpkin show with towering walls of jack-o'-lanterns, pumpkin-carving contests, pumpkin weighing and, of course, the ever-popular pumpkin bowl.

 WHERE TO STAY

Historic **Bretton Woods** (p125) is a classy spot and was part of the famous Bretton Woods Agreement, signed in 1944 as a way to prevent another Great Depression. Appalachian Trail fans should look for the **Notch Hostel**, with its Tibetan prayer flags and sauna for those crisp NH nights. Families with kids will appreciate the **Golden Gables**, which has an expansive back lawn for kiddos to run off leash. No matter where you go in New Hampshire, you'll never have to look too hard to find a place where everyone can have a great time.

Resources

Union Leader
(*unionleader.com*)
The Granite State's largest newspaper, with local news, events, listings and activity suggestions.

Visit New Hampshire
(*visitnh.gov*)
This state tourism site posts seasonal planning guides, suggestions for kid-friendly detours, as well as places to stay and eat.

20

NEW HAMPSHIRE

White Mountains Loop

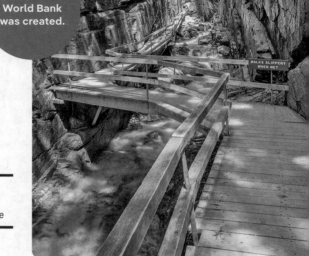

BEST FOR HISTORY

Bretton Woods, where the World Bank was created.

Flume Gorge

DURATION	DISTANCE	GREAT FOR
3 days	135 miles / 217km	Families, history & nature

BEST TIME TO GO	Visit from May to October for warm days and full foliage.

Hikers, lace up your boots and grab your walking sticks. The White Mountain National Forest, with help from the Appalachian Mountain Club, is home to one of the most impressive trail networks in the nation. You'll experience waterfalls crashing through gorges, streams rippling past an abandoned settlement and mountain huts serving up meals and beds. Not a hiker? Train rides through leafy terrain and a fairy-tale theme park bring the adventure to you.

Link Your Trip

21 Connecticut River Byway

Drive toward Littleton on I-93 north from Franconia Notch to start a pastoral drive along the Connecticut River.

22 Lake Winnipesaukee

Leave the mountains behind and discover New Hampshire's beautiful lakes region; from Lincoln, it's a 45-minute drive to Weirs Beach via I-93 and NH 104.

01 LINCOLN & NORTH WOODSTOCK

Outdoor shops, an adventure outfitter and a gob-smacking array of pizza joints line the Kancamagus Hwy on its run through Lincoln and nearby North Woodstock. Start at the **White Mountains Visitor Center** (visitwhitemountains.com), where a stuffed moose sets a mood for adventure. This is also the place to grab brochures and trail maps and purchase a White Mountain National Forest Recreation Pass ($5 day pass), which is required for extended stops at some national forest trailheads.

Want to leave the planning to others? Try **Alpine Adventures** (alpinezipline.com) a few doors down.

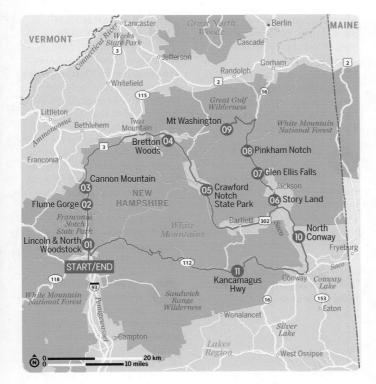

These knowledgeable folks lead backwoods safaris and zipline tours.

THE DRIVE
Drive 4 miles north on I-93 to exit 34A and follow the signs 0.5 miles further to Flume Gorge.

02 FRANCONIA NOTCH STATE PARK: FLUME GORGE

Expect crowds at **Flume Gorge** (flumegorge.com), a natural granite sluice with 90ft walls in Franconia Notch State Park. But don't let elbow jostling keep you away – the verdant, moss-covered cliffs and rushing stream are worth it. The trail has a sturdy walkway, making it accessible for everyone. If you plan to ride

the **Cannon Mountain Aerial Tramway**, buy the Discovery Pass, which covers the flume and the tram at a reduced rate.

Take a walk or a bike ride on the 8-mile **Recreation Trail** beside the Pemigewasset River or stroll 500ft to the **Basin**, the first of several waterfalls accessed from the Basin parking lot north of the Flume Gorge Visitor Center.

THE DRIVE
Follow US 3 for 1 mile north to join I-93, then continue 4.5 miles north to exit 34B. Here in the heart of Franconia Notch State Park, I-93 and US 3 merge into a single highway, flanked closely on either side by the Kinsman and Franconia mountain ranges.

03 FRANCONIA NOTCH STATE PARK: CANNON MOUNTAIN

A short drive north, the **Cannon Mountain Aerial Tramway** (cannonmt.com) whisks you to a lookout point so lofty that you'll feel you've sprouted wings.

Every New Hampshirite mourns the **Old Man of the Mountain**, a rock formation that remains the state symbol despite its collapse in May 2003. Near the Tramway Valley Station, the departure point for the tram, you'll find the **Old Man of the Mountain Museum**, where there are forensically accurate diagrams of 'the Profile's' collapse, and tributes to this beloved bit of state history.

THE DRIVE
Follow I-93 north to exit 35, taking US 3 north to Twin Mountain, where you'll pass a prison-striped moose at the police station. Fill up the tank at Foster's Crossroads, then follow US 302 east. The drive is 17 miles.

04 BRETTON WOODS

From July 1 to July 22, 1944, the **Mt Washington Hotel** hosted the Bretton Woods International Monetary Conference. This history-making summit established the World Bank and helped stabilize the global economy as WWII ended. World leaders were determined to avoid the disastrous economic fallout that occurred after WWI. Today, spend a sumptuous night in one of the resort's 200 rooms or simply stop by to wander past the historic photographs beside the lobby. A drink on the veranda with its view of Mt Washington is also a pleasant diversion.

THE DRIVE
Follow US 302 south 4 miles to the park.

05 CRAWFORD NOTCH STATE PARK

The **Pond Loop** and **Sam Tilley** trails are two easy riverside hikes in this **state park** (nhstateparks.org) at the base of the White Mountains. For details about local trails, stop by the **AMC Highland Center** (outdoors.org), one of the country's best launchpads for outdoor exploration. There's an information desk, a dining room and a small outdoor retail shop. Overnight lodging is also available, and hikers can link to the AMC's popular hut-to-hut trail system from here. The huts are lodge-like dorms offering meals, bunks and stellar views. The Highland Center is just north of the park.

The Conway Scenic Railroad's Notch Train stops at the nearby 1891 **Crawford Depot & Visitor Center** (outdoors.org), which contains a small but good collection of train-related history.

THE DRIVE
Continue east on US 302 for 16 miles, passing Dry River Campground and the Crawford Notch General Store. Turn left at NH 16, and continue 0.25 miles to Story Land.

06 STORY LAND

With its bright, off-kilter facade, **Story Land** (storylandnh.com) is like a Venus flytrap, luring families in for a closer look, then preventing escape with scenes of kiddie-minded fun just beyond its protective wall. What's inside this roadside theme park? Shows, games, costumed characters and 20 rides based on

fairy tales and make-believe. This popular place gets a thumbs-up from kids and parents alike.

THE DRIVE
Drive north on NH 16. In 2 miles, take a photo break at the covered bridge in tiny Jackson. Continue 8 miles to the trailhead for Glen Ellis Falls.

07 GLEN ELLIS FALLS

Only a stone's throw off NH 16, stop at Glen Ellis Falls for a few snapshots. This easy walk brings you 0.3 miles to a 60ft waterfall, one of the prettiest in the region. Most can make the hike without breaking a sweat.

THE DRIVE
Continue north almost 1 mile to the visitor center.

TOP TIP:
Hiker Shuttle

Need transportation before or after a strenuous one-way hike in the White Mountains region? Use the **AMC hiker shuttle** (outdoors.org/shuttle) system for your pick-up or drop-off. These shuttles run daily from June to mid-September, then on weekends to mid-October. One-way rides cost $24 ($20 for AMC members) and are best reserved in advance.

---

08 PINKHAM NOTCH VISITOR CENTER

Hikers tackling Mt Washington should stop by the **Pinkham Notch Visitor Center** (facebook.com/pg/JoeDodge Lodge) for information, maps and a diorama that spotlights area trails. The 4.2-mile **Tuckerman Ravine Trail** to the summit starts behind the visitor center. Appropriate preparation for this brutal climb – which can be deadly in bad weather – is imperative.

THE DRIVE
Drive 3 miles north to the entrance to Auto Rd. From here it's 7.6 miles to the summit.

09 MT WASHINGTON

Welcome to Mt Washington, New England's highest peak and the site of the world's second-highest recorded wind gust: 231mph (and the highest ever observed by humans). To reach the summit, pay the toll for the **Mt Washington Auto Road** (mt-washington.com) then hold tight to the wheel as you twist 7.6 miles to the summit on a narrow road with steep drop-offs and no guard rails. But the views of the Presidential Range are superb. Guided tours are also available if you want to leave the driving to someone else.

Up top, stop in for souvenirs, refreshments, views from the observation deck and a visit to the **Extreme Mt Washington** (mountwashington.org/visit-us) museum, where you can contemplate Mt Washington's claim as 'home of the world's worst weather' and learn how scientists track climate conditions year-round despite hurricane-force winds and Arctic temperatures.

Aspiring athletes take note: a handful of runners have reached the top in less than one hour (!) during the annual Mt Washington Road Race.

THE DRIVE
Backtrack to the junction of NH 16 and US 302. Follow US 302/NH 16 southeast for 5 miles to North Conway, stopping at the Intervale Scenic Vista for views, brochures and restrooms.

10 NORTH CONWAY
North Conway is the perfect mountain town: lively pubs, top-notch breakfast joints and numerous quaint inns. Shopaholics can pop into one of the 80 outlet stores (including LL Bean) at **Settlers Green** (settlersgreen.com). North Conway is also home to the **Conway Scenic Railroad** (conwayscenic. com), which runs half-day train trips up into Crawford Notch. On sunny days they may attach the open-air coach car, a restored Pullman with no glass in the windows that's perfect for shutterbugs.

Photo Opportunity
Capture presidential peaks from the CL Graham Wangan Grounds Overlook.

THE DRIVE
US 302 splits from NH 16 south of downtown. Follow NH 16 heading south for 2.5 miles, taking it through Conway, then hop onto NH 112, which is better known as the Kancamagus Hwy.

11 KANCAMAGUS HIGHWAY
Roll down the windows and slip on your shades. It's time to drive. This 34.5-mile byway, named for a peace-seeking Native American chief, rolls through the **White Mountain National Forest** unhampered by commercial distractions or pesky stoplights – although you do need to gauge your speed and watch for wildlife.

Stop by the **Saco Ranger District Office** (fs.usda.gov/recarea/white mountain/recreation/camping-cabins/recarea) for maps, information and a recreation pass if you plan to park and explore. National park passes work too.

Fifteen miles west, pull over at **Sabbaday Falls** for an easy climb to flumes cascading through granite channels and small pools. After the falls, the road starts rising and leafy maples are replaced by dark conifers. The serene view at **Kancamagus Pass** (elevation 2855ft) can be beat only by Mt Washington. For camera-ready panoramas, stop at the **CL Graham Wangan Grounds Overlook** just east of the pass, or the **Pemi Overlook** just west.

The **Lincoln Woods Trail** (fs. usda.gov) at the parking area further west follows the Pemigewasset River for 2.9 miles. Kids enjoy the suspension bridge beside the visitor center.

THE DRIVE
From here, drive west on NH 112 to return to Lincoln and North Woodstock.

WANGKUN JIA/SHUTTERSTOCK ©

Kancamagus Highway

21

NEW HAMPSHIRE

Connecticut River Byway

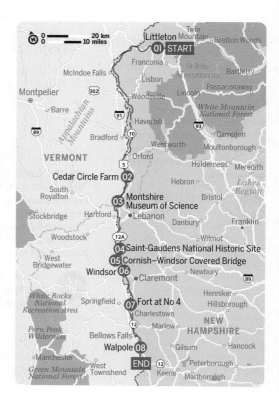

DURATION	DISTANCE	GREAT FOR
2 days	132 miles / 212km	History, nature, food & drink

BEST TIME TO GO	April to November for spring flowers, summer greenery and fall foliage.

Taking this leisurely, winding road trip through the Connecticut River's Upper Valley is like earning a liberal arts degree in one weekend. There's the Colonial history of the Fort at No 4, natural sciences at the Montshire Museum and a mini-session in the arts among the sculpture-dotted grounds of Saint-Gaudens. Along the way, you'll be greeted by lush farms and maple-covered hillsides rolling down to meet New England's longest river.

Link Your Trip

03 Ivy League Tour

Cross the river near the Montshire museum to tour Dartmouth College.

23 Monadnock Villages

From Walpole, take NH 12 to Keene for a stroll through downtown.

 LITTLETON, NEW HAMPSHIRE

Littleton may be off the beaten path, but it's an inspirational place to start this trip. The White Mountains hover to the southeast, the Ammonoosuc River churns through town, a towering steeple overlooks Main St and the world's longest candy counter beckons with a rainbow's array of sweets at **Chutters** (chutters.com).

On Main St, the **Littleton Chamber of Commerce Welcome Center** (littletonareachamber.com) provides a walking-tour brochure with a stop at the **Littleton Grist Mill**. Built in 1797, it's back

BEST FOR FOODIES

Dig into fancy chocolates and savory fare at Burdick Chocolates in Walpole.

DENISTANGNEYJR/ISTOCK/GETTY IMAGES ©

Covered bridge, Littleton

in service as a mill after renovations initiated in the 1990s. The adjacent Ammonoosuc drops 144ft as it crashes through town. The **covered bridge** here, built in 2004, looks like it's barely hanging onto the riverbank – but it's perfectly safe for walking.

 THE DRIVE
Take I-93 north to exit 44 and NH 135 south. This bucolic road passes fields, red barns and cattle-crossing signs as it hugs the river. Snap a photo of the covered bridge in Woodsville, then continue south on NH 10. In Orford, look left for the impressive Seven Ridge Houses, built in the Bullfinch style by local craftspeople between 1773 and 1839. Cross the bridge to Fairlee (VT) and continue south along US 5,

following the Connecticut River down to East Thetford. The drive is 58 miles.

02 CEDAR CIRCLE FARM, EAST THETFORD, VERMONT

With its vast fields stretching out toward the banks of the Connecticut River and bins overflowing with homegrown organic produce, **Cedar Circle Farm** (cedarcirclefarm.org) is like a roadside farm stand on steroids. Wander through the lush fields of produce, pick your own berries, flowers and pumpkins, lounge in an Adirondack chair by the river, or simply stop in at the cafe to pick up a snack for the road ahead. Summer and

fall events include dinners in the field, workshops on canning and freezing, and strawberry (June) and pumpkin (October) festivals.

 THE DRIVE
Follow US 5 south for 11 miles to Norwich, VT, then take Montshire Rd to the Montshire Museum.

03 MONTSHIRE MUSEUM OF SCIENCE, NORWICH, VERMONT

Rub the tooth of a mastodon. View current images from the Hubble telescope. Watch leafcutter ants at work. But whatever you do at the **Montshire** (montshire.org), don't park your car near the planet Neptune – it's part of a model solar system that stretches the length of the parking lot and beyond (and Neptune is way, way out there).

Located on a 110-acre site beside the Connecticut River, this kid-friendly museum offers exhibits covering ecology, technology, and the natural and physical sciences. It's also the regional visitor center for the **Silvio Conte National Fish & Wildlife Refuge** – look for the life-size moose and the displays that highlight local flora and fauna. In summer, water-focused and sensory exhibits in the Montshire's outdoor Science Park will fascinate younger kids.

THE DRIVE
Cross the river back to Hanover, NH, taking NH 10 past the strip-mall wasteland of West Lebanon, where you pick up NH 12A south to Saint-Gaudens; the drive is 18 miles. (For variety, the river can be tracked along

Photo Opportunity

The Cornish–Windsor Covered Bridge linking Vermont and New Hampshire.

US 5 in Vermont between a village or two, with regular bridges connecting New Hampshire and Vermont until you reach Walpole.)

04 SAINT-GAUDENS NATIONAL HISTORIC SITE

In the summer of 1885, the sculptor Augustus Saint-Gaudens rented an old inn near the town of Cornish and came to this beautiful spot to work. He

returned summer after summer and eventually bought the place in 1892. The **estate** (nps.gov/saga), where he lived until his death in 1907, is now open to the public.

Saint-Gaudens is best known for his public monuments, including the Robert Gold Shaw Memorial across from the state house in Boston. Recasts of his greatest sculptures dot the beautiful grounds. Visitors can also tour his home and wander the studios, where artists-in-residence sculpt. Exhibit buildings are closed in winter, but the visitor center is usually open 9am to 4pm weekdays.

THE DRIVE
Head 1.5 miles south on NH 12A to reach the Cornish–Windsor Covered Bridge.

Cornish–Windsor Covered Bridge

05 CORNISH–WINDSOR COVERED BRIDGE

Built in 1866, this 449ft-long beauty is the longest wooden covered bridge in the United States and you can still drive across it! One bit of trivia, in case you were wondering: the whole thing belongs to the state of New Hampshire, so you won't actually cross into Vermont until you touch the riverbank on the far side.

LOCAL KNOWLEDGE

Shopping & Strolling Downtown Littleton

Lined with 19th- and early-20th-century buildings, Littleton's Main St is a delightful place to stroll, with some attractive, independently owned stores. For outdoor gear and clothing, step into **Lahout's** (lahouts.com), America's oldest ski shop. A few doors down, the **League of New Hampshire Craftsmen** (littleton. nhcrafts.org) runs a gallery that sells jewelry, pottery and other New Hampshire–made arts and crafts. For lunch and a slice of local life, grab a seat at the **Coffee Pot** (thecoffee potrestaurant.com) on Main St, or head round the corner to the 18th-century grist mill by the Ammonoosuc River, where you can soak up river views over craft brews and pizza at **Schilling Beer Co**.

 THE DRIVE

Cross the covered bridge into Windsor, VT, then take US 5 north to the Old Constitution House at 16 N Main St.

06 WINDSOR, VERMONT

Affectionately known as the 'Birthplace of Vermont,' Windsor is home to the **Old Constitution House State Historic Site** (historicsites. vermont.gov/constitution-house). This small museum occupies the former tavern where a devoted band of Vermonters – rejecting the competing claims of New York and New Hampshire to their territory – officially declared Vermont's independence in July 1777. The groundbreaking constitution signed here was the first in the New World to outlaw slavery, create a free public education system for both men and women, and give every man (regardless of property ownership) the right to vote.

Vermont held its ground as an independent republic for 14 years (eat your heart out, Texas!) before finally joining the Union as the 14th state in 1791. Visitors can tour the museum here and learn about Vermont's early history on weekends from Memorial Day to Columbus Day.

 THE DRIVE

Bop back into New Hampshire via the Cornish–Windsor Bridge and turn right to follow the Connecticut River downstream. Not quite 1 mile south, bear left onto Town House Rd at the fork for two more covered bridges, then continue south for another 17 miles on NH 12A, which soon rejoins NH 12, to Charlestown.

07 FORT AT NO 4, CHARLESTOWN

Named for a 1700s land grant, the original fort was built in the 1740s to protect pioneer farmers from Native Americans and the French. The original fort, which was no longer needed by the late 1770s and no longer exists, was reconstructed in the 1960s as a **living history museum** (fortat4.org), with a layout based on a detailed drawing sketched in 1746.

Visitors can explore the different rooms of the fort, wander the riverside grounds and watch historical re-enactors, whose activities vary from weekend to weekend. Check the Facebook page for current activities.

 THE DRIVE

Rolling mountains, as well as fields, train tracks, river views and a sugar house, decorate the 14-mile drive on NH 12 south to Walpole.

08 WALPOLE

The carefully crafted desserts at **Burdick Chocolates** look like they attended finishing school – no slovenly lava cakes or naughty whoopee pies here. But you'll find more than just rich chocolate indulgences. The adjoining bistro serves creative new American dishes, plus artisanal cheeses and top-notch wines; the creamy quiche is fantastic.

Purchase local art and crafts across the street at the **Walpole Artists Cooperative** (walpole artisans.org).

22

NEW HAMPSHIRE

BEST FOR WILDLIFE

Visit Squam Lakes Natural Science Center for critter-watching and live animal demos.

Lake Winnipesaukee

DURATION	DISTANCE	GREAT FOR
2 days	85 miles / 137km	Nature & families

BEST TIME TO GO	June to September: school's out and the weather is warm.

Winnipesaukee Scenic Railroad

Across the lake, Bailey's Bubble has scooped ice cream for generations of appreciative families. Summer camps in the area have thrived for decades too. There's something special about this mountain-ringed lake, a place that summons people back year after year. But it's not just the beauty. It's the little moments of family fun and summer camaraderie that make it truly magical.

Link Your Trip

03 Ivy League Tour

Follow I-93 to the Ivies for guided tours about history and traditions.

20 White Mountains Loop

From Holderness, drive north to the Notches for trains, hiking and cascades.

01 **WEIRS BEACH**

A word of warning: if you're traveling with kids, they're going to want to stay here all day. With its colorful distractions – video arcades, slippery waterslides, souvenir stands and a bustling boardwalk – Weirs Beach is the lake region's center of tacky fun. Escape the hoopla on the **Winnipesaukee Scenic Railroad** (hoborr.com), whose '20s and '30s train cars travel to the lake's southern tip at Alton Bay and back – kids love the ice-cream-parlor car. The train depot is also the departure point for MS *Mt Washington*.

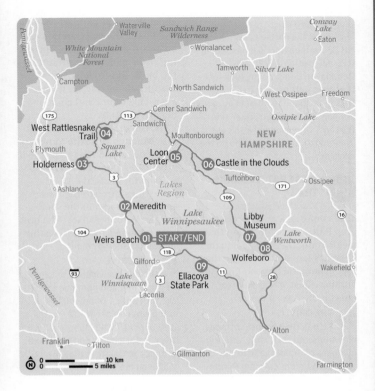

Cruising on MS Mt Washington

Boasting 183 miles of coastline, Lake Winnipesaukee is prime cruising territory. The classic MS *Mt Washington* (cruisenh. com) steams out of Weirs Beach on a relaxing 2½-hour scenic lake cruise, departing twice daily in July, August and late September to mid-October (reduced schedule May, June and early September).

Special trips include the Sunday champagne brunch cruise and the evening sunset, plus fall foliage and theme cruises (tribute to Elvis, Lobsterfest etc) running throughout summer and fall. From late June through August, the boat stops in Meredith on Monday and in Wolfeboro daily from Tuesday to Saturday (Monday through Saturday in Wolfeboro in September and October).

THE DRIVE

Go north on US 3/Endicott St, which runs parallel to the lake. Soon after passing the high-flying ropes course at Monkey Trunks (monkeytrunks.com), US 3's local name changes to Daniel Webster Hwy. Meredith is 5 miles north of Weirs Beach.

02 MEREDITH

Upscale Meredith is a lively lakeside town with attractive Colonial and Victorian homes flanking a commercial center. In Meredith village, boutiques, art and craft stores, galleries and restaurants line US 3 and Main St.

Just south of the village roundabout, stop in at **Mill Falls Marketplace** (millfalls.com/shop), a restored linen mill that houses a dozen shops and restaurants.

The Winnipesaukee Scenic Railroad and the MS *Mt Washington* boat (Monday only July and August) both stop in Meredith.

THE DRIVE

From Meredith, continue 5 miles north on woodsy, easy-driving US 3. Don't be surprised if you see lots of motorcyclists. Squam Lake soon nudges into view to the northeast.

03 HOLDERNESS

The site of the movie *On Golden Pond*, Squam Lake and Holderness remain placid and peaceful, perfect for a pair of waders and fly-fishing, or for plopping your butt in a beach chair and soaking up the sun. If you hike in the shady forests you'll frequently surprise deer, moose and even a black bear or two.

It's all about the wildlife at **Squam Lakes Natural Science Center** (nhnature.org), where four nature paths weave through the woods and around the marsh. The 0.75-mile **Gephardt Trail** is a highlight, leading past large trailside enclosures that hold bobcats, mountain lions, river otters and raptors. (Most of the animals were orphaned or injured and are unable to live on their own in the wild.) The center also offers informative 90-minute tours of the lake and educational live animal demonstrations.

The Great Pumpkin Was Here

One of the state's quirkiest annual gatherings, the **New Hampshire Pumpkin Festival** (facebook.com/NHPumpkin Festival), held on the third or fourth Saturday in October, draws in thousands of visitors to admire the world's largest tower of jack-o'-lanterns. Started in 1991 by merchants in Keene, the event exploded over the years, with the town's 2003 tally of nearly 29,000 pumpkins setting a Guinness world record. In 2015 the festival moved to Laconia, about 7 miles south of Weirs Beach.

In addition to gazing into the eyes of the plump, artfully carved orange fruit, visitors can enjoy a craft fair, a costume parade, seed-spitting contests and fireworks. Live bands play on the surrounding streets as local merchants dish up clam chowder, fried sausages, mulled cider and plenty of pumpkin pie.

THE DRIVE
From the nature center, follow NH 113 northeast for 5 miles. About 0.25 miles after the 'Rockywold Deephaven Camps' sign, look for the 'West Rattlesnake Trail' sign. Park in the parking lot or in a permissible space on either side of the road, wherever you don't see a 'No Parking' sign. The trail is on the lakeside.

04 WEST RATTLESNAKE TRAIL
The West Rattlesnake Trail climbs to a rocky outcrop atop Rattlesnake Mountain that yields stunning views of Squam Lake. It's less than a mile to the top, making this a good hike for families. (Just watch younger kids on the rocks.)

THE DRIVE
RNH 113 twists past cottages, pine trees and rock walls, offering glimpses of Squam Lake to the southeast before entering Center Sandwich. From this white clapboard village, pick up NH 109 south for 4.5 miles to NH 25/Whittier Hwy. Turn right onto NH 25 and follow it about 0.5 miles to Blake Rd and turn left. Follow Blake Rd to Lees Mill Rd and turn right.

05 LOON CENTER
Loons may be waterbirds, but their closest relatives are actually penguins, not ducks or geese. Known for their unique and varied calls (the wail sounds like a howling wolf), loons experienced a sharp decline in the 1970s.

The Loon Preservation Committee monitors the birds and works to restore a strong, healthy population. At its secluded **Loon Center** (loon.org), wildlife enthusiasts can learn

about the birds' plumage, habitat and distinctive calls, and watch an award-winning video. There are also details about protecting the birds. Kid-friendly activities include interactive games, a scavenger hunt and a junior biologist's guide.

The center sits within the 200-acre **Markus Wildlife Sanctuary** (loon.org/markus-wls). The sanctuary's **Loon Nest Trail** is a haven for birds: the 1.7-mile path winds through the forest and past a marsh to the shores of Lake Winnipesaukee. The best time for loon-spotting is nesting season, in June and July.

THE DRIVE
Follow Lees Mill Rd to Lee Rd. Turn right and continue to NH 109. Turn right. Continue 1.2 miles to the junction of NH 109 and the start of NH 171/Old Mountain Rd. Drive about 2 miles on NH 171. The entrance to Castle in the Clouds will be on the left.

06 CASTLE IN THE CLOUDS
Perched on high like a king surveying his territory, the arts-and-crafts-style **Castle in the Clouds** (castleintheclouds. org) wows with its stone walls and exposed-timber beams, but it's the views of lakes and valleys that draw the crowds – in fall the kaleidoscope of rust, red and yellow beats any postcard. The 5500-acre estate features gardens, ponds and a path leading to a small waterfall. Admission includes the 2-mile scenic road to the mansion and stories about the eccentric millionaire, Thomas Plant, who built it.

From late June to late August, make reservations for sunset music performances with dinner

Common Loon, Lake Winnipesaukee

on Monday and Thursday nights. Check the online calendar for other events, ranging from yoga on the lawn to stargazing.

THE DRIVE
Return to NH 109 south, following a woodsy route that tracks Lake Winnipesaukee (although you won't always be able to see the water). After Melvin Village, cross Mirror Lake on a pinch of land before hitting the outskirts of Wolfeboro. The drive is 10 miles.

07 LIBBY MUSEUM
At the age of 40, Henry Forrest Libby, a local doctor, began collecting things. In 1912 he built a home for his collections, which later became the eccentric little **Libby Museum** (libbymuseum.org). Starting with butterflies and moths, the amateur naturalist built up a private natural-history collection that now includes numerous stuffed mammals and birds. Other collections followed, including Abenaki relics and early American farm and home implements. The museum sits in a lovely spot across from Winter Harbor on Lake Winnipesaukee.

THE DRIVE
Drive 3.2 miles southeast on NH 109 to downtown Wolfeboro.

Photo Opportunity
The Weirs
Beach Boardwalk –
it's a classic!

08 WOLFEBORO
The self-proclaimed 'Oldest Resort in America' is a nice place to wander for a few hours. The waterfront is picturesque, with a grassy lakeside park, and in summer there are lots of free concerts and art events. (It's also garnered fame as the site of Republican presidential candidate Mitt Romney's summer home.)

Stretch your legs on the **Cotton Valley Rail Trail** (cottonvalley railtrail.org), which runs for 12 miles along a former train track. It passes two lakes, climbs through Cotton Valley, and winds through forests and fields. The trail starts behind the **Wolfeboro Chamber of Commerce** (wolfeborochamber.com), inside the former train depot, which carries a fantastic map detailing the walk. Before leaving, buy a scoop of ice cream downtown

from **Bailey's Bubble** (baileysbubble.com), where they've served generations of families.

THE DRIVE
Leave NH 109 in Wolfeboro, picking up NH 28 east just south of downtown. Summer camps dot the 10-mile drive toward Alton. Turn right on Old Bay Rd to pick up NH 11 north and drive for another 10 miles, passing the trailhead for the Mt Major Trail, a 1.5-mile one-way path leading to big views of the lake.

09 ELLACOYA STATE PARK
This has been a busy trip, so if you're ready to relax in a lovely setting, unpack your beach towel for a sunny day at lakeside **Ellacoya State Park** (nhstateparks.org/find-parks-trails/ellacoya-state-park), which has a 600ft-wide beach with gorgeous views across the lake to the Sandwich and Ossipee Mountains. This is an excellent place for swimming, fishing and canoeing. If your timing is right you might even see the MS *Mt Washington* cruising across the still waters – it's a pretty scene!

THE DRIVE
To complete the loop, return to Weirs Beach by taking NH 11 and NH 11B north for 7 miles.

23

NEW HAMPSHIRE

BEST FOR OUTDOORS

A hike to the summit of Mt Monadnock – views are superb!

Monadnock Villages

DURATION	DISTANCE	GREAT FOR
2 days	89 miles / 143km	Nature, food & drink

BEST TIME TO GO	April through October for festivals, foliage and hiking.

Miller State Park

Striking peaks, birch-lined streams, white-painted villages – it's no wonder artists and writers such as Henry David Thoreau, Willa Cather and Thornton Wilder found inspiration here. But the camaraderie in the towns, with their attractive communal spaces, surely added oomph to their oohs and aahs. This convivial spirit continues today, from the shared sense of adventure on the White Dot Trail to the ice-cream fans toughing out the winds on a chilly day at Kimball Farm.

Link Your Trip

03 Ivy League Tour

Head north from Keene to Hanover via NH 12 and I-91 for a tour of New England's most legendary colleges.

21 Connecticut River Byway

Swoop west from Keene on NH 12 to join the beautiful valley of the Connecticut River.

01 **MILLER STATE PARK**

If Mt Monadnock is the main course, then **Pack Monadnock** is the appetizer. Just 4 miles east of Peterborough, this 2290ft mountain is the heart of **Miller State Park** (nhstateparks. org/find-parks-trails/miller-state-park). Established in 1891, the park is New Hampshire's oldest, and a good one to visit if you're traveling with young children and pets. Two separate trails, the **Womack Trail** and the **Marion Davis Trail**, lead 1.4 miles from the parking lot to the summit, where you can climb a **fire tower** (built in 1939) for sweeping

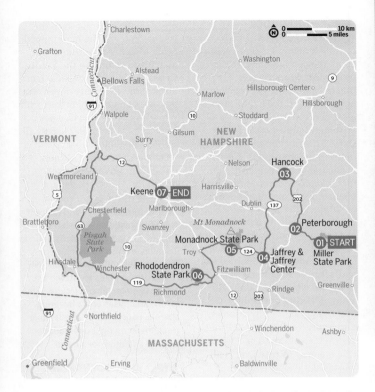

Attention: Artists at Work!

The **MacDowell Colony**, Peterborough's century-old art colony, draws more than 250 poets, composers, writers, architects and playwrights to the Monadnock region each year.

Playwright Thornton Wilder wrote *Our Town*, a play openly inspired by Peterborough, while at the colony. On the first Friday of every month between March and November, MacDowell fellows share their work through the MacDowell Downtown program, a series of free performances and panel discussions open to the general public.

views. Short on time? Drive the 1.3-mile paved road to the top.

THE DRIVE
Take NH 101 west for 4 miles into Peterborough.

02 PETERBOROUGH
This charming village of redbrick houses and tree-lined streets, with the idyllic Nabasuit River coursing through its historic center, is a particularly nice place for an extended stop. Its atmosphere is enhanced by the artistic influence of the nearby MacDowell Colony.

Pop into the **Mariposa Museum** (mariposamuseum.org) for folk art and folklore from around the world. It's a 'please touch'

kind of place, and kids are encouraged to try on costumes and play the musical instruments. Visit during one of the periodic interactive performances featuring musicians and storytellers. The indie bookstore **Toadstool Bookshop** (toadbooks.com) has a welcoming vibe and a good selection of books. Its small cafe, **Aesop's Tables** (facebook.com/aesopstablescafe), has a few patio tables and sells coffee, quiches, salads and sandwiches.

THE DRIVE
From Peterborough, drive 9 miles northwest on US 202/NH 123, along a woodsy route also popular with motorcyclists.

03 HANCOCK
In the first half of the 1800s, wandering artists would paint colorful landscape murals on bedroom walls in homes and inns throughout New England. Rufus Porter, an inventor who started *Scientific American* magazine, was one of the most famous of these traveling artists; unfortunately, many of his stencils and paintings were subsequently covered, and ruined, by wallpaper. Two murals are still visible inside the **Hancock Inn**, a three-story B&B in the heart of town. The inn is the oldest in New Hampshire and has been in continuous operation since 1789 – when George Washington was president! Although the murals are in guest rooms, you can enjoy a Porter-style mural – with a cocktail – in the inn's

sitting room before a meal at the restaurant.

THE DRIVE

NH 137 winds past marshes, stone walls and lichen-covered rocks on its way to NH 101, which is 6.5 miles south. Continue south on NH 137 for 7 miles to Jaffrey or, if you need to break for a meal, turn left and continue to Peterborough, then head south to Jaffrey on US 202.

04 JAFFREY & JAFFREY CENTER

Jaffrey Center, 2 miles west of Jaffrey, is another tiny, picture-perfect village of serene lanes, 18th-century homes and a dramatic white-steepled meetinghouse. All of its historic sites are clustered around the wee historic district, located on both sides of Gilmore Pond Rd off NH 124. The most intriguing sights include the towering 1775 **meetinghouse** (townofjaffrey. com), the frozen-in-time **Little Red School House** and the **Melville Academy** (townof jaffrey.com), which houses a one-room museum of rural artifacts. Willa Cather, a frequent visitor to Jaffrey, is buried in the **Old Burying Ground** behind the meetinghouse, with a quote from *My Antonia* gracing the headstone.

Jaffrey is perhaps best known as the home of Kimball Farm, an ice-cream shop that is favored by Mt Monadnock hikers.

THE DRIVE
From Jaffrey Center, drive under a half-mile on NH 124 and turn right on Dublin Rd. Pass a church camp and follow the signs to the park.

05 MONADNOCK STATE PARK

Roughly 125,000 people climb the commanding 3165ft peak of **Mt Monadnock** (nhstateparks.org) every year, helping it earn the honor of the most-climbed peak in the USA. Writer and philosopher Henry David Thoreau climbed it several times in the mid-1800s. Displays inside the visitor center explain that *monadnock* comes from the Abenaki word meaning 'special' or 'unique.' The word is now used geologically to describe a residual hill that rises alone from a plain.

Twelve miles of ungroomed **ski trails** lure cross-country skiers in winter, while more than 40 miles of **hiking paths** draw the trail-hungry hordes in summer. Numerous combinations of trails lead to the summit. The 1.9-mile one-way **White Dot Trail** (nhstateparks.org) is the most

LOCAL KNOWLEDGE

Kimball Farm

After a hike to the summit of Mt Monadnock, everyone knows that the best reward is ice cream from **Kimball Farm** (kimball farm.com). Consider the 40 flavors, order at the window, then find a seat at a picnic table out front. Perennial favorites include maple walnut, vanilla peanut butter, raspberry chocolate chip and coffee Oreo. Take note: the scoops are huge.

direct route, running from the visitor center to the bare-topped peak; it's a 3.9-mile round-trip hike if you return on the **White Cross Trail**, and the whole trip takes about 3½ hours. Most people ascend on the slightly shorter White Dot Trail. On clear days, you can gaze 100 miles across all six New England states.

The park's seasonal **Gilson Pond Campground** is well placed for a sunrise ascent.

THE DRIVE
Return to NH 124 and follow it 4.5 miles west, then bear left onto Troy Rd/Monadnock St and continue 2.5 miles west to join NH 12 near Troy. Turn left onto southbound NH 12 and drive 4 miles to Fitzwilliam, whose town green is surrounded by lovely old houses and a towering steeple. Follow NH 119 about 1 mile west, then turn right on Rhododendron Rd and drive for 2 miles.

06 RHODODENDRON STATE PARK

The 16-acre rhododendron grove in this serene **park** (nhstateparks.org) is the largest in New England. It makes for a nice stroll in mid-July, when thick stands of the giant plant (*Rhododendron maximum*) bloom white and pink along the 0.6-mile **Rhododendron Trail** circling the grove. The blooms can last for weeks and the final blossoms may occur as the leaves are turning. Listen for songbirds in the foliage while on the trail. The trail is also accessible to people with disabilities.

Hikers can hook onto the adjacent **Wildflower Trail**, where they may see mountain laurel blooms in June and berries in the fall. More ambitious ramblers can link from the Rhododendron

Trail to the **Little Monadnock Mountain Trail**, which climbs to the 1883ft summit of Little Monadnock Mountain. On the way it joins the 117-mile **MetaComet–Monadnock Trail** (nicknamed the M&M Trail), which continues to the summit of Mt Monadnock.

THE DRIVE
Drive west on NH 119, crossing NH 32 before heading into Winchester. Continue west on NH 119, passing one entrance to Pisgah State Park. Turn right on NH 63 for a bucolic spin past cows and red barns. Cross NH 9 to begin a particularly scenic drive past Spofford Lake, pine trees and the startlingly impressive Park Hill Meeting House. Turn right on NH 12 at Stuart & John's Sugar House and drive toward Keene. The drive is 47 miles.

Photo Opportunity

From Kimball Farm, photograph Mt Monadnock, then order your ice cream.

07 **KEENE**
Keene is like the hub of a giant wheel, with a half-dozen spokes linking to dozens of outlying villages that encircle the city, providing an endless supply of scenic loops. You really can't go wrong with any of them.

Keene itself is a great place to explore, particularly along its pleasant and lively Main St, which is lined with indie shops and cozy eateries. For local crafts, foodstuffs and gifts, stop by **Hannah Grimes Marketplace** (hannah grimes market place.com).

Main St is crowned by a small tree-filled plaza with a fountain at one end. The elegant, redbrick **Keene State College** (keene. edu) anchors the western end of Main St and the students inject downtown with an energetic vibe, as well as a youthful, artistic sensibility. The spacious, skylit halls at the **Thorne-Sagendorph Art Gallery** (keene.edu/tsag) showcase rotating exhibits of regional and national artists. The small permanent collection includes pieces by national artists who have been drawn to the Monadnock region since the 1800s.

In the evening, see what's doing at the 90-year-old **Colonial Theater** (thecolonial.org), which offers a diverse lineup of entertainment.

Central Square, Keene

24

NEW HAMPSHIRE

Woodland Heritage Trail

DURATION	DISTANCE	GREAT FOR
2 days	90 miles / 145km	Families, history & nature

BEST TIME TO GO	June to October for warm weather, fall foliage and open attractions.

Water Wheel, Jefferson

Why is northern New Hampshire so wild? Because a forward-thinking US senator from the Granite State, John W Weeks, introduced a bill in 1909 that birthed the modern national forest system. This trip makes the most of his vision by circling the White Mountain National Forest's rugged Kilkenny District, plunked dramatically between the Connecticut and Androscoggin Rivers and the Presidential Range. But it's not all lumberjacks and moose – Santa himself has somehow muscled onto the landscape.

Link Your Trip

20 White Mountains Loop

From Gorham drive south to Mt Washington, New England's highest peak.

21 Connecticut River Byway

Vistas are bucolic on the Connecticut River Byway, which rolls south from Lancaster.

01 WATER WHEEL

This trip starts with blueberry buttermilk pancakes and pure maple syrup at the appropriately named Water Wheel – look for the big red wheel, or at least half of one. You can also stock up on New Hampshire gifts at this cozy place.

THE DRIVE

From the Water Wheel, look both ways for logging trucks, then turn right on US 2 and head to Jefferson, 3 miles away.

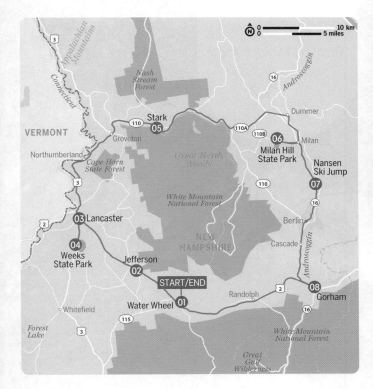

Live Free or Die

New Hampshire is the most politically conservative state in New England, with a libertarian streak that runs deep. It's tough and rugged, and its citizens still cling with pride to the famous words uttered by General John Stark, victor at the crucial Battle of Bennington: 'Live Free or Die!' The famous saying graces local license plates and appears all over the state.

02 JEFFERSON

Just west of mountain-ringed Jefferson is every child's dream: **Santa's Village** (santasvillage.com). Inside this cheery theme park, look for Santa's 26 elves as you enjoy the kiddie-focused rides, a Ferris wheel and the *Jingle Bell Express* train. Kids can even visit Santa himself, usually found relaxing at home. The attached water park, **Ho Ho H2O**, is open from late May into early October. The park also opens weekends in December for holiday visits.

THE DRIVE

Continue west 7 miles from Santa's Village to Lancaster, passing clapboard homes, logging trucks and commanding views of the Presidential Range.

03 LANCASTER

Photo op! Substitute your face for Paul Bunyan's at the **Great North Woods Welcome Center** (northern gatewaychamber.org) in downtown Lancaster. Here you can pick up maps and brochures before wandering past the boutiques and antique stores lining nearby Main St.

THE DRIVE

Follow US 3 for 3 miles south out of downtown Lancaster. The Weeks State Park entrance is on the left, across the street from a scenic pull-off.

04 WEEKS STATE PARK

Named for US senator John Weeks, **Weeks State Park** (nhstateparks.org) sits atop Mt Prospect. Weeks was a Lancaster native who introduced legislation in 1909 that helped to stem the degradation of local lands caused by unregulated logging, with legislation that became known as the Weeks Act. By authorizing the federal government to purchase land at the head of navigable streams, the act kick-started the national forest system, adding more than 19 million acres of land to the nation's holdings.

The park encompasses the 420-acre **Weeks estate**, where you can drive the 1.5-mile scenic road, explore the Weeks home and enjoy 360-degree mountain views from the property's stone **fire tower**.

THE DRIVE

From Lancaster, drive north on US 3, also known as the Daniel Webster Hwy, through Coos Junction, passing bogs and paralleling the

Photo Opportunity

Stark Covered Bridge, which anchors a picturesque village.

train tracks. In Groveton, 10 miles north, snap a photo of the covered bridge before continuing east on NH 110 for 21 miles to Stark.

 05 STARK

Fans of George RR Martin's novel *A Game of Thrones* can't be blamed if they ask directions to Winterfell, the northern holdfast of the Stark family that sits on the fringes of the lonely Wolfswood. But there aren't any wildling or wargs in this roadside village (that we saw, anyway), just the impossibly picturesque **Stark Covered Bridge**. This white, 134ft Paddleford truss bridge – constructed in 1862 and subsequently rebuilt and strengthened – spans the Upper Ammonoosuc River. It's flanked by the white **Union Church** (1850) and a white schoolhouse, making for an eye-catching photo. General John Stark was a famous commander during the American Revolution.

Two miles east, pull over for the **Camp Stark Roadside Marker**, which describes the WWII prisoner-of-war camp located nearby, where prisoners were put to work cutting pulpwood. It was the only war camp in New Hampshire.

🚗 **THE DRIVE**
Continue east for 2.7 miles. Make a sharp left onto NH 110A at the junction of NH 110 and NH 110A. Drive just over 3.5 miles (you'll pass 110B) to NH 16 and a view of the mighty Androscoggin River. Turn right and follow NH 16 south toward Berlin for 4 miles. Turn right at 110B for a short drive to Milan Hill State Park.

06 MILAN HILL STATE PARK

How often do you get to spend the night in a purple yurt? Yep, that's an option at **Milan Hill State Park** (nhstateparks.org), also known for its cross-country skiing and snowshoe trails. The 45ft **fire tower** provides expansive views of New Hampshire's mountains, as well as of mountain ranges in Vermont, Maine and Canada. The park is pet-friendly, so bring Fido for a walk or picnic. It's open year-round but only staffed seasonally; no day-use fee is collected in the low season.

The park is just south of New Hampshire's **13 Mile Woods Scenic Area**, which stretches along NH 16 and the Androscoggin River a few miles north and is known to be a popular strip for free-ranging moose.

🚗 **THE DRIVE**
Continue south on NH 16 from Milan for 4 miles, keeping your eyes open for moose, particularly in the morning and early evening. The road hugs the western side of the

Boom Piers

Driving south on NH 16 from Milan to Gorham, it's hard to miss the compact clusters of wood that rise from the middle of the river. Are they beaver dams? Small islands? Nope, those eye-catching clusters are boom piers, human-made islands that were used by lumbermen to separate logs by owner during the annual log drives. (Stamps that identified the owners were hammered into the end of the logs.) The log drives ended in 1963.

birch-lined Androscoggin River, a log-carrying highway in the first half of the 20th century.

07 NANSEN SKI JUMP

South of Milan, on the way to Gorham, pull over at the historic marker describing the Nansen Ski Jump, which is visible on the adjacent hill as you look north. This 171ft ski jump, first used in 1936, was the site of Olympic ski-jump trials in 1938. It was last used in 1982.

🚗 **THE DRIVE**
Continue another 11 miles south on NH 16 to reach Gorham.

08 GORHAM

Gorham is a regional crossroads, linking roads flowing in from the North Woods, from Mt Washington and North Conway, and from the Rangeley Lakes region of northwestern Maine. Stop here for one of the area's best restaurants, **Libby's Bistro**. Housed in an old bank building, it has a relaxed, speakeasy feel and uses local produce, in-season vegetables and New Hampshire seafood. Original wall safes speak of the building's banking past.

By this point, you've probably seen several moose-crossing signs dotting the route. If you still haven't seen an actual moose, join a moose safari with **Gorham Moose Tours** (gorhammoosetours.org). These determined folks know where the moose are and have a 93% to 97% moose-spotting success rate (and, yes, they've done the math!)

🚗 **THE DRIVE**
Complete the loop by returning to Jefferson, just west of the junction of US 2 and NH 115.

Left: Stark

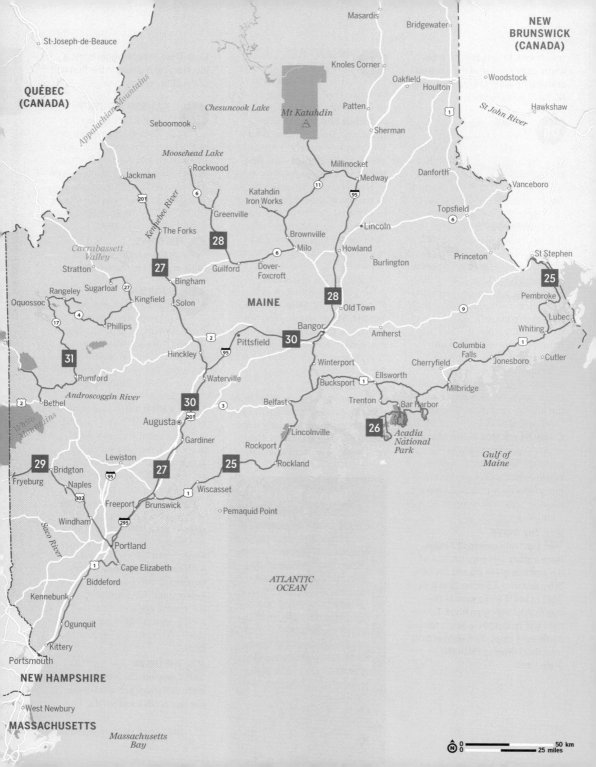

ERIC URQUHART/SHUTTERSTOCK ©

Sand Beach (p158)

Maine

Explore
Maine

Maine is a driver's delight, though with the main animal attraction (moose) sometimes crossing the road, you'll want to keep your foot from getting too heavy on the gas pedal, especially at night. These drives take you through the best of the best: inland villages and tiny coastal towns, where the seafood is wonderful. As with the rest of New England, Maine's forests resemble a bonfire in autumn; they're beautiful to behold, but they do draw thousands of others, so plan ahead. Also note: Maine is *biiiiig*, taking a full eight hours to drive Portsmouth to Edmundston, including traffic.

Bangor

Bangor sits slightly north of the midpoint of Maine's stretch of I-95, which traverses the state. On the placid banks of the Penobscot River, this is the last city on the map before the North Woods and it makes a good stopping point for those wanting to bypass the capital of Augusta. Like the latter, Bangor is an old working-class mill town that got its start with logging and trapping. Today it's a quiet, artsy spot with great dining options and access to just about everywhere in the state.

Bar Harbor

The largest town on Mount Desert Island, Bar Harbor has a lot going for it...and a lot of famous celebs going to it as well. Susan Sarandon, Paul Newman, Martha Stewart and the Vanderbilts have all visited or called this spot home. If you're coming from the inland rural parts, a stop at Bar Harbor will open your eyes, and empty your pocketbook. Expect to pay New York City prices for anything you buy or eat here. But it's hard to argue with the gorgeous scenery, the water, the boats and the placid conifer trees overlooking the rugged, rocky coastline. If Bar Harbor seems too extra for you, consider another coastal town like Camden or Boothbay Harbor, which have their own charms.

Augusta

Maine's capital is a great spot to base yourself in between trips. While its central location means you won't be on the coast – a downside for many folks – it's a boon if you're heading to the

WHEN TO GO

Like all of New England, there are four distinct seasons here, but in Maine the snows last longer and the summer is shorter. Likewise, fall arrives sooner than in the more southerly spots.

Leaf peeping begins around mid-September, depending on the year. Watch for slippery road conditions in winter, especially around curves.

north or west of the state. The pretty Kennebec River and the mix of old Victorian buildings and brick row houses makes Augusta a photogenic place. There are several historic sites in town, you'll find all the outfitting staples you'll need and there's even an airport, so you can fly here directly if you don't want to drive.

Sugarloaf

Winter drivers will be hard-pressed to find a better spot to stop and put the skis on than Sugarloaf, one of New England's classic ski resorts that's northerly enough (even with climate change) to have reliable powder throughout the season. Come to ski, hang out in chalets and sip hot cocoa or relax with a cognac or brandy by the fire. In the summer, take the lifts to the summit

for great views and hiking, ride the mountain-bike trails or play a round of Frisbee golf.

Resources

Visit Maine
(*visitmaine.com*)
Maine's official tourism website has helpful info about where to go, what to see and where to stay.

Maine Tourism Association
(*mainetourism.com*)
Helpful planning tips and a whole lot more.

Maine Bureau of Parks & Lands
(*maine.gov/dacf/parks*)
Oversees 48 state parks and historic sites.

WHAT'S ON

Blueberry Festival

This mid-summer celebration of the juicy blueberry is a great way to enjoy Maine's bounty. There are multitudes of blueberry-related events, pie contests, a 'Blueberry Princess' and even oxen-pulling competitions.

Maine Lobster Fest

What better way to celebrate the world's best-tasting crustacean than a festival in Rockland. Enjoy lobster, sample new recipes, listen to live music, sip craft beers and learn everything you ever wanted to know about pirates.

TRANSPORTATION

The starting points for many of the road trips in this chapter are not easily accessible by public transportation; renting a car is advised. Augusta and Bangor have rental offices, but many other towns in Maine do not, so plan carefully. Maine's largest airport is Portland International Jetport, at the southern end of the state.

WHERE TO STAY

Maine has accommodations for all budgets, from simple rustic farmhouses and cheap motels all the way up to five-star resorts that regularly host A-list celebrities. Atmospheric family guesthouses are often set in historic buildings, and vary from midrange to luxurious. Expect prices to increase dramatically in the summer and during ski season (November to April). Plenty of campgrounds and inexpensive roadside motels in the middle of nowhere make overnights affordable for everyone, but be sure to reserve well in advance in order to secure a campsite or room for your dates.

25

MAINE

Maritime Maine

DURATION	DISTANCE	GREAT FOR
5 days	285 miles / 459km	Nature, history & families

BEST TIME TO GO	Summer is great, but you'll shake the crowds in September and October.

Portland Head Light

The rugged complexity of the Maine coast hits home at Rockland's visitor center, where a giant state map – complete with lighthouses – sprawls across the floor. Islands, peninsulas, harbors – it's no wonder this state has such a strong maritime heritage. And it's this heritage that makes the trip memorable. The sunrises and rocky coasts are lovely, but it's the stories about lighthouse-keepers, brave captains and shipyard Rosie the Riveters that make this coastal drive unique.

Link Your Trip

27 Old Canada Road

From Bath, drive to Brunswick to wander a museum about Arctic explorers, then continue the route north along the stunning Kennebec River.

30 Mainely Art

In Rockland, join a cultural loop of Maine's artistic heritage and contemporary culture.

01 **KITTERY**

The drive to **Fort Foster Park** (fortfoster. weebly.com) twists past flowers, Victorian homes and tantalizing ocean glimpses. The seaside park is a nice place to walk some trails, have a picnic and play in rocky tide pools. Look out to sea for **Whaleback Ledge** (1831), the first lighthouse on this trip.

To get here from US 1, take ME 103 for 5 miles, then cross a small channel to Gerrish Island. Follow Pocahontas Dr through the woods.

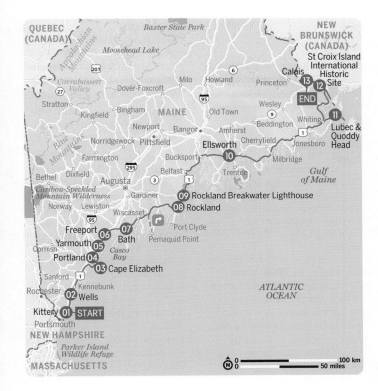

late-19th-century artillery base, and check out WWII bunkers and gun emplacements (a German U-boat was spotted in Casco Bay in 1942). The fort guarded the entrance to the bay until 1964.

A favorite feature of the park is the **Portland Head Light** (portlandheadlight.com), the oldest of Maine's 52 functioning lighthouses. Commissioned by George Washington in 1791, it was staffed until 1989, when machines took over. The keeper's house is now a museum, which traces the maritime and military history of the region.

THE DRIVE

Drive north 1 mile on Shore Rd, then turn right onto Preble St. Drive another mile, then turn right on Broadway then left onto Breakwater Dr. Just ahead, turn right onto Madison St.

04 PORTLAND

Maine's largest city and port is graced by a handful of handsome lights, including the 1875 **Portland Breakwater Light**, with Corinthian columns. Dubbed the 'Bug Light' because of its tiny size, it sits in a small park in South Portland with a panoramic view of downtown across the harbor. You can't enter the Bug Light, but you can traipse over the stone breakwater and walk around the light's exterior. The **Liberty Ship memorial**, across the park from the Bug Light, describes the site's history as a shipyard during WWII, when more than 30,000 people, including about 3750 women, were employed here to build cargo vessels, called Liberty Ships.

THE DRIVE

Continue north on US 1. There's a nice but potentially crowded sand beach at Ogunquit. Seven miles north of Ogunquit, turn right onto Laudholm Farm Rd.

02 WELLS

Wildlife-lovers, bird-watchers and families enjoy wandering the 7 miles of trails at the 2250-acre **Wells National Estuarine Research Reserve** (wellsreserve.org), a protected coastal ecosystem (no pets permitted). Down the road, the **Rachel Carson National Wildlife Reserve** (fws.gov/refuge/rachel_carson) holds more than 14,000 acres of protected coastal areas, with four trails scattered along 50 miles of shoreline. The 1-mile, pet-friendly **Carson Trail** meanders along tidal creeks and salt marshes.

THE DRIVE

Follow US 1 north, passing through Saco. In Scarborough, turn right onto ME 207. Follow it almost 3 miles to ME 77 and turn left. Drive just over 7 miles, passing Two Lights Rd, to Shore Rd. Turn right.

03 CAPE ELIZABETH

Good photo opportunities abound at **Fort Williams Park** (fortwilliams.org), where you can explore the ruins of the fort, which was a

THE DRIVE
Follow I-295 north and take exit 17. DeLorme cartographic company will be on your right off the ramp (signed 'Global Village'). You can also follow US 1 north from Portland.

05 YARMOUTH
On the way to the stores of Freeport, geography buffs shouldn't miss a visit to the DeLorme cartographic company – its lofty office atrium is home to a giant rotating globe named **Eartha**. Eartha has a diameter of 41.5ft and has been acknowledged by the Guinness Book of Records as the world's largest revolving and rotating globe. The detail on it is impressive (it took two years to build), as is the

---

WHY THIS IS A CLASSIC TRIP

Amy Balfour, Writer

There's a certain thrill in joining the crowds at the iconic spots along the coast. In Freeport, I was directed down to the marina to feast on lobster at the iconic red-painted seafood shack of the **Harraseeket Lunch & Lobster Co** (harraseeketlunchandlobster. com). If it's nice out, you can grab a picnic table – or just do like the locals and sit on the roof of your car. Make sure you finish with a slice of blueberry pie. And be there early to beat the crowds. It's BYOB and cash only, so come prepared.

---

opportunity for visitors to stop by for a look.

THE DRIVE
Follow US 1 north 4.5 miles past outlet stores and motels to LL Bean. There's a large parking lot on the left between Howard Pl and Nathan Nye St.

06 FREEPORT
A century ago Leon Leonwood Bean opened a shop here to sell equipment and provisions to hunters and fishers. His success lured other retailers and today nearly 200 stores line US 1, leading to traffic jams in summer.

Fronted by a 16ft hunting boot, the flagship **LL Bean store** (llbean.com) is a Maine must-see. In 1951 Bean himself removed the locks from the doors, deciding to stay open 24 hours a day, 365 days a year. With almost three million visitors annually, the store is one of the state's most popular attractions. There's a 3500-gallon aquarium and trout pond, a stuffed moose, and eating outlets – not to mention outdoor clothing and gear, spread over a small campus of stores (one dedicated to hunting and fishing, another to bike, boat and ski, and another to home furnishings).

Two 'Bootmobiles' travel the country on a mission to inspire people to get outside. The **LL Bean Outdoor Discovery School** (llbeanoutdoors.com) offers an array of courses, from in-store bike-maintenance clinics to first aid, plus fantastic excursions, tours and classes locally and across the state – from archery to snowshoeing by way of fly-fishing and bird-watching.

THE DRIVE
Follow US 1 north 18 miles through Brunswick to Bath. Pass Middle St, turn right on Washington St and drive 1.2 miles to the maritime museum.

07 BATH
This quaint Kennebec River town was once home to more than 20 shipyards producing more than a quarter of early America's wooden ships. **Bath Iron Works**, founded in 1884, is still one of the largest and most productive shipyards in the nation.

On the western bank of the Kennebec, the **Maine Maritime Museum** (mainemaritime museum.org) preserves the town's traditions with paintings, models and exhibits that tell the tale of the last 400 years of seafaring. Landlubbers and old salts alike will find something of interest, whether it's an 1849 ship's log describing the power of a hurricane or a hands-on tugboat pilot's house. On the grounds, look for the remains of the *Snow Squall*, a three-mast 1851 clipper ship that foundered near the Falkland Islands, and a life-size sculpture of the *Wyoming*, the largest wooden sailing vessel ever built.

In summer, the museum offers a variety of **boat cruises**, taking in assorted lighthouses and bird-rich bays ($34 to $50 per person, including museum admission). It also has a trolley tour that gives an insider's perspective of the Bath Iron Works.

THE DRIVE
Return to US 1 and continue north 40 miles, taking a moment to ogle the long line at Red's, a popular lobster shack in Wiscasset known for its lobster rolls. Continue north to Rockland.

Right: Maine Maritime Museum

Detour
Pemaquid Point
Start: **07** **Bath**

Maine's most famous lighthouse these days is the 1827 Pemaquid Point Light, which was featured on the special-edition Maine quarter. It's perched dramatically above rock-crashing surf in **Pemaquid Lighthouse Park** (bristolmaine.org/parks-recreation/pemaquid-point-lighthouse-park). The keeper's house now serves as the **Fisherman's Museum** (thefishermens museum.org). Staffed by volunteers (so with occasionally irregular hours), it displays fishing paraphernalia and photos. From Damariscotta, between Wiscasset and Waldoboro, follow ME 130 south.

Photo Opportunity

Stand on the rocks for a photo of Pemaquid lighthouse.

08 ROCKLAND

This thriving commercial port boasts a large fishing fleet and a proud year-round population. Settled in 1769, it was once an important shipbuilding center and a transportation hub for river cargo. Today, tall-masted ships still fill the harbor because Rockland (along with nearby Camden) is a center for Maine's **windjammer cruises** (sailmainecoast.com), which are multiday sailings on wind-powered schooners.

A map of Maine's coast, with all of its lighthouses, spreads across the floor of the **Penobscot Bay Regional Chamber of Commerce** (camdenrockland.com) beside Rockland Harbor. Ask for the list that identifies the lighthouses on the map. The chamber of commerce shares a roof with the **Maine Lighthouse Museum** (mainelighthousemuseum. org), which exhibits vintage Fresnel lenses, foghorns, marine instruments and ship models.

THE DRIVE
Follow Main St/US 1 north just over 1 mile from downtown to Waldo Ave. Turn right and drive half

Pemaquid lighthouse

a mile. Turn right onto Samoset Rd, following it to a small parking lot.

09 ROCKLAND BREAKWATER LIGHTHOUSE

Feeling adventurous? Tackle the rugged stone breakwater that stretches almost 1 mile into Rockland Harbor from Jameson Point at the harbor's northern shore. Made of granite blocks, this 'walkway' – which took 18 years to build – ends at the **Rockland Breakwater Lighthouse** (rocklandharborlights. org). Older kids should be fine; just watch for slippery rocks and ankle-twisting gaps between stones. Bring a sweater, and don't hike if a storm is on the horizon.

🚗 THE DRIVE
US 1 hugs the coast as it swoops north past the artsy enclaves of Rockport, Camden and Belfast, curving east through Bucksport before landing in Ellsworth, about 60 miles from Rockland.

10 ELLSWORTH
Cooks and coffee-lovers, this stop's for you. In old-school Ellsworth, pull over for **Rooster Brother** (rooster brother.com), a kitchenware boutique that also sells amazing roasted coffee. Step downstairs from the retail store for a coffee sample – but be careful, you'll likely end up buying a full cup or a pound to go. Check out the excellent fresh cookies, especially the super-tasty ginger and molasses. Wine, chocolate, cheese and fresh bread are also for sale.

🚗 THE DRIVE
From Ellsworth, drive east on US 1. Consider taking ME 182, the most direct route north, but it's a more scenic option to follow US 1 south onto the Schoodic Peninsula. ME 182 hooks back onto US 1 at Cherryfield. From here, enter 'Down East' Maine, an unspoiled region dotted with traditional fishing villages. For a good meal and convenient lodging, stop in Machias.

11 LUBEC & QUODDY HEAD
Lubec is a small fishing village that makes its living off transborder traffic with Canada and a bit of tourism. South of town, a walking trail winds along towering, jagged cliffs at the 541-acre **Quoddy Head State Park** (maine.gov/quoddyhead), a moody place when the mist is thick and the foghorn blasts its lonely wail. The tides here are dramatic, fluctuating 16ft in six hours. Look for whales migrating along the coast in summer. The park is also the site of the 1858 **West Quoddy Light**, which looks like a barber's pole.

🚗 THE DRIVE
Return to US 1 north, passing Pembroke and Perry. About 3 miles north of Perry look for a pull-off on the left marking the 45th parallel, the halfway point between the North Pole and the equator. Continue 8.5 miles north.

12 ST CROIX ISLAND INTERNATIONAL HISTORIC SITE

The site of one of the first European settlements in the New World is visible from this **historic park** (nps.gov/sacr), 8 miles southeast of Calais. In 1604 a company of settlers sailed from France to establish a French claim in North America. They built a settlement on a small island in Passamaquoddy Bay, between Maine and New Brunswick, Canada. The settlers were ill-prepared for winter, and icy waters essentially trapped them on the island with limited food until spring. Many perished. The settlement was abandoned in 1605 and a new home was established in Port Royal, Nova Scotia. A short trail at the park winds past bronze statues and historic displays; a visitor center is staffed from mid-May to mid-October.

🚗 THE DRIVE
Return to US 1 and drive 5 miles north to a rest area on your right. If you end up in Canada – or pass the local high school – you've gone too far.

13 CALAIS
Maine's northernmost lighthouse is **Whitlocks Mill Light** (stcroixhistorical. com), visible from a rest area 3.5 miles south of Calais. To spot the lighthouse, look for the sign, walk down to the fence and look north.

26

MAINE

Acadia National Park

DURATION	DISTANCE	GREAT FOR
3 days	112 miles / 180km	Nature, history, families

BEST TIME TO GO	May through October for good weather and open facilities.

Lupines, Acadia National Park

Drivers and hikers can thank John D Rockefeller Jr and other wealthy landowners for the aesthetically pleasing bridges, overlooks and stone steps that give Acadia National Park its artistic oomph. Rockefeller in particular worked diligently with architects and masons to ensure that the infrastructure complemented the surrounding landscape. Today, park explorers can put Rockefeller's planning to good use – tour the wonderful Park Loop Rd by car, but be sure to explore on foot and by bike wherever you can.

Link Your Trip

25 Maritime Maine

Enjoy Bass lighthouse? Hop on US 1 for more photogenic beacons.

30 Mainely Art

Take US 1 south to Rockland for galleries, museums and local artists.

01 ACADIA NATIONAL PARK HULLS COVE VISITOR CENTER

Whoa, whoa, whoa. Before zooming into Bar Harbor on ME 3, stop at the **park visitor center** (nps.gov/acad) to get the lay of the land and pay the admission fee. Inside, head directly to the large diorama, which provides a helpful overview of Mount Desert Island (MDI). As you'll see, Acadia National Park shares the island with several non-park communities, which are tucked here and there beside Acadia's borders.

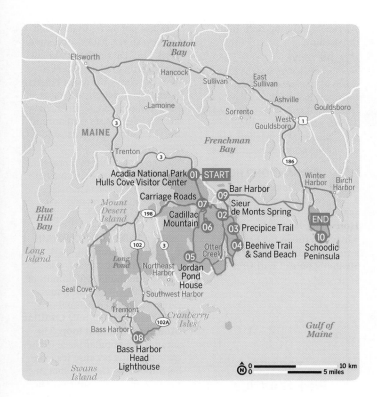

WHY THIS IS A CLASSIC TRIP

Benedict Walker, Writer

New England's one-and-only national park turned 100 in 2016 and continues to live up to its celebrity status — around two million visitors each year make it one of the most popular parks in the USA. The best way to get oriented is to drive Park Loop Rd, but don't be afraid to venture off the beaten track, or take the 'other' loop to explore the scenic Schoodic Peninsula. You'll find pristine inlets and sleepy coves on the 'Quietside,' the occasional working lobster shack, and nature, the star performer, thriving at every turn.

From the visitor center, the best initiation to the park is to drive the 27-mile **Park Loop Road**, which links the park's highlights in the eastern section of MDI. It's one way (traveling clockwise) for most of its length.

 THE DRIVE
From the visitor center, turn right onto the Park Loop Rd, not ME 3 (which leads into Bar Harbor). Take in a nice view of Frenchman Bay on your left before passing the spur to ME 233. A short distance ahead, turn left to begin the one-way loop on the Park Loop Rd.

02 SIEUR DE MONTS SPRING
Nature-lovers and history buffs will enjoy a stop at the Sieur de Monts Spring area at the intersection of ME 3 and the Park Loop Rd. Here you'll find a nature center and the summer-only branch of the **Abbe Museum** (abbemuseum. org; closed for maintenance at time of research), which sits in a lush, nature-like setting. Twelve of Acadia's biospheres are displayed in miniature at the **Wild Gardens of Acadia**, from bog to coniferous woods to meadow. Botany enthusiasts will appreciate the plant labels. There are also some amazing stone-step

trails here, appearing out of the talus as if by magic.

 THE DRIVE
If you wish to avoid driving the full park loop, you can follow ME 3 from here into Bar Harbor. Push on for the full experience – you won't regret it.

03 PRECIPICE TRAIL
What's the most exciting way to get a bird's-eye view of the park? By climbing up to where the birds are. Two 'ladder trails' cling to the sides of exposed cliffs on the northeastern section of the Park Loop Rd, dubbed Ocean Dr. If you're fit and the season's right, tackle the first of the ladder trails,

the steep, challenging 1.6-mile Precipice Trail, which climbs the east face of Champlain Mountain on iron rungs and ladders. (Note that the trail is typically closed late spring to mid-August because it's a nesting area for peregrine falcons. If it is closed, you might catch volunteers and staff monitoring the birds through scopes from the trail-head parking lot.) Skip the trail on rainy days.

 THE DRIVE
Continue south on the Park Loop Rd. The Beehive Trail starts 100ft north of the Sand Beach parking area.

04 **BEEHIVE TRAIL & SAND BEACH**
Another good ladder trail is the **Beehive Trail**. The 0.8-mile climb includes ladders, rungs, narrow wooden bridges and scrambling – with steep drop-offs. As with the Precipice Trail, it's recommended that you descend via a nearby walking route, rather than climbing down.

Don't let the crowds keep you away from **Sand Beach**. It's home to one of the few sandy shorelines in the park, and it's a don't-miss spot. But you don't have to visit in the middle of the day to appreciate its charms. Beat the crowds early in the morning, or visit at night, especially for the **Stars over Sand Beach program**. During these free one-hour talks, lie on the beach, look up at the sky and listen to rangers share stories and science about the stars. Even if you miss the talk, the eastern coastline along Ocean Dr is worth checking out at night, when you can watch the Milky

Way seemingly slip right into the ocean.

 THE DRIVE
Swoop south past the crashing waves of Thunder Hole. If you want to exit the loop road, turn right onto Otter Cliff Rd, which hooks up to ME 3 north into Bar Harbor. Otherwise, pass Otter Point then follow the road inland past Wildwood Stables.

05 **JORDAN POND HOUSE**
Share hiking stories with other nature-lovers at the lodge-like **Jordan Pond House** (jordanpondhouse.com), where afternoon tea has been a tradition since the late 1800s. Steaming pots of Earl Grey come

---

TOP TIP:

Park Shuttles

With millions of visitors coming to the park each summer, traffic and parking can be a hassle. On arrival, drive the Park Loop Rd straight through for the views and the driving experience. Then leave the driving to others by using the **Island Explorer** (exploreacadia. com), which is free with park admission. Shuttles run along nine routes that connect visitors to trails, carriage roads, beaches, campgrounds and in-town destinations. They can even carry mountain bikes.

---

with hot popovers (hollow rolls made with egg batter) and strawberry jam. Eat on the broad lawn overlooking the lake. On clear days the glassy waters of 176-acre Jordan Pond reflect the image of Mt Penobscot like a mirror. Take the 3.2-mile nature trail around the pond after finishing your tea.

 THE DRIVE
Look up for the rock precariously perched atop South Bubble from the pull-off almost 2 miles north. Continue north to access Cadillac Mountain Rd.

06 **CADILLAC MOUNTAIN**
Don't leave the park without driving – or hiking – to the 1530ft summit of Cadillac Mountain. For panoramic views of Frenchman Bay, walk the paved 0.5-mile **Cadillac Mountain Summit loop**. The summit is a popular place in the early morning because it's long been touted as the first spot in the USA to see the sunrise. The truth? It is, but only between October 7 and March 6. The crown is passed to northern coastal towns the rest of the year because of the tilt of the earth. But, hey, the sunset is always a good bet.

 THE DRIVE
Drunk on the views, you can complete the loop road and exit the park, heading for your accommodations or next destination. But consider finding a parking lot and tackling walking trails, or heading to Bar Harbor to hire bikes.

07 **CARRIAGE ROADS**
John D Rockefeller Jr, a lover of old-fashioned horse carriages, gifted Acadia some 45 miles of crisscrossing carriage roads. Made from

Right: Cadillac Mountain

Photo Opportunity

Capture that sea-and-sunrise panorama from atop Cadillac Mountain.

Bass Harbor Head Lighthouse

crushed stone, the roads are free of cars and are popular with cyclists, hikers and equestrians. Several of them fan out from Jordan Pond House, but if the lot is too crowded continue north to the parking area at **Eagle Lake** on US 233 to link to the carriage-road network. If you're planning to explore by bike, the Bicycle Express Shuttle runs to Eagle Lake from the Bar Harbor Village Green from late June through September. Pick up a *Carriage Road User's Map* at the visitor center.

THE DRIVE

Still in the mood for cruising? Before you head for the bright lights of Bar Harbor, take a detour: drive ME 233 toward the western part of MDI, connecting to ME 198 west, then drop south on ME 102 toward Southwest Harbor. Pass Echo Lake Beach and Southwest Harbor, then bear left onto ME 102A for a dramatic rise up and back into the park near the seawall.

08 BASS HARBOR HEAD LIGHTHOUSE

There is only one lighthouse on Mount Desert Island, and it sits in the somnolent village of Bass Harbor in the far southwest corner of the park. Built in 1858, the 36ft lighthouse still has a Fresnel lens from 1902. It's in a beautiful location that's a photographers' favorite. The lighthouse is a coast guard residence, so you can't go inside, but you can take photos. You can also stroll to the coast on two easy trails near the property: the **Ship Harbor Trail**, a 1.2-mile loop, and the **Wonderland Trail**, a 1.4-mile round trip. These trails are spectacular ways to get through the forest and to the coast, which looks different to the coast on Ocean Dr.

THE DRIVE

For a lollipop loop, return on ME 102A to ME 102 through the village of Bass Harbor. Follow ME 102 then ME 233 all the way to Bar Harbor.

09 BAR HARBOR

Tucked on the rugged coast in the shadows of Acadia's mountains, Bar Harbor is a busy gateway town with a J Crew joie de vivre. Restaurants, taverns and boutiques are scattered along Main St, Mt Desert St and Cottage St. Shops sell everything from books and camping gear to handicrafts and art. For a fascinating collection of natural artifacts related to Maine's Native American heritage, visit the **Abbe Museum** (abbemuseum.org). The collection holds more than 50,000 objects, such as pottery, tools, combs and fishing instruments spanning the last 2000 years, including contemporary pieces. (There's a smaller summer-only branch in Sieur de Monts Spring.)

Done browsing? Spend the rest of the afternoon, or early evening, exploring the area by water. Sign up in Bar Harbor for a half-day or sunset sea-kayaking trip. **Coastal**

Kayaking Tours (acadiafun. com) offers guided trips along the jagged coast.

🚗 THE DRIVE

There's another part of the park you haven't yet explored. Reaching it involves a 44-mile drive (north on Rte 3 to US 1, following it about 17 miles to ME 186 S). ME 186 passes through Winter Harbor and then links to Schoodic Point Loop Rd. It's about an hour's drive one way. Alternatively, hop on a Downeast Windjammer ferry from the pier beside the Bar Harbor Inn.

10 SCHOODIC PENINSULA

The Schoodic Peninsula is the only section of Acadia National Park that's part of the mainland. It's also home to the Park Loop Rd, a rugged, woodsy drive with splendid views of Mount Desert Island and Cadillac Mountain. You're more likely to see a moose here than on MDI – what moose wants to cross a bridge?

Much of the drive is one way. There's the excellent **Schoodic Woods Campground** (recreation.gov) near the entrance, then a picnic area at **Frazer Point**. Further along the loop, turn right for a short ride to **Schoodic Point**, a 440ft-high promontory with ocean views.

The full loop from Winter Harbor is 11.5 miles. If you're planning to come by ferry, you could rent a bike beforehand at **Bar Harbor Bicycle Shop** (barharborbike.com) – the Park Loop Rd's smooth surface and easy hills make it ideal for cycling.

In July and August, the Island Explorer Schoodic shuttle bus runs from Winter Harbor to the peninsula ferry terminal and around the Park Loop Rd.

VLAD G/SHUTTERSTOCK ©

Acadia National Park

ISLAND VISIT PLANNER

Acadia National Park

ORIENTATION & FEES

Park admission is $30 per vehicle (including passengers), $20 per motorcycle and $12 for walk-ins and cyclists. Admission is valid for seven days.

CAMPING

There are two great rustic campgrounds on Mount Desert Island, with nearly 500 sites between them. Both are densely wooded and near the coast; reservations are essential (except in winter at Blackwoods). **Seawall** (recreation.gov) is 4 miles south of Southwest Harbor on the 'Quietside' of Mount Desert Island, while **Blackwoods** (recreation.gov) is closer to Bar Harbor (5 miles south, on ME 3).

Bar Harbor & Mount Desert Island

Before your trip, check lodging availability at the **Bar Harbor Chamber of Commerce** (visitbarharbor.com). Staff can mail you a copy of the visitor guide. Otherwise, stop by the welcome center for lodging brochures, maps and local information. It's located north of the bridge onto Mount Desert Island. There is a second **visitor center** (visitbarharbor.com) in Bar Harbor itself.

27

MAINE

Old Canada Road

BEST FOR OUTDOORS

White-water rafting trips launch onto the Kennebec and Dead Rivers near The Forks.

DURATION	DISTANCE	GREAT FOR
2 days	139 miles / 224km	Nature, history & families

BEST TIME TO GO	July to October for top rafting and hiking.

The Old Canada Rd is a 'hands-on' museum for history buffs. Stretching north from Hallowell to the Canadian border along US 201, it tracks the Kennebec River for most of the drive, passing farms, old ports, private timberlands and rafting companies – all of the industries that have sustained the region over the last few centuries. You're also following the trail of Benedict Arnold, who marched this way for George Washington during the Revolutionary War.

Link Your Trip

28 Great North Woods

From Jackman, take ME 6 east to Rockwood to tour Maine's largest lake.

30 Mainely Art

Visit the Bowdoin College Museum of Art in Brunswick, then stroll through galleries along the coast.

01 BRUNSWICK

What better place to start a road trip than a museum dedicated to an intrepid explorer? On the campus of Bowdoin College, the **Peary-MacMillan Arctic Museum** (bowdoin.edu/arctic-museum) displays memorabilia from the expeditions of Robert Peary and Donald MacMillan, who were among the first explorers to reach the North Pole – or a spot pretty darn close to it. Exhibits include an oak-and-rawhide sledge used to carry the expedition to the pole and Peary's journal entry reading 'The pole at last!' Also notable are

RANDY DUCHAINE/ALAMY STOCK PHOTO ©

Peary-MacMillan Arctic Museum

MacMillan's black-and-white Arctic photos and displays examining the Inuit people and Arctic wildlife. The stuffed polar bears look...not so cuddly.

The surrounding town of Brunswick, which sits on the banks of the Androscoggin River, is a handsome, well-kept community with a pretty village green and historic homes tucked along its tree-lined streets.

THE DRIVE
Follow US 201 north past meadows, fruit stands, old Chevy pickup trucks and Dunkin' Donuts (they're everywhere!) on this 30-mile stretch.

02 HALLOWELL
Hallowell, a major river port for many years, thrived on the transportation of granite, ice and timber. There's a nice view of the town and the Kennebec River from the **Kennebec-Chaudière International Corridor Information Panel**, located at a small pull-off south of town and describing the 233-mile international heritage trail between Québec City and coastal Maine. Hallowell dates from 1726, and it's a sociable place, dubbed 'the New Orleans of the North.' The compact downtown is home to numerous historic buildings, antique stores, cafes and an easygoing pub, the **Liberal Cup**.

THE DRIVE
From Hallowell, follow US 201 just 1.5 miles north to downtown Augusta and the State Capitol complex.

03 AUGUSTA
What happens when a moose and his rival lock horns in mortal combat? Their interlocked racks end up in the Cabinet of Curiosities at the **Maine State Museum** (maine statemuseum.org) in Augusta, the state capital. The museum, a four-storey ode to all things Maine, is situated around a multistory mill that churns by waterpower. The newest permanent exhibit, 'At Home in Maine,' looks at homes throughout the years;

in the mod 1970s house you can watch a family filmstrip and dial a rotary phone.

Across the parking lot, take a tour (guided or self-guided) of the **State House** (legislature. maine.gov/lio), built in 1832 and enlarged in 1909. It was designed by Boston architect Charles Bulfinch, the same architect behind the nation's Capitol building in Washington, DC.

THE DRIVE
On the 19-mile drive to Winslow you'll cross the river and pass a barn or two, a taxidermy shop, pine trees, creeks and small churches.

04 WATERVILLE & WINSLOW
The oldest blockhouse fortification in the USA is located at the **Fort Halifax State Historic Site**, in a small park on the banks of the Kennebec River in Winslow. The log blockhouse is all that remains of a larger palisaded garrison built by British Americans in 1754, designed to guard against attacks by the French and their allied Native American tribes. In 1987 the blockhouse's logs came apart during a flood and floated downstream. They were recovered, and the fortification was rebuilt. It sits in pretty Fort Halifax Park on US 201, a mile south of the Winslow–Waterville Bridge (well hidden among gas stations).

THE DRIVE
Cross the Winslow–Waterville Bridge and continue on US 201 north through downtown Waterville. From here it's a 9-mile drive. Look out for logging trucks as the road approaches Hinckley.

05 LC BATES MUSEUM
Any road trip worth its stripes includes at least one eccentricity. This one earns its stripes – and its spots and feathers – with the nicely nonconformist **LC Bates Museum** (gwh.org). Housed in a 1903 brick school building on the Good Will-Hinckley educational complex south of Hinckley, the museum embraces the concept of the 20th-century Cabinet of Curiosities, with a huge assortment of natural, geologic and artistic artifacts. On the 1st floor, look for an amazing array of taxidermied birds. The basement holds stuffed mammals (including one of the last caribou shot in Maine), rocks, minerals and fossils. There are treasures here, and staff members are glad to point out the more interesting finds and answer questions. **Nature trails** meander through the forest out back.

THE DRIVE
The Kennebec stays in the picture on the 10-mile drive to Skowhegan, former home of Margaret Chase Smith, the first woman elected to both the US House of Representatives and Senate.

06 SKOWHEGAN
At Skowhegan's hard-to-resist ice-cream stand **Gifford's** (giffordsicecream. com), every flavor sounds delicious, from Maine Wild Blueberry to Caramel Caribou to Moose Tracks, made with peanut-butter cups and fudge. If you don't pull over for a scoop, you'll never hear the end of it if you've got kids or a co-pilot on board. But don't worry, these creamy concoctions are delicious. Plus: if you need a real leg-stretch,

North Woods River-Rafting Trips

Some of the best white water in America rushes through Maine's North Woods. From early May to mid-October, dozens of companies run organized rafting trips on the Kennebec, Dead and Penobscot Rivers. Bingham and The Forks serve as bases for rafting companies, and trips range in difficulty from Class II to Class V. For a one-day trip on the Kennebec, expect to pay between $69 and $129, with prices at their highest in July and August.

The following recommended rafting companies, all with lodges for accommodations and meals, plus other outdoor activities on offer (including river tubing, fishing, wildlife-spotting and winter snowmobiling), are all based in The Forks. **Crab Apple Whitewater** (crabapplewhitewater.com) **Northern Outdoors** (northernoutdoors.com) **Three Rivers Whitewater** (threeriverswhitewater.com)

there's a mini-golf course here too.

THE DRIVE
From Skowhegan, drive 10 miles north to the junction of US 201 and ME 43, which marks the start of the Old Canada Rd National Scenic Byway – a particularly lovely stretch of the longer Old Canada Rd.

Left: White-water rafting, Kennebec River

07 ROBBINS HILL SCENIC AREA

Take a picnic and your camera to the overlook at Robbins Hill near the start of the national byway. Look west for views of Saddleback Mountain, Mt Abraham and other mountains in Maine's Rangeley Lakes region. Signboards detail the history of the communities along the Old Canada Rd, from the region's agricultural beginnings in the late 1700s to the effects of the railroad and the arrival of the timber industry.

THE DRIVE
Pass white clapboard houses in Solon and another roadside pull-off, this one overlooking the Kennebec River. Here you'll find informational plaques about the railroad and the logging industries, including a picture of the last American log drive here in 1976. Continue past anglers' cabins, rafting businesses and brewpubs.

08 THE FORKS

After passing through Bingham and Moscow, US 201 follows a gorgeous stretch of river into The Forks. At this dot on the map, the Dead River joins the Kennebec River, setting the stage for excellent white-water rafting. At the junction of US 201 and Lake Moxie Rd, there's a small rest area with picnic tables, an information kiosk and a footbridge over the Kennebec River. From here, drive 2 miles east on Lake Moxie Rd to the trailhead for the easy walk (0.6 miles one way) to the dramatic **Moxie Falls**. At 90ft, this is one of the highest waterfalls in the state.

THE DRIVE
On this 20-mile push, you'll ascend Johnson Mountain before reaching the Lake Parlin overlook, where there are details about the American moose – which can reach speeds of 35mph.

09 JACKMAN

Jackman knows how to throw out the welcome mat. Just south of town, the **Attean View Overlook** greets road-trippers with a dramatic view of Attean Lake and distant mountains – a landscape that sweeps into Canada.

The lake and overlook are named for Joseph Attean, a Penobscot Indian leader who guided Henry David Thoreau on trips through the Maine woods in 1853 and 1857. Attean died during a log drive on July 4, 1870. Legend says that his boots were hung from a pine knot near where his body was found, a tradition for river drivers killed while working the water-way. Today, Jackman is a good base for outdoor fun, including fishing, canoeing, hiking, biking, snow-mobiling and cross-country skiing. Its ATV trails are considered some of the state's best.

Benedict Arnold Slept Here

About 12 miles north of Bingham, on the left side of the road, a small stone memorial marks the spot where Benedict Arnold and his soldiers left the Kennebec River in October 1775 during the Revolutionary War. Arnold, at the time still loyal to America, had been placed in command of 1100 men by George Washington. His mission? To follow the Kennebec and Dead Rivers north to defeat the British forces at Québec. The soldiers used bateaux (shallow-draft river boats) to travel up the Kennebec and encountered numerous difficulties along the way. Many men were lost through desertion and illness. A weakened force of about 500 reached Québec, where they were ultimately defeated.

Right: Benedict Arnold memorial, Kennebec River

Photo Opportunity

From the Attean View Overlook, take a sunset shot of Attean Lake and distant mountains.

THIS TABLET MARKS THE PLACE
WHERE COLONEL BENEDICT ARNOLD
WITH HIS SOLDIERS LEFT THE KENNEBEC
RIVER OCTOBER 1775 AND MARCHED
FROM THE WEST SHORE IN A NORTH-
WESTERLY DIRECTION TO DEAD RIVER
ON THEIR WAY TO QUEBEC

PLACED BY THE KENNEBEC CHAPTER
OF THE DAUGHTERS OF THE AMERICAN REVOLUTION
1916

28

MAINE

Great North Woods

Statue of Paul Bunyan, Bangor

DURATION	DISTANCE	GREAT FOR
3 days	3250 miles / 402km	Nature & families

BEST TIME TO GO	July and August brings warm weather and no blackflies.

Texts. Tweets. Twenty-four hours of breaking news. If you need a respite from the modern world, grab your map – a paper one! – and drive directly to the Maine highlands, part of the sprawling North Woods. What will you find? Silence and solitude. Water and pines. The unfettered wildness of Baxter State Park. And access to 175,000 acres of private forest thrown open for public recreation.

Link Your Trip

27 Old Canada Road

Head west to US 201 from Rockwood for rafting and riverside history.

30 Mainely Art

In Bangor, kick-start a loop of Maine's finest art and culture with a visit to the University of Maine Museum of Art.

01 BANGOR

Bangor is the last city on the map before the North Woods. So it seems appropriate that a towering **statue of Paul Bunyan** stands near the center of downtown. The 31ft statue has watched over Bangor since the 1950s, but the ax-wielding lumberman isn't getting much love these days. His view of the Penobscot River is now blocked by a casino, and a new multipurpose arena has risen behind him.

But Paul's not the only star in town. **Stephen King**, the mega-best-selling author of horror novels such as *Carrie* and *The Shining*, resides in an

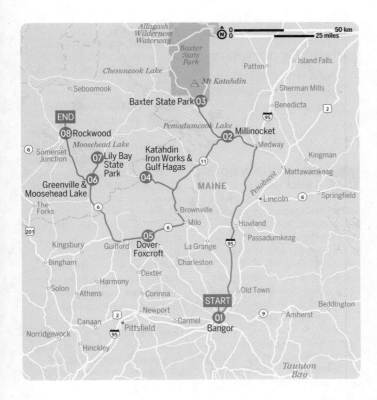

Baxter Practicalities

● No pets are permitted inside the park boundaries.

● Bring insect repellent. Blackflies and no-see-ums bite in the spring and mosquitoes appear in June. Green deer flies and black moose flies can also bite in the middle of summer.

● Pack warm clothes, even in summer, as well as water, a flashlight and rain protection.

● There are no treated water sources inside the park, so bring your own or carry purifying tablets.

● Cell phones and iPads don't work in the park. Handheld GPS devices work with reasonable accuracy, but always hike with a map and compass. Vehicle GPS units can be less reliable. Use written directions after Millinocket Lake, near the south entrance. See: baxterstateparkauthority. com/maps/directions.htm

---

appropriately Gothic red Victorian house off Hammond St. You can't go inside, but you can snap a photo of his splendidly creepy wrought-iron front fence, adorned with spiderwebs and bats. The house is in a residential neighborhood, so please keep your shrieking to a minimum.

THE DRIVE

The 60-mile drive on I-95 north to exit 244 for Millinocket isn't that interesting. But it's efficient, and the rest of the drive will blow this ho-hum stretch from your memory. From exit 244, drive northwest on ME 11/157.

02 MILLINOCKET

Baxter State Park is far, far off the beaten path, and many of its rules and policies differ from those at other Maine state parks – so do a bit of planning before driving out here. The town of Millinocket, with its motels, inns and eating outlets, works well as a base camp. Eighteen miles from the park, it's also the closest town to the southern entrance. For park information and a copy of *Windnotes*, the helpful park visitor guide, stop by the **Baxter State Park Authority Headquarters** (baxterstateparkauthority.com); it's just beside the McDonald's.

THE DRIVE
The drive from Millinocket to Baxter State Park takes in bogs, birches and pine trees, and then some very narrow roads. Gape at Katahdin from the Keep Maine Beautiful sign, then continue to Togue Pond gate.

03 BAXTER STATE PARK
In the 1930s Governor Percival Baxter began buying land for **Baxter State Park** (baxterstatepark.org), using his own money. By the time of his death in 1969, he had given, in trust, more than 200,000 acres to the park as a gift to the people of Maine. **Mt Katahdin** is the park's crowning glory. At 5267ft it is Maine's tallest mountain and the northern endpoint of the 2190-mile Appalachian Trail.

Baxter also left an endowment fund for the support and maintenance of the park. His greatest desire was for the land to remain wild and to serve as a 'sanctuary for beasts and birds.' To ensure that his vision is followed, the park is kept in a primitive state and there is very little infrastructure inside its boundaries. And what a difference this makes. Baxter is Maine at its most primeval: the wind whips around dozens of peaks, black bears root through the underbrush, and hikers go for miles without seeing another soul.

THE DRIVE

From Millinocket, follow ME 11 south for about 25 miles. Turn right onto Katahdin Iron Works Rd, and drive 6.3 miles on a dirt road. If you get to Brownsville Junction on ME 11, you missed Katahdin Iron Works Rd.

Photo Opportunity
Capture Mt Katahdin rising behind Baxter State Park's southern entrance.

04 KATAHDIN IRON WORKS & GULF HAGAS
A reminder of a time when blast furnaces and charcoal kilns smelted iron all day, the **iron works** (maine.gov/katahdinironworks) were built in 1843. Eventually the costs of operating in such isolation meant the facility was unable to compete with foundries in Pennsylvania and other states, and it closed in 1890.

From here, Katahdin Iron Works Rd leads another 6.5 miles to the trailhead for **Gulf Hagas** (northmainewoods.org), dubbed the Grand Canyon of Maine. The gorge features a stunning 500ft drop studded with waterfalls over the course of its 3 miles. Carved over five million years by water eroding the slate bedrock, the gulf is a national natural landmark and is surrounded by some of Maine's oldest white pines. An 8-mile rim-trail hiking loop is remote and challenging, so come very prepared. Gulf Hagas is within the KI-Jo Mary Multiple-Use Forest, which is owned and managed by private timber interests but allows public use. Pay the entrance fee at the checkpoint across from Katahdin Iron Works. Visit the website for maps as well as details about access and trails at Gulf Hagas.

THE DRIVE
From Brownville, south of Brownsville Junction, continue south on ME 11. Take ME 6 west to Dover-Foxcroft.

05 DOVER-FOXCROFT
It's a bit of a haul between the iron works and Greenville. This route swings below the private logging roads of the North Woods. Take a break for **Butterfield's Ice Cream** in Dover-Foxcroft. Walk up to the window, choose your scoop, grab a seat and enjoy your licks beside the smiling cow.

THE DRIVE

Follow ME 6 west through Guilford and Abbot Village. North of Monson, look for a pull-off on your right beside the Appalachian Trail. From this trailhead it's 112 miles north to Katahdin. This trailhead marks the southern start of a very remote section of the trail. The pull-off is about 11 miles south of Greenville.

06 GREENVILLE & MOOSEHEAD LAKE
Silver-blue and dotted with islands, Moosehead Lake sprawls over 120 sq miles of North Woods wilderness. Named, some say, after its shape from the air, it's one of the state's most glorious places. Greenville is the main settlement of the region.

Owned and maintained by the Moosehead Marine Museum, the steamboat **SS *Katahdin*** (katahdincruises.com) was built in 1914. It still makes the rounds on Moosehead Lake from Greenville's center, just like it did in Greenville's heyday. The lake's colorful history is preserved in the **Moosehead Marine Museum** (katahdincruises.com/museum), next to the dock. For moose-spotting safaris, white-water rafting, ATV tours, guided fishing trips and canoe adventures, stop by **Northwoods Outfitters** (maineoutfitter.com) in the center of town. It also rents and sells outdoor gear.

The **Moosehead Lake Region Chamber of Commerce** (destinationmooseheadlake.com) runs a useful visitor center located south of downtown.

Baxter State Park

🚗 THE DRIVE
Tantalizing glimpses of Moosehead Lake peek through the trees on the 8-mile drive from Greenville on Lily Bay Rd, culminating in grand views from Blair Hill.

07 LILY BAY STATE PARK
To camp on the shores of Moosehead Lake, pitch your tent at one of the 90 campsites at this lovely, 925-acre **park** (maine.gov/lilybay). Relax on the sandy beach, bird-watch and stroll the 2-mile shoreline trail.

🚗 THE DRIVE
Return to Greenville, then drive 20 miles north on ME 6, passing the Lavigne Memorial Bridge and marker, memorializing a local son who died in WWII.

08 ROCKWOOD
The distinctive Mt Kineo is a 1769ft rhyolite mountain rising from the bottom of Moosehead Lake. For a good silhouette of its steep, towering face, which juts more than 700ft above the lake, pull over in the village of Rockwood north of Greenville. From Rockwood, return to Greenville or continue 26 miles through the woods on a lovely ribbon of road with lake views to US 201 near Jackman.

BAXTER STATE PARK PLANNER

ADMISSION

In order to protect the park from overuse, day-use is limited by the capacity of trailhead parking lots. Parking lots for the most popular Katahdin-access trailheads fill very early (by 6:30am) on sunny summer weekends.

Parking space at the most popular day-use parking lots is reservable ($5) under the park's Day Use Parking Reservation (DUPR) system – see the website baxterstateparkauthority.com. Reservations can be made up to two weeks before your visit.

Baxter's two main gates are **Togue Pond gate** in the south and **Matagamon gate** in the north. Both are generally open 6am to 10pm from mid-May to mid-October.

Togue Pond is 18 miles from Millinocket; there's a visitor center (offering canoe rental) just south of the gate. The less-popular access point at Matagamon is 26 miles from the town of Patten.

There is a $16 admission fee per vehicle per day (free for Maine residents).

CAMPING

Winter Campsites $18, two-person cabin $60

Summer Campsites $34, two-person cabin $60

HIKING

Read the park's website thoroughly. To hike, you need a car-parking reservation. A few spots may be available on a first-come, first-served basis, but don't count on that on a summer weekend. Make a DUPR booking online.

For an easy day in the southern part of the park, try the mile-long walk to **Katahdin Stream** falls or the pleasant 2-mile nature path around **Daicey Pond**. See the park's website for maps and details about hiking **Mt Katahdin**.

29

MAINE

Lakes Tour

BEST FOR
FAMILIES

Spend a lazy afternoon canoeing the Saco River near Fryeburg.

DURATION	DISTANCE	GREAT FOR
2 days	60 miles / 97km	Nature & families

BEST TIME TO GO	To enjoy swimming and boating, visit from May to October.

Fryeburg Fair

US 302 in southeast Maine is the quickest link between North Conway's outlet stores and the LL Bean store just north of Portland, but the road is also the lifeline for the stunning Lakes region. Filled with glacier-made lakes and ponds, this summer hot spot is home to the state's most popular campground as well as a beloved paddle wheeler and the family-friendly Saco River. Lovely B&Bs encourage lingering with water views and scrumptious breakfasts.

Link Your Trip

20 White Mountains Loop

Take US 302 west to North Conway, NH, to hop a train ride to the Presidential Range.

30 Mainely Art

For cultural inspiration, join this gallery-filled route, starting with the American landscapes at the Portland Museum of Art.

01 FRYEBURG VISITOR INFORMATION CENTER

Just east of the Maine state line, this state-run visitor center can prepare you for an adventure anywhere in the Pine Tree State. It's well stocked with brochures, and the staff are very helpful. Want to stretch your legs? A 4.2-mile section of the new **Mountain Division Trail** begins just behind the visitor center. If all goes to plan, the hiking and biking trail will eventually extend 52 miles from Fryeburg to Portland.

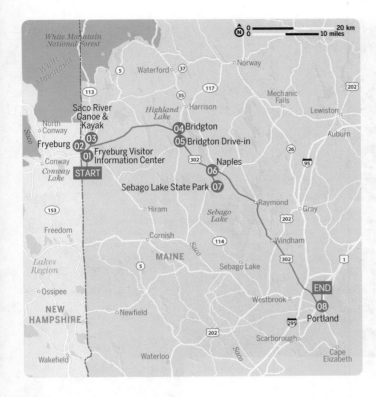

03 SACO RIVER CANOE & KAYAK

Ready to get out on the water? The friendly folks at **Saco River Canoe & Kayak** (sacorivercanoe.com), who've run self-guided trips for more than 40 years, will set you up on the family-friendly Saco River. The river flows about 120 miles from Saco Lake in New Hampshire's upper White Mountains through Crawford Notch and into Maine. In Maine, the Saco runs parallel to US 302 as it makes its way to the Gulf of Maine southwest of Portland. The river is particularly pleasant around Fryeburg, with leafy banks and sandy shores, mountain views and gentle conditions. Trips can range from one hour to several days. Canoe and kayak rentals run from $33 to $45 per day, depending on watercraft and season. Delivery and pick-up services are charged separately, and cost $7 to $16 per trip (minimum charge from $15). Service to the nearby Swans Fall access point is free.

THE DRIVE
US 302 passes Christmas-tree farms and diamond-blue lakes on its 15-mile run east to Bridgton.

04 BRIDGTON

Bridgton is prime digs for a weekend getaway. Main St runs for 1.5 miles past a museum, a movie house, an inviting park and an eclectic array of indie shops. The well-regarded **Rufus Porter Museum** (rufusportermuseum.org) looks at the work of 19th-century Renaissance man Rufus Porter. Porter is recognized throughout New England for the landscape murals he painted in hundreds

---

THE DRIVE
From the visitor center, follow US 302 east into downtown.

02 FRYEBURG

Sitting prettily on the banks of the Saco River, Fryeburg is best known for hosting the annual **Fryeburg Fair** (fryeburgfair.org), an eight-day state agricultural fair that started in 1851. Today it attracts more than 300,000 people. Events and attractions include everything from livestock and flower shows to a whoopie-pie contest, a pig scramble (local pigs only, please), a horse-pulling contest and Woodsmen's Day, when male and female lumberjacks chisel poles

of timber with their chainsaws and hurl their mighty axes.

The rest of the year, the big draw is the Saco River. If you want to feel the sand under your feet after hiking through the White Mountains in next-door New Hampshire, relax on **Weston's Beach**. To get there, take a left onto ME 113/River Rd just before entering Fryeburg from the visitor center. Parking is ahead on the right after crossing the river.

THE DRIVE
Follow ME 5 north for half a mile from the junction of US 302 and ME 5, where signs advertising chowder suppers and community dinners tempt weary travelers.

WHITNEY HAYWARD/PORTLAND PORTLAND PRESS HERALD VIA GETTY IMAGES ©

Bridgton Twin Drive-in

of houses in the region between 1825 and 1845. Also an inventor, he sold the concept of the revolving rifle to Samuel Colt in 1844, and created *Scientific American* magazine.

Take a moment to walk through the photogenic Bob Dunning Memorial Bridge – built by district craftspeople in 2007 to honor a local conservationist. It marks the northern entrance to **Pondicherry Park** (lelt.org), a 66-acre woodland park filled with trails and wildlife. The park sits behind the **Magic Lantern** (magiclanternmovies.com), a beloved community movie house – and the site of a tannery in the 1800s – that anchors downtown.

Congenial staff, a pub with a 23ft screen and three themed theaters make this a pleasant spot to catch a blockbuster, an indie flick or the big game.

🛞 **THE DRIVE**
From downtown Bridgton drive 1 mile east on US 302.

05 **BRIDGTON TWIN DRIVE-IN**
One of just six drive-ins remaining in the state, Bridgton Twin Drive-in has been going strong for some 60 years. It shows movies on two screens, and is a popular choice with families. Visit its Facebook page to see what's playing.

Shops of Bridgton

Welcoming proprietors and an eclectic mix of shops in close proximity make downtown Bridgton a great spot for an hour or two of shopping.

Bridgton Books (bridgtonbooks.com) There's a large inventory of new and used books in this independent bookstore, and helpful staff.

Gallery 302 (gallery302.com) This co-op with 60 member artists displays and sells art in all its forms.

Renys (renys.com) A discount mini department store found throughout Maine, with 17 locations. They sell clothing, housewares and lots of outdoor essentials for Maine adventures.

THE DRIVE
US 302 rolls east out of Bridgton, turning in a more southerly direction as it approaches Naples, 8 miles to the south.

06 NAPLES
Restaurants and shops cluster around the Causeway in downtown Naples, which sits on a spit of land between Long Lake and Brandy Pond. A walk along the Causeway affords grand views of bright blue Long Lake. The big draw here, beyond the eating outlets and bars with lake views, is the red-and-white ***Songo River Queen II*** (songoriverqueen2. com), a 93ft paddle wheeler with a covered upper deck. The boat churns up the east coast of the lake, then comes back down the west side (or vice versa). You'll get a look at Mt Washington and the Presidential Range during the cruise. The *Songo* holds 350 people, so reservations are not typically needed.

THE DRIVE
From the Causeway, turn left onto ME 114 and drive 2 miles south. Turn left onto State Park Dr and take a woodsy cruise to the park entrance.

Photo Opportunity
Stake your position on the Naples causeway for sweet pics of Long Lake.

07 SEBAGO LAKE STATE PARK
With 250 campsites scattered throughout the woods beside the sandy shores of Sebago Lake, this 1500-acre **state park** (maine.gov/sebagolake) is a popular and scenic place to swim, picnic and camp on the way to Portland. Sebago Lake is Maine's second-largest lake, at 45 sq miles. Visitors can enjoy the beaches (Songo Beach is a pearl), grills and picnic tables, and if the beach gets too crowded, just step into the woods, where you can wander several miles of easy to moderate trails or bike the roadways. There's also a nature center. In summer, rangers lead talks, hikes and canoe trips; look for details on the bulletin board at the park entrance. Pets are not allowed on the beaches or in the campground.

THE DRIVE
Continue southeast on US 302, passing through Windham. Suburbia and development creep in as Portland approaches.

08 PORTLAND
Well, hello there. Is that a brew house at the eastern end of US 302, on the fringes of downtown Portland? Yes? Cheers, we say! And welcome to the **Great Lost Bear** (greatlostbear.com), a fun and quirky place in a fun and quirky city. Decked out in Christmas lights and flea-market kitsch, this rambling bar and restaurant is a Portland institution. Seventy-eight taps serve primarily Northeastern brews, including 40 from Maine, making the GLB one of America's best regional beer bars. The atmosphere is family friendly (at least early in the evening), with a massive menu of burgers, quesadillas and other bar nibbles. It's the perfect fuel-stop before further explorations of Portland's museums, mansions and working wharves.

30

MAINE

Galleries,
museums
and a mural
keep Portland
cutting-edge.

Mainely Art

DURATION	DISTANCE	GREAT FOR
3 days	200 miles / 322km	History, food & drink

BEST TIME TO GO	May through October is high season for art walks.

PORTLAND MUSEUM *of* ART

Portland Museum of Art

Art museums in Maine spotlight native sons and daughters and other American artists who found inspiration here. It's a talented bunch that includes Winslow Homer, George Bellows, Edward Hopper, Louise Nevelson and the Wyeths. But really injecting energy into the contemporary art scene are the fantastic special exhibits that explore the issues of our day, from conservation and urban planning to social networking, in unexpected but thought-provoking works.

Link Your Trip

28 Great North Woods

From Bangor, a short drive on I-95 leads to the North Woods and Mt Katahdin.

29 Lakes Tour

Hop on US 302 in Portland and head northwest for a bright-blue lake-dappled landscape.

01 **PORTLAND**

A great introduction to Maine's artistic treasure trove is found in the **Portland Museum of Art** (portlandmuseum.org), founded in 1882. This well-respected museum houses an outstanding collection of American works. Maine artists are particularly well represented. You'll also find a few paintings by European masters. From here, some of the city's coolest highlights are within easy walking distance.

THE DRIVE

If you want to make good time, hop on I-295 and drive 25 miles north to Brunswick. For LL Bean and the

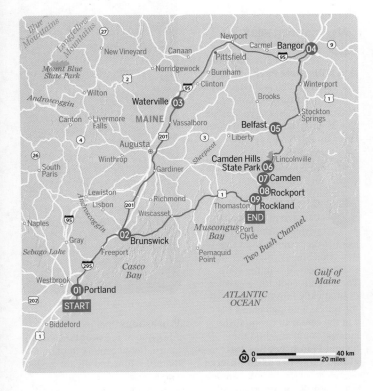

of a 26,000-sq-ft glass pavilion. The space displays works from a nearly 500-piece collection gifted to Colby by longtime benefactors Peter and Paula Lunder. It is one of the largest gifts of art to a liberal-arts college; highlights of the collection are numerous, with works by James McNeill Whistler, Winslow Homer and Georgia O'Keeffe, among others, and a focus on American and contemporary art.

THE DRIVE
From Waterville, I-95 swoops along the edges of the Maine highlands as it angles north and then east on its 55-mile swing to Bangor.

04 BANGOR
The small **University of Maine Museum of Art** (zam.umaine.edu) in Bangor is the northernmost art museum on the **Maine Art Museum Trail** (maineartmuseums.org). It's not the largest or most impressive collection in the state, but Bangor is a pleasant gateway for exploring the moody Maine highlands to the north and the Midcoast art towns just south. The university's collection spotlights mid-century modern American artists as well as contemporary pieces by David Hockney, Roy Lichtenstein, Andy Warhol and others. The special exhibits can really shine, so check the online calendar to see what's on display.

THE DRIVE
This 45-mile jaunt south on US 1A west to US 1 south passes the Paul Bunyan statue in downtown Bangor then tracks the Penobscot River, passing the informative Penobscot Marine Museum in Searsport.

outlet stores, make a detour onto US 1 at Freeport.

02 BRUNSWICK
Tidy Brunswick, with its well-kept central green and dramatic perch over the Androscoggin River, is a landscape painting come to life. The view stays inspiring on the Bowdoin College campus, where stately buildings surround a tree-dotted quad. The dramatic glass entrance pavilion at the **Bowdoin College Museum of Art** (bowdoin.edu/art-museum) injects this pastoral scene with a bit of modernity, and sets a compelling tone for further exploration. The 20,000-piece

collection is particularly strong in the works of 19th- and 20th-century European and American painters, with some surprising antiquities, too.

THE DRIVE
For inspiring views of the Kennebec River and time on the historic Old Canada Rd, follow US 201 north. The quickest route for the 50-mile drive is I-295 north to I-95 north.

03 WATERVILLE
Another bucolic college campus, another outstanding art collection – this time, it's the **Colby College Museum of Art** (museum.colby.edu), fresh from a marvelous expansion and the addition

05 BELFAST

There aren't any art museums in Belfast, but this working-class community with Scots-Irish roots does have an inviting downtown with 12 or so galleries and studios. The oceanfront town is also the site of the nation's oldest shoe store, **Colburn Shoe**, which opened in 1832! The art-deco **Colonial Theatre** (colonialtheatre.com) has shown movies since 1912, luring moviegoers with a neon sign and a rooftop elephant. See what's happening at **Waterfall Arts** (waterfallarts.org), a non-profit contemporary arts center that hosts exhibitions, lectures, art classes, musical performances, film screenings and more.

 THE DRIVE
Follow US 1 south for 16 miles, mostly along the coast, passing Ducktrap and Lincolnville.

TOP TIP:
Gallery Guide & Art News

For a list of galleries and studios throughout the state, pick up the free **Maine Gallery & Studio Guide** (mainegalleryguide.com) at art museums and galleries. It's also available online at cafedesartistes.

---

06 CAMDEN HILLS STATE PARK

A favorite hike in **Camden Hills State Park** (maine.gov/camdenhills) is the half-mile climb up **Mt Battie**, offering outstanding views of Penobscot Bay. Feeling sluggish? You can drive up the mountain, too.

THE DRIVE
Drive 2 miles south on US 1 to downtown Camden.

07 CAMDEN

Camden and its picture-perfect harbor, framed against the mountains of Camden Hills State Park, is one of the prettiest sites in the state. The Megunticook River crashes dramatically into the sea beside the public landing behind US 1 in the center of town. At the landing you'll also find the helpful **Penobscot Bay Regional Chamber of Commerce** (camdenrockland.com). Camden offers **windjammer cruises** (sailmainecoast.com) – anything from two-hour rides to multiday journeys up the coast. There are also galleries, fine seafood restaurants and back alleys for exploring. Enjoy a good meal at **Fresh & Co** (freshcamden.com).

THE DRIVE
By the time you get your seatbelt buckled you're almost in Rockport, just a 2-mile drive south on US 1.

08 ROCKPORT

Photographers flock to Rockport, a sleepy harborside town, for more than just the picturesque coast. Rockport is the home of the world-renowned **Maine Media**

Workshops (mainemedia.edu), one of the world's leading instructional centers in photography, film and digital media. The institute offers hundreds of workshops and master classes throughout the year. Student and faculty works are displayed in a gallery at 18 Central St.

But let's not forget the most important attraction in town: the granite statue of **Andre the Seal**, about half a mile off US 1 via Main St. Andre was a crowd-pleasing showboat who swam to the harbor from Boston every summer from the 1970s until his death in the mid-'80s. He was the subject of a children's book, *z*, and a 1994 movie.

 THE DRIVE
Leave Andre behind as you turn left onto Pascal Ave, following it to US 1. Rockland is 6 miles to the south.

09 ROCKLAND

Rockland is a cool little town. Its commercial port adds vibrancy, and its bustling Main St is a window into the city's sociocultural diversity, with working-class diners, bohemian cafes and high-end bistros beside galleries and old-fashioned storefronts.

Just off Main St, the **Farnsworth Art Museum** (farnsworthmuseum.org) is one of the country's best small regional museums, with works spanning 200 years of American art. The 'Maine in America' collections spotlight artists who have lived or worked in the state. Exhibits about the Wyeths – Andrew, NC and Jamie – are housed in galleries throughout the museum and in the Wyeth Center, a former Methodist church across the garden.

Photo Opportunity

Capture all of island-dotted Penobscot Bay from the top of Mt Battie in Camden Hills State Park.

The wonderful **Archipelago Fine Arts** (thearchipelago.net) sells jewelry, paintings and arts and crafts by artists living on Maine's islands and coast. It works in partnership with the **Island Institute** (islandinstitute.org), an organization whose goal is to support Maine's remote coastal and island communities.

THE DRIVE

From Rockland, continue south along the coast on US 1 to loop back to Brunswick.

E J JOHNSON PHOTOGRAPHY/SHUTTERSTOCK ©

Mt Battie, Camden Hills State Park

31

MAINE

Moose & Mountains: Western Maine

BEST FOR WILDLIFE

ME 16 between Rangeley and Stratton is a local moose alley.

DURATION	DISTANCE	GREAT FOR
2 days	160 miles / 257km	Nature

BEST TIME TO GO	June through March is good for hiking, leaf-peeping and skiing.

Screw Auger Falls

The first time you see a moose standing on the side of the road, it doesn't seem unusual. You've been prepped by all of the moose-crossing signs. But then it registers. 'Hey, that's a moose!' And you simultaneously swerve, slam on the brakes and speed up. Control these impulses. Simply slow your speed and enjoy the gift of wildlife.

Link Your Trip

24 Woodland Heritage Trail

Take US 2 west to learn the history of logging on the Androscoggin River.

29 Lakes Tour

Follow the Pequawket Trail Scenic Byway along ME 113 to a riverside beach in Fryeburg and more lakes beyond.

01 **BETHEL**

If you glance at the map, tiny Bethel doesn't seem much different from the other towns scattered across this alpine region. But look more closely. The town is cocooned between two powerful rivers, and several ski resorts and ski centers call the community home. Four state and national scenic byways begin within an 85-mile drive.

Of the ski resorts, **Sunday River** (sundayriver. com) is the biggest draw, luring skiers with eight interconnected peaks, 135 trails and a host of winter activities. From July until early October, the resort opens 25 mountain-bike trails and runs trips up to North Peak on its fast-moving **Chondola**. Several

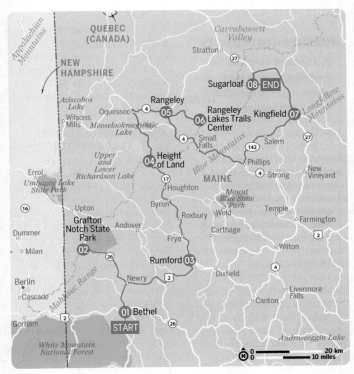

Scenic Byways in the Lakes & Mountains Region

Read more at exploremaine.org/byways.

Grafton Notch Scenic Byway
From Bethel, follow US 2 north, then turn left at Newry and take ME 26 through Grafton Notch State Park.

Pequawket Trail Scenic Byway
Follow the Androscoggin River west from Bethel on US 2. Turn south onto ME 113 at Gilead and follow it to Fryeburg.

State Route 27 Scenic Byway
From stop seven, in Kingfield, follow ME 16/27 to Sugarloaf, then continue north on ME 27 to Canada.

Rangeley Lakes National Scenic Byway
Drive east on US 2 from Rumford to Mexico, then turn north on US 17. The byway begins about 15 miles north, just beyond the town of Byron.

---

outdoor centers, including **Carter's X-C Ski Center** (cartersxcski.com), are base camps for cross-country skiing and snowshoeing, with 'fat biking' growing in popularity.

THE DRIVE
Follow ME 5/ME 26/US 2 north from Bethel, tracking the Sunday River about 6 miles north. Keep left on NH 26 as it leaves ME 5/US 2 and becomes Bear River Rd, which leads to the park 11 miles west.

02 GRAFTON NOTCH STATE PARK

Sitting astride the Grafton Notch Scenic Byway within the Mahoosuc Range, this rugged **park** (maine.gov/grafton notch) is a stunner. Carved by a glacier that retreated 12,000

years ago, the notch is a four-season playground, chock-full of waterfalls, gorges, lofty viewpoints and hiking trails, including over 20 miles of the Appalachian Trail. Peregrine falcons build nests in the cliffs, helping the park earn its spot on the **Maine Birding Trail** (mainebirding trail.com); the best viewing is May to October. Cross-country skiers and snowshoers enjoy the park in winter. If you're short on time, simply wander the path beside **Screw Auger Falls**, off the main parking lot. This 23ft waterfall crashes dramatically through a narrow gorge. If you have more time, try the 2.4-mile round-trip hike up to **Table Rock overlook** or the 2.2-mile **Eyebrow Loop**

Trail. There are excellent picnicking opportunities within the park – the Spruce Meadow picnic area is signed off ME 26.

THE DRIVE
Return to US 2 north. On the 16-mile drive, you'll pass stone walls and antique stores, and enjoy the Androscoggin River tagging along on your right.

03 RUMFORD

How do you know you've arrived? When the giant, ax-wielding **Paul Bunyan** says 'Hey there.' According to legend, the red-shirted lumberman was born in Maine but was later sent west by his parents. Today, he stands tall beside the **River Valley Chamber of Commerce Visitor Center** (rivervalley chamber.com). Walk a few steps beyond the building for a fantastic view of the wild and woolly **Rumford Falls**. The highest falls east of Niagara, they drop 176ft over a granite ledge. The small park here holds a black marble memorial honoring local son and former US senator Edmund Muskie, who authored the Clean Water Act.

THE DRIVE

Leave Rumford and US 2, picking up ME 17 north in Mexico. From here ME 17 runs parallel to pines, farms, meadows and the rocky Swift River. Snap a photo of the river barreling through metamorphic rock at the Coos Canyon Rest Area in Byron, then head north, picking up the Rangeley Lakes National Scenic Byway north of Houghton.

04 HEIGHT OF LAND

The entrance to this photogenic **overlook** sneaks up on you – it's on the left as you round a bend on Brimstone Mountain, just after a hiker warning sign. But don't slam on your brakes and swerve across the grass divider if you miss the turn (we saw this happen), because there's another entrance just north. But you *should* pull over. The expansive view of island-dotted **Mooselookmeguntic Lake**, the largest of the Rangeley region's lakes, as it sweeps north toward

Photo Opportunity

Frame a shot of Mooselookmeguntic Lake from the Height of Land overlook.

distant mountains is astounding. Views of undeveloped forest stretch for up to 100 miles; you can even see the White Mountains in New Hampshire. The dogged Appalachian Trail runs alongside the viewpoint, and an interpretive sign shares a few details about the 2190-mile footpath.

THE DRIVE

Drive north to the village of Oquossoc, then turn right onto ME 4/16. Take a photo at the Rangeley Scenic Overlook, where there is a panoramic view of Rangeley Lake. This overlook is about 5.5 miles from Height of Land. From here, continue east.

05 RANGELEY

An adventure hub, with tidy inns and down-home restaurants, Rangeley makes a useful base for skiing, hiking, white-water rafting and mountain biking in the nearby mountains. Snowmobilers can zoom across 150 miles of trails. For information, stop by the **Rangeley Lakes Chamber of Commerce** (rangeleymaine.com), which has handouts about restaurants, lodging options, local trails and moose-watching. Just behind the visitor center, **Rangeley Town Cove Park** is a nice spot to enjoy a picnic by the lake. On rainy days, ask at the chamber of commerce about the local museums.

THE DRIVE

ME 4 breaks from ME 16 in downtown Rangeley. From the chamber of commerce, follow ME 4 east. Turn left onto Dallas Hill Rd, then in 2.5 miles bear right on Saddleback Mountain Rd and continue another 2.5 miles.

06 RANGELEY LAKES TRAILS CENTER

A green yurt marks your arrival at the **Rangeley Lakes Trails Center** (rangeleylakestrailscenter.org), a four-season trail system covering gorgeous woodland terrain beside Saddleback Lake. Here there are more than 40 miles of trails for cross-country skiing and snowshoeing during snow season (rental equipment is available inside the yurt, along with hot soup!). In summer, the cross-country trails double as hiking trails, and the snowshoe trails allow single-track biking. The yurt is closed in summer, but trail maps are available from an information board (or from the chamber of commerce in Rangeley).

THE DRIVE

Follow ME 4 southeast, passing another Rangeley Lake overlook. Continue southeast. You'll pass another Appalachian Trail crossing before entering prime moose country. Follow ME 12 east to NE 16/27 north.

07 KINGFIELD

If you enjoy hiking and cross-country skiing, but not backpacking, consider a hut-to-hut trip through **Maine Huts & Trails** (mainehuts.org), a wonderful nonprofit organization based in Kingfield that operates four ecolodges along an 80-mile

Sugarloaf

trail system near Sugarloaf (with more huts planned). Choose a dorm bed or a private bunkroom and enjoy three meals (including a packed lunch) and pretty plush off-the-grid relaxation. Pillows and blankets are provided, but not bedding. Winter and summer are peak popularity for the huts; in the off-season you can still stay overnight, but without meal service (and with reduced prices). There is no vehicle access to the lodges (two are less than 2 miles from a trailhead).

🚗 **THE DRIVE**
From Kingfield, NH 16 joins ME 27, unfurling beneath the pines, with the Carrabassett River tumbling merrily alongside.

08 SUGARLOAF
The Rangeley area's most popular **ski resort** (sugarloaf.com), Sugarloaf has a vertical drop of 2820ft, with 162 trails and glades, and 13 lifts. This is Maine's second-highest peak (4237ft). Summer activities include lift rides, ziplines and

golf. The resort village complex has an enormous mountain lodge, an inn and rental condos. Nearby towns of Kingfield and Stratton are also good bases.

Near Sugarloaf's slopes, the **Sugarloaf Outdoor Center** has 56 miles of groomed cross-country trails, plus guided snowshoeing safaris and public ice-skating on an NHL-size rink.

TOOLKIT

The chapters in this section cover the most important topics you'll need to know about in New England. They're full of nuts-and-bolts information and valuable insights to help you understand and navigate New England and get the most out of your trip.

Arriving
p186

Getting Around
p187

Accommodations
p188

Cars
p189

Health & Safe Travel
p190

Responsible Travel
p191

Nuts & Bolts
p192

Nantucket Harbor (p43), Massachusetts
(PBOKIC BOJAN/SHUTTERSTOCK ©

Arriving

Driving or flying to Boston are the two most common ways to reach New England, though Amtrak's Acela express, which serves the northeast corridor, and private bus services from New York City are two other possibilities. Boston's Logan International Airport is the largest in New England; it's a modern, easy-to-navigate hub. Smaller regional airports are found throughout the region.

Car Rental at Airports

At many times of the year you'll have no problem renting a car without a reservation at one of the many agencies at Boston's Logan International. However, during holidays and leaf-peeping season (when the fall foliage is at its best), vehicles will be scarce – reserve in advance. At the rental desk you'll be asked if you want to pre-pay for gas (thus avoiding the hassle of finding a station when you return) but the rates are usually pricier than if you filled up on your own. Your car includes the minimum legal insurance, so you do not need to add additional coverage unless you want to. Most agencies are somewhat cheaper if you rent and return from their non-airport locations, but the convenience of an airport rental is hard to beat. Some agencies offer fully electric options, but not all.

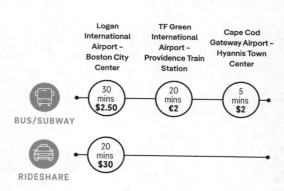

	Logan International Airport – Boston City Center	TF Green International Airport – Providence Train Station	Cape Cod Gateway Airport – Hyannis Town Center
BUS/SUBWAY	30 mins $2.50	20 mins €2	5 mins $2
RIDESHARE	20 mins $30		

VISAS

Generally not required for stays of 90 days or less for citizens of the Visa Waiver Program countries, following ESTA approval (esta.cbp.dhs.gov). Apply for ESTA authorization at least 72 hours in advance.

MONEY

ATMS are widely available, but credit cards are required for car and hotel reservations. Tipping in the US is customary, not optional. Cashless payments are increasingly common, but smaller stores may be cash only.

CELL PHONE COVERAGE

Don't expect data to be available everywhere, especially if you have an international carrier. In many mountain regions service can drop, so download hiking trail maps or plan for alternate directions just in case.

WI-FI

Airports such as Boston's Logan have free wi-fi available, though connections are not secure and require no password. Do not do any banking or enter any sensitive information over public wi-fi.

Getting Around

The busiest driving corridors in New England tend to be federal interstates and state highways, although always expect traffic in and around Boston and along popular coastal roads.

DRIVING INFO

Drive on the right.

Many toll roads use transponders only.

.08

Blood alcohol limit is 0.8g/L.

PUBLIC TRANSPORTATION

Big cities like Boston, Hartford and Providence have public transportation, but don't count on it for smaller towns. Rideshare apps are uber-convenient but local taxis are also available.

RVs & Campers

Chances are that even if you're not in a bus-sized house on wheels, you'll be sharing the road with folks who are. Some roads require extreme caution; many steeper ones are impassable in RVs.

TRAVEL COSTS

Car rental
$600/week

Gas
$3.50/gallon

EV charging
$15–30

Train fare DC to Boston
$150

Electric Vehicles

Electric charging stations are relatively common and easy to find using online services, apps or even the car itself. Drivers of EVs don't have to worry too much about range anxiety.

Rotaries & Roundabouts

Many non-local drivers are confused about rotaries (aka traffic circles or roundabouts). Drivers must yield to traffic already within the circle. The inner lane is for continuing around the circle; the outer lane is for exiting.

FLASHING HEADLIGHTS

In New England, flashing your headlights is the accepted way of indicating to someone, 'You go first.' If you're at a four-way stop, it's first in, first out, but you can tell someone to go ahead by flashing your lights. At night, a quick flash means you've forgotten to turn off your brights...or that your low-beams are so bright they're blinding other drivers.

Accommodations

☆ **RESERVATIONS**

Online reservation websites take a hefty cut from participating hotels – sometimes as much as 30%. Rather than booking your stay through one of these middlemen, try buying local by calling or reserving a room online directly from the business itself.

HOW MUCH FOR A NIGHT IN A...

beachfront cabin in Provincetown
$500/day

double motel room off the highway
$90/day

room at a waterfront Maine resort
$500/day

Mom & Pop Hotels

You'll find that this region has plenty of chain motels and hotels to suit every possible budget, but the best stays are always ones where you know you're helping a small business. It's not hard to find family-owned and -run options, and they will often give you better rates if you pay in cash.

Air-Conditioning

Summer cottages and smaller family-run motels may not have A/C. The region is breezy, temperatures rarely climb into the insufferable range and prices are better for rooms with fans. However, heat waves can turn a fan-cooled stay into a sauna, so you may want to opt for A/C even if you don't end up needing it.

Cabins

Many visitors to New England thrill at the idea of a cabin stay. These small, independent buildings are often no bigger than a hotel room, and usually include an en-suite bathroom and sometimes an outside deck. They're delightful, but they fill up quickly.

Book ahead by up to six months to ensure you get the overnight you're dreaming of.

CAMPING & BOONDOCKING

Camping is generally only allowed in designated camping areas or on private land with the owner's explicit permission. You can be arrested for trespassing or told to move on by police if you're in the wrong area. The exception is the White Mountains, where you can set up camp in whatever spot seems suitable, unless signs are posted otherwise.

☆ **BRINGING FIDO**

Many hotels and motels allow pets, but the rules and regulations are almost as varied as dog breeds, so check carefully beforehand that your accommodations allows your animal. Small dogs are defined as 20lb and under, and nearly all places have a clause that lets them evict guests whose dogs bark or disturb guests. If your pup soils the rug, expect to pay a hefty-to-exorbitant cleaning fee. Make sure to keep your dog leashed at all times between your room and your vehicle.

Cars

HOW MUCH TO HIRE A...

small car
from $35/day

EV
from $100/day

large SUV
from $150/day

Car Rental

Car rental companies are mostly ubiquitous chains but a few places, such as Nantucket and Martha's Vineyard, have local agencies, often including over-sand vehicle permits in the (hefty) rental fee.

Many expressways only accept toll transponders, so you will be billed by the rental company if you don't have one. This too is often included now, or at the very least is an available option.

US citizens will need a valid drivers license and major credit card, and if your country's language is non-Latin, you'll need a notarized translation or International Drivers Permit as well as your passport.

Expect to spend at least 30 minutes for handover; most airport agencies have a shuttle to/from the terminals.

EVs

Electric vehicles are increasingly common and are beginning to make their way to the rental market, but recent pushback (mostly from drivers unfamiliar with how to use them) has dented their appeal. EV charging stations are everywhere thanks to Tesla's popularity. Highways have dedicated fast chargers, and many malls, department stores and even convenience stores have charging stations. Apps and websites list their locations, making them easy to find. If you're not going to be charging overnight, keep in mind that a fast charge will get you mostly juiced in 10 to 15 minutes, depending on the type of charger and your car. Plug in and grab some lunch, and by the time you're paying the bill you'll be ready to drive again.

OTHER GEAR

Child seats, booster seats and infant carriers are usually available, sometimes free of charge, but bringing your own ensures safety, comfort and peace of mind. Airlines often allow seats and strollers to be checked for free. If you will be renting child seats with your vehicle, make sure you pre-book the extras.

Health & Safe Travel

Emergencies

If you have an emergency of any kind, dial 911 immediately. Cell phones, especially international ones, may not be able to share your location automatically, so be ready to communicate your address or location to the dispatcher. Rescue teams can take hours, even days, to reach hikers in the backcountry, and cell coverage may not extend to all regions.

Animals

In upper New England, the biggest danger while driving is hitting a moose at high speed. People are routinely killed when this happens – even hitting a deer can be fatal. Use extreme care when driving at night and remember that a quadruped could leap in front of you at any moment. Serious tick-borne illnesses such as Lyme disease are common. If you find a tick on your body followed by a concentric 'bull's-eye' rash around the bite, see a doctor.

Weather

New England weather can go from great to ghastly in the blink of an eye. Be prepared, make sure you've got proper clothes, water and supplies, and have a plan B for those inconvenient rainy days.

Security

While keeping valuables out of sight is always wise, smash-n-grabs are uncommon even in big cities, and very rare in smaller towns. Minimize the risks by storing purses, bags, suitcases and cameras in the trunk. Beach theft is a possibility, though the culprits are often opportunistic seagulls who may carry off unattended food, clothing or even cell phones and keys.

CAR BREAKDOWN

Your rental agency will give you a toll-free number to call if you experience a breakdown. This is often covered but if you're found to be at fault, such as driving on the beach without proper permits, you'll pay in full. Tow trucks may take an hour or more to arrive. AAA (aaa.com) offers roadside assistance plans that can supplement whatever the agency offers.

Responsible Travel

Climate Change

It's impossible to ignore the impact we have when traveling, and the importance of making changes where we can. Lonely Planet urges all travelers to engage with their travel carbon footprint. There are many carbon calculators online that allow travelers to estimate the carbon emissions generated by their journey; try resurgence.org/resources/carbon-calulator.html. Many airlines and booking sites offer travelers the option of offsetting the impact of greenhouse gas emissions by contributing to climate-friendly initiatives around the world. We continue to offset the carbon footprint of all Lonely Planet staff travel, while recognizing this is a mitigation more than a solution.

Visit New England

visitnewengland.com
Sustainable, responsible New England travel.

Visit Maine

visitmaine.com
Make your visit a climate-friendly one.

Ethos

the-ethos.co
Eco-friendly biodegradable soaps and sustainable meals.

REDUCE, REUSE, REFILL

Single-use plastic such as water bottles is a scourge. People often inadvertently leave bottles where they blow away or are forgotten. Tap water's good here; you'll be able to refill bottles easily.

BUY LOCAL

Buy fresh produce, fruit, meat, honey and other products at farm stands instead of the big supermarket chains. The produce will be delicious and local veggies means a lower carbon footprint.

PACK IT OUT

Picking up trash isn't only about bear safety, it's about the health of the planet. If you spot a discarded water bottle or wrapper, consider packing it out even if it's not yours.

Nuts & Bolts

CURRENCY:
US DOLLAR ($)

Tap Water

New England has great-tasting tap water; it is potable unless marked otherwise.

Gotta Go, Gotta Go

Urinating in public is prohibited and can be prosecuted. Many beaches have portable toilets; some have full restroom buildings. Gas stations and rest areas often have facilities.

ELECTRICITY
120V/60Hz

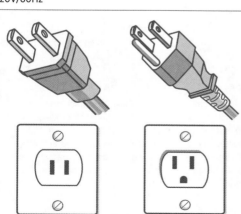

Type A
120V/60Hz

Type B
120V/60Hz

Cash or Credit?

Nearly all establishments except some small vendors accept credit cards, though each transaction costs them a 1.5% to 3.5% processing fee. Send more of your money to the little guys by paying in cash. Many restaurants and stores also accept phone-based transactions.

The Ben Franklin Dilemma

While good ole Ben (the face of the $100 bill) is worth a bit less these days, smaller businesses are still less likely to break a $100, especially if you're making a small purchase. Plan to have a range of bills on hand if you're paying in cash.

Tipping Etiquette

Always, always tip waitstaff unless the tip has already been added into your bill (often 18% or more for groups). Waitstaff earn well below legal minimum wage because they are supposed to make it up in tips. For OK to great service, tip 15% to 25%.

Smoking

Smoking is prohibited at beaches and inside most businesses and hotels.

PEMIGEWASSET
RIVER

·1886·

DANGER
PEDESTRIANS
KEEP OUT
BUS BRIDGE

Franconia Notch State Park (p125), New Hampshire
BORIS BUJAK/SHUTTERSTOCK ©

Index

Notes

THE WRITERS

This is the 6th edition of Lonely Planet's *Best Road Trips New England* guidebook, updated with new material by Ray Bartlett. Writers on previous editions whose work also appears in this book are included below.

Ray Bartlett

Ray is a travel writer and novelist with over 100 Lonely Planet titles to his credit. Find him on Instagram at @kaisoradotcom or at www.kaisora.com

Contributing writers

Isabel Albiston, Amy C Balfour, Robert Balkovich, Gregor Clark, Adam Karlin, Brian Kluepfel, Regis St Louis, Mara Vorhees, Benedict Walker

SEND US YOUR FEEDBACK

We love to hear from travelers – your comments keep us on our toes and help make our books better. Our well-traveled team reads every word on what you loved or loathed about this book. Although we cannot reply individually to your submissions, we always guarantee that your feedback goes straight to the appropriate writers, in time for the next edition. Each person who sends us information is thanked in the next edition.

Visit **lonelyplanet.com/contact** to submit your updates and suggestions or to ask for help. Our award-winning website also features inspirational travel stories and news.

Note: We may edit, reproduce and incorporate your comments in Lonely Planet products such as guidebooks, websites and digital products, so let us know if you are happy to have your name acknowledged. For a copy of our privacy policy visit **lonelyplanet.com/legal**.

BEHIND THE SCENES

This book was produced by the following:

Commissioning Editor
Caroline Trefler

Production Editor
Jennifer McCann

Book Designer
Clara Monitto

Cartographer
Bohumil Ptáček

Assisting Editors
James Appleton, Janet Austin, Alex Conroy, Kate Mathews, Jenna Myers, Christopher Pitts

Cover Researcher
Marc Backwell, Kat Marsh

Thanks to
Karen Henderson, Daniela Machová, Darren O'Connell

Product Development
Amy Lynch, Marc Backwell, Katerina Pavkova, Fergal Condon, Ania Bartoszek

ACKNOWLEDGMENTS

Cover photograph
Pemaquid Point Light, Pemaquid Point, Maine; Susanne Kremer/4Corner Images ©